Adjudicating International Human Rights

Sandy Ghandhi

Adjudicating International Human Rights

Essays in Honour of Sandy Ghandhi

Edited by

James A. Green
Christopher P.M. Waters

with a Foreword by

Dame Rosalyn Higgins

BRILL
NIJHOFF

LEIDEN | BOSTON

Cover illustration: Adam John Green.

Library of Congress Cataloging-in-Publication Data

Adjudicating international human rights : essays in honour of Sandy Ghandhi / edited by James A. Green, Christopher P.M. Waters.
pages cm
Includes bibliographical references and index.
ISBN 978-90-04-26117-4 (hardback : alk. paper) -- ISBN 978-90-04-26118-1 (e-book) 1. Human rights. I. Green, James A., 1981- editor. II. Waters, Christopher P. M. (Christopher Peter Michael), 1968- editor. III. Ghandhi, P. R., 1951- honouree.

K3240.A33845 2015
341.4'8--dc23

2014035131

This publication has been typeset in the multilingual "Brill" typeface. With over 5,100 characters covering Latin, IPA, Greek, and Cyrillic, this typeface is especially suitable for use in the humanities. For more information, please see http://www.brill.com/brill-typeface.

ISBN 978-90-04-26117-4 (hardback)
ISBN 978-90-04-26118-1 (e-book)

This book is printed on acid-free paper.

Contents

Foreword

It is in every way appropriate that Brill Nijhoff, a leading publisher in international law, should be bringing out this book of essays in honour of Sandy Ghandhi.

Sandy has his BA and MA from New College, Oxford, and then an LLM from King's College London. All of his teaching life he has been at the University of Reading, to which he has given extraordinary service since 1979.

He is, of course, best known to a wider public for his writings on international human rights law, and in particular the law and practice relating to the International Covenant on Civil and Political Rights. I was a Member of the Human Rights Committee under that Covenant from 1985 to 1995 and it was during that time that I first met Sandy. He was then preparing his outstanding book on *The Human Rights Committee and the Right of Individual Communication*, which was published in 1998. I found it exceptional that a book with so much insight and appreciation of the legal complexities could be written by one who was not actually present at the various closed meetings on the case law.

We have been friends ever since and I have seen his many chapters in books covering various aspects of human rights law, often with a special emphasis on the Human Rights Committee. He has also written on *Al-Skeini*, the ICJ *Georgia v. The Russian Federation* case, and family and child rights. From 2000 to 2012 he was responsible for Oxford University Press' *International Human Rights Documents*, essential for students and scholars alike. Less well known are the Reports he has been asked to prepare for the Law Society on different human rights issues. While many academic international lawyers were also active, and highly visible, at the Bar, Sandy has, over the years, given important service to the Law Society.

I think this fact has typified the man. He has never sought to draw attention to himself, leaving his writings to do the talking. That this self-effacing individual is widely appreciated by his peers is evidenced by the distinction of those who have contributed chapters to this volume. The list of contributors, as well as the wide variety of topics within the field of human rights covered, reflect the scholar that they honour.

Not only has this quiet man been appreciated for his work, but also for his qualities of character. He has been an exemplary colleague at Reading, doing everything asked of him, and more. He was a caring and knowledgeable teacher, giving time and all support to his students. He also willingly took on a large number of administrative duties and it is clear that Sandy was very highly regarded by his colleagues, not only for his scholarship but for the exceptional overall contribution he had made over the years to the Law School and the University.

This kind and gentle man has other qualities which make ever more appropriate this volume to honour him. Family and friendship reflect his nature. He and his wife Jennifer, with her many skills, have throughout the years helped each other and given every support to their children. It is entirely typical that Sandy and Jennifer wish now, in retirement, to help their parents in any way possible. Sandy is also a great nurturer of his friendships. He remains in close touch and readily brings his friends into the news-circle of his many activities.

Dame Rosalyn Higgins

Preface

This volume has been prepared to honour the career of Professor Sandy Ghandhi on the occasion of his retirement. It has been an absolute privilege for me to have been involved as an editor and contributor to this work. Sandy's influence on the field of international human rights law has been immense, and it is only fitting that it be recognised by a collection such as this.

My co-editor, Chris Waters, has examined Sandy's significant contribution to international human rights law in this volume's Introduction, so I will not dwell on that here. I just want to highlight in this preface the fact that Sandy's impact within his profession goes far beyond his contribution to his chosen field, hugely significant though that has been. He has also tirelessly worked to support colleagues and fellow researchers (especially junior colleagues/researchers), striven to continue to improve the Law School at the University of Reading in all respects and – crucially – provided the best possible teaching environment for his students, year-on-year.

Sandy first taught me when I was 18, as an undergraduate student, and he has been a constant positive presence in my life ever since. Following my appointment to the academic staff at Reading in 2006, his mentorship with regard to all aspects of my job has been invaluable to me. His constant support has played a significant role in my development as an academic, and I know that I will continue to benefit from the guidance he has given me in the future. Of course, I am far from alone in this regard; many of the contributors to this volume were also mentored at various stages of their career by Sandy, and there are countless other students and academics that he has similarly supported over the years.

This volume is intended as a tribute to Sandy's work in the field of international human rights law, but Chris and I hope that it also goes some way to thanking him more generally on behalf of all of those that he has helped during a wonderful career.

To me, he has been a teacher and a mentor, and will always remain a great friend.

James A. Green

Contributors

Dr Tawhida Ahmed

Tawhida Ahmed is an Associate Professor in the School of Law, University of Reading. She specialises in human rights protection and the EU. She has written widely on a range of human rights issues, including the EU's relationship with international and European law, minority rights protection in EU and international law, as well on topics such as cultural rights, linguistic rights and the freedom of religion. Tawhida is the author of *The Impact of EU Law on Minority Rights* (Hart, 2011). She is Associate Fellow of the Human Rights Consortium, University of London and is a founding member of the UK Network on Human Rights and Minority Groups.

Professor J. Craig Barker

Craig Barker took up a Chair in Law at the Sussex Law School, University of Sussex in 2004 where he served as Head of Department from 2009–2012. Previously he was Lecturer and then Senior Lecturer in the School of Law at the University of Reading (1993–2004). He has written extensively on immunities from jurisdiction, including two monographs on diplomatic immunity, as well as a number of articles on the Pinochet litigation. Craig has also written a monograph examining the relationship between international law and international relations and is co-author of *The Encyclopaedic Dictionary of International Law* (Oxford University Press, 3rd edition, 2009). More recently he has been writing about the *Germany v. Italy Immunity Case*, as well as the concept of responsibility to protect. He is International Tribunals editor of the *International and Comparative Law Quarterly* and book reviews editor of the *British Yearbook of International Law.*

Dr Robert P. Barnidge, Jr.

Robert P. Barnidge, Jr., is Lecturer and Coordinator of International Relations in the Department of History, Politics, and International Relations at Webster University. Prior to arriving at Webster, he was an Associate Professor and Honorary Visiting Fellow at OP Jindal Global University in India (2013) and Lecturer in the School of Law at the University of Reading (2007–2012). Robert has been a visiting lecturer at the Interdisciplinary Center Herzliya, Uppsala University, Koç University and The Hague University. He has been awarded academic fellowships from the British Academy, the Leverhulme Trust, Brandeis University, the Society of Legal Scholars, and the Foundation for Defense of Democracies. He is the author of *Non-State Actors and Terrorism:*

Applying the Law of State Responsibility and the Due Diligence Principle (TMC Asser Press, 2008) and editor of *The Liberal Way of War: Legal Perspectives* (Ashgate Publishing, 2013). His next monograph, which is provisionally entitled *Self-Determination, Statehood, and the Law of Negotiation: The Case of Palestine*, will be published in 2015 by Hart Publishing.

Dr Alison Bisset

Alison Bisset is a Lecturer in Law at the University of Reading, where she teaches International Children's Rights, International Human Rights Law and International Criminal Law. Her research arises in the area of transitional justice, with a particular focus on the theoretical and practical dilemmas of cooperation between different transitional justice mechanisms. Her doctoral research explored the coexistence of truth commissions and criminal courts, a topic on which she has published in the *Journal of International Criminal Justice* and *International Criminal Law Review*. She is the author of *Truth Commissions and Criminal Courts* (Cambridge University Press, 2012), the first multi-level analysis of the relationship between truth commissions and prosecutorial institutions.

Professor Malcolm D. Evans

Malcolm D. Evans, OBE, is Professor of Public International Law at Bristol University. He has worked in the area of torture prevention for over 20 years. He has written widely on the work and practice of the European Convention for the Prevention of Torture; since 2009 he has been an elected member of the UN Subcommittee for the Prevention of Torture (the SPT) and since 2011 has been its Chair. He is currently Vice Chair and Chair-elect of the Meeting of Chairs of Human Rights Treaty Bodies. He also works extensively on issues concerning the international protection of the freedom of religion or belief and since 2010 has been a member of the UK Foreign Secretary's Human Rights Advisory Group. He is the author or co-author of several books on the subject of torture, including *Preventing Torture* (Oxford University Press, 1997), *Combating Torture in Europe* (Council of Europe, 2001); and *The Optional Protocol to the UNCAT* (Oxford University Press, 2011), as well as many articles and chapters. He is also editor of *International Law* (4th edition, Oxford University Press, 2014) and General Editor of the *International and Comparative Law Quarterly*.

Dr James A. Green

James A. Green is Associate Professor of Public International Law at the University of Reading, where he has been a member of staff since 2006.

Previously, he studied for his doctorate at the University of Nottingham and, in 2005, was a visiting research scholar at the University of Michigan. He is the author of *The International Court of Justice and Self-Defence in International Law* (Hart Publishing, 2009), which was the winner of the Francis Lieber Prize, awarded by the American Society of International Law's Lieber Society, as well as the co-editor of *Conflict in the Caucasus: Implications for International Order* (with C.P.M. Waters, Palgrave, 2010). He has published numerous articles on international law in leading journals. James is co-editor-in-chief of the *Journal on the Use of Force and International Law* and is a member of the International Law Association Committee on the Use of Force. His next monograph, *The Persistent Objector Rule in International Law*, will be published in 2015 by Oxford University Press.

Dame Rosalyn Higgins

Rosalyn Higgins, DBE, QC, is the former President of the International Court of Justice (member 1995–2009; President 2006–2009). She was previously professor of international law at the University of London (1981–1995), and prior to that held positions at the Royal Institute of International Affairs, the London School of Economics and the University of Kent. Dame Rosalyn practiced public international law and petroleum law in the English courts and before various international courts and tribunals. Having held numerous adjudicative, academic and professional roles in an illustrious career, it is of particular note in the context of this volume that she was a member of the Committee on Human Rights under the International Covenant on Civil and Political Rights, including acting as its Special Rapporteur for new cases (member, 1985–1995; Special Rapporteur, 1989–1991). Dame Rosalyn has published numerous seminal works and articles on various aspects of public international law. She is the President of the British Institute of International and Comparative Law and, in October 2009, was appointed advisor on international law to the UK government's inquiry into the Iraq war ('Chilcot Inquiry').

Nora Honkala

Nora Honkala is a final-year PhD candidate at the University of Reading. Sandy Ghandhi was one of her supervisors until his retirement in September 2013. Nora's thesis examines the extent and the ways in which the domestic application of international law plays a role in the protection of the rights of asylum seeker women in forced marriage cases. Her doctoral research is funded by the Economic and Social Research Council. She holds an LLB from University of Melbourne (2006) and an LLM in International Law and World Order from University of Reading (2009).

David Leary

David Leary is a final-year PhD candidate at the University of Reading. Sandy Ghandhi was one of his supervisors. David's doctoral research focuses on the impact of counter-terrorism requirements dictated by the Security Council under Chapter VII of the UN Charter on the application of States' duties under international human rights and refugee law. He previously completed a degree in Law at the University of Bristol and an LLM in International Business Law at the University of Liverpool.

Professor Javaid Rehman

Javaid Rehman is a Professor of Islamic Law and Muslim Constitutionalism at Brunel Law School. He obtained an LLB (Hons) from the University of Reading and was then awarded LLM and PhD degrees from the University of Hull. He is a former Head of Brunel Law School, Brunel University, London (2009–2013) and currently directs the Brunel University Research Centre of Security, Media and Human Rights (SHRM). Professor Rehman is a member of the International Law Association (ILA) and is the co-rapporteur of the ILA's *Islamic Law and International Law Committee*. Professor Rehman has been invited to provide legal opinions in a number of high profile cases involving Islamic law, international terrorism and human rights law. He has written extensively on the subject of Islamic Law, international human rights and minority rights, with over one hundred publications. His recent works include *International Human Rights Law* (Longman, 2010); *Islamic State Practices, International Law and the Threat from Terrorism* (Hart Publishing, 2005); and *Religion, Human Rights and International Law* (with S.C. Breau, Brill, 2007).

Professor Sir Nigel Rodley

Nigel Rodley, KBE, PhD (Essex), is Professor of Law and Chair of the Human Rights Centre at the University of Essex where he has taught since 1990. He is the current Chairperson of the UN Human Rights Committee (member since 2001) and a former UN Special Rapporteur on Torture (1993–2001). He is President of the International Commission of Jurists. The Chair of the Board of Trustees of the International Centre for Prison Studies, he is also a Patron of the Freedom from Torture (former Medical Foundation for the Care of Victims of Torture and a Patron of REDRESS. He is a member of Foreign Secretary's Advisory Group on Human Rights (established November 2010). Sir Nigel is Co-Editor-in-Chief of the *Israel Law Review*. His publications include the landmark and now standard work *The Treatment of Prisoners under International Law* (with Matt Pollard, Oxford University Press, 3rd edition, 2009).

Professor Christopher P.M. Waters

Christopher Waters is Professor at the Faculty of Law, University of Windsor, Canada. He joined the Faculty in 2007 and served as Associate Dean from 2009–2012. His previous academic post was at the School of Law of the University of Reading. In 2012–2013 he was a visiting scholar at the Centre d'Etudes et de Recherche Internationales et Communautaires at Aix-Marseille Université. Dr Waters teaches and researches on various aspects of public international law, with an emphasis on international humanitarian law. His publications include the following books: *A Guide to International Law Careers* (with A. Smit, British Institute of International and Comparative Law, 2nd edition, 2014); *Conflict in the Caucasus: Implications for International Order* (with J.A. Green, Palgrave 2010); *British and Canadian Perspectives on International Law* (Martinus Nijhoff, 2006); *The State of Law in the South Caucasus* (Palgrave, 2005); and *Counsel in the Caucasus: Professionalization and Law in Georgia* (Martinus Nijhoff, 2004). He has extensive field experience with international organizations in Eastern Europe and the former Soviet Union.

Introduction

Christopher P.M. Waters

1 Ghandhi the Generalist

This book brings together established and emerging scholars to honour Professor Sandy Ghandhi on his retirement. It does so through a series of essays probing the framework and adequacy of international human rights adjudication. Our emphasis on human rights adjudication is inspired by Ghandhi's impressive scholarship, as well as his teaching and advocacy, in this field.[1] However, it should be pointed out that while Ghandhi is best known for his human rights work, he has published in a variety of areas. These areas include general public international law, tort law, damages, European Union law, marital rape, blasphemy, family law, environmental law, highway law, water law and employment law. That Ghandhi's intellectual curiosity has taken him across diverse legal fields is perhaps most evident in the subject matter of a case comment which he co-wrote with his spouse, fellow law professor Jennifer James, on the protection of cultural property. The case involved the recovery of cultural artefacts where one of the claimants was the Sivalingam, "a sculpted stone phallus from a defunct temple."[2] Though the Sivalingam did not appear in his later scholarship, Ghandhi's generalist base allowed him to draw jurisprudential connections, including in his human rights scholarship, which others might have missed. For example, in a comment on the *Al Skeini* case at the European Court of Human Rights (EctHR) on the extraterritorial reach of the European Convention on Human Rights (ECHR),[3] Ghandhi wrote: "[t]his appears to be a case where the Court, faced with an entirely new factual

1 While this book focuses on Ghandhi's scholarship, we would be remiss in not pointing out that his human rights work also took place in numerous teaching and advocacy fora. At the University of Reading he taught international human rights to countless undergraduate and graduate students and his edited compilation of human rights instruments for law students reached thousands more: Sandy Ghandhi, *Blackstone's International Human Rights Documents* (8th ed., United Kingdom: Oxford University Press, 2012). Many of the contributors to this book are former students or mentees. In terms of advocacy he laboured, without fanfare, with several organisations, including the Human Rights Committee of the Law Society of England and Wales.

2 Sandy Ghandhi and Jennifer James, "The God That Won," *International Journal of Cultural Property* 1 (1992): 369, 370.

3 *Al Skeini v. United Kingdom*, 53 EHRR 18 (ECHR 2011).

 | DOI 10.1163/9789004261181_002

matrix, felt bound to find in favour of the applicants on the basis of vulnerability for reasons of broad Council of Europe Public policy by straining both logic and precedent."[4] Drawing an analogy to a decision where the English Court of Appeal expanded the notion of negligence on subjective policy grounds (in a manner rejected by the House of Lords in subsequent cases), he added: "[t]he approach of the Grand Chamber to dealing with the role of policy factors in determining liability in novel factual situations is remarkably similar to the approach adopted by Lord Denning MR in *Dutton v. Bognor Regis Urban District Council*..."[5]

2 Ghandhi's Approach to International Human Rights Adjudication

Turning now to the theme of this volume, it is necessary to define the scope of what we intend by the term "adjudication" in the human rights context. Lon Fuller defined adjudication broadly. In a posthumously published paper, he wrote:

> [I]t includes a father attempting to assume the role of judge in a dispute between his children over possession of a toy. At the other extreme it embraces the most formal and even awesome exercises of adjudicative power...[I]ts application is not restricted to tribunals functioning as part of an established government. It includes adjudicative bodies which owe their powers to the consent of the litigants expressed in an agreement of submission, as in labor relations and in international law.[6]

Similarly, this book addresses international human rights adjudication in a broad sense. Although, as noted above, Ghandhi had a generalist base, his primary and abiding interest was human rights protection through legal institutions. In particular, he was interested in what remedy would be available when a human rights breach occurred. Dinah Shelton has pointed out that the term

4 Sandy Ghandhi, "*Al Skeini* and the Extra-Territorial Application of the European Convention on Human Rights," in *Judge and Jurist: Essays in Memory of Lord Rodger of Earlsferry*, edited by Andrew Burrows, David Johnston and Reinhard Zimmermann (Oxford: OUP, 2013), 575, 582.

5 *Ibid.*, at note 36.

6 Lon L. Fuller, "The Forms and Limits of Adjudication," *Harvard Law Review* 92, 2 (1978): 353, 353–354.

"remedy" has two meanings, one procedural and one substantive: "[i]n the first sense, remedies are the processes by which arguable claims of human rights violations are heard and decided, whether by courts administrative agencies, or other competent bodies. The second notion of remedies refers to the outcome of the proceedings, the relief afforded to the successful claimant."[7] Ghandhi was particularly interested in the first, *procedural*, notion of remedy, although much of his work, including his writing on the death penalty and interim measures of protection, crossed these conceptual boundaries. Throughout his career, Ghandhi's scholarship consistently asked an academic lawyer's questions: through what mechanism or process can international human rights standards be made real? How can an individual or group access human rights justice?

To address these questions, Ghandhi took a keen and detailed view of the institutional design and procedures of bodies charged with adjudicating human rights. Procedure is relatively neglected in the legal academy,[8] but Ghandhi was of the view that proper procedures made all the difference when it came to both the protection of an individual complainant and the credibility of the adjudicative body in the eyes of States and other actors. It must be stressed that Ghandhi's view of processes extended beyond the rules of procedure and the working methods of human rights institutions, important as those features are. He was convinced that careful, well-reasoned decision making by human rights bodies, along the lines of a sound common law court's reasoning, would result in greater long-term compliance by States with their obligations. Accordingly, his analysis would often probe the quality of jurisprudence.[9] His scrutiny of the jurisprudence was not so much to better understand the normative scope of a particular right, although he was interested in that too, but rather to gauge how well the institution could further human protection within the confines of the relevant treaty or legislation.

---

7 Dinah Shelton, *Remedies in Rights Law* (Oxford: OUP, 2005), 7.

8 Jeremy Waldron, "The Rule of Law and the Importance of Procedure," in *Getting to the Rule of Law*, edited by James E. Fleming (New York: New York University Press, 2011), 3–31.

9 For example, in his book, P.R. Ghandhi, *The Human Rights Committee and the Right of Individual Communication: Law and Practice* (Aldershot: Ashgate Publishing Co, 1998), 395 [hereinafter *The Human Rights Committee*], Ghandhi wrote that, while the Human Rights Committee is not a court, "it is well aware that, for its authority under the O.P. to be respected by both States Parties and authors alike, it must be seen to be acting in a manner which approximates, as nearly as possible to the way in which a court acts, when exercising its functions under the O.P. Accordingly, the Committee strives to make its decisions conform to a judicial pattern, to produce cogent *rationes decidendi* and develop a consistent jurisprudence."

As is clear from its chapter titles, this volume does not confine itself to the adjudication of human rights in any particular human rights institution or system (such as, for example, that of the United Nations). Rather, it encompasses adjudication emanating from all manner of courts, boards, commissions, and treaty bodies which are charged with interpreting and applying international human rights law. Ghandhi's view has been that human rights protection needs to be pressed on every adjudicative front reasonably available. While cognizant of the concerns about the fragmentation of international law, Ghandhi suggests that human rights adjudication as a part of a global conversation across legal institutions, including within the United Nations system, is a workable way forward.[10]

Ghandhi is perhaps best known for his work on the United Nations Human Rights Committee, the treaty enforcement mechanism established under the International Covenant on Civil and Political Rights (ICCPR).[11] The Committee, a body of independent experts, considers State reports on compliance with the ICCPR, which currently has 167 parties, and issues General Comments on thematic issues. The Committee also considers individual complaints emanating from the 114 parties to the First Optional Protocol to the ICCPR.[12] The ICCPR system has been described as "the most serious machinery ever for the realization of human rights."[13] Not surprisingly, therefore, the ICCPR and the Committee have received a great deal of scholarly attention.[14]

Although now two and a half decades old, Ghandhi's book, *The Human Rights Committee and the Right of Individual Communication: Law and Practice*, remains a leading text on the Committee and the right of individuals to petition the Committee following the exhaustion of domestic remedies.[15] Various

---

10 Sandy Ghandhi, "Human Rights and the International Court of Justice in the *Ahmadou Sadio Diallo* Case," *Human Rights Law Review* 11, 3 (2011): 536.

11 Office of the High Commissioner for Human Rights, *International Covenant on Civil and Political Rights*, adopted by U.N. General Assembly resolution 2200A (XXI), New York, 16 December 1966.

12 Office of the High Commissioner for Human Rights, *Optional Protocol to the International Covenant on Civil and Political Rights*, adopted by U.N. General Assembly resolution 2200A (XXI), New York, 16 December 1966.

13 Alfred de Zayas, "The Potential for the United States Joining the Covenant Family," *Georgia Journal of International and Comparative Law* 20 (1990): 299, 309–310.

14 Two recent studies are Yogesh Tyagi, *The UN Human Rights Committee Practice and Procedure* (Cambridge: Cambridge University Press, 2011); and Jakob Th. Möller and Alfred de Zayas, *The United Nations Human Rights Committee Case Law 1977–2008: A Handbook* (Kehl: N.P. Engel, 2009).

15 *The Human Rights Committee*, *supra* note 9. For a recent study citing Ghandhi's book see Tyagi, *supra* note 14, 4, at note 20.

aspects of the Committee's procedures, doctrines and jurisprudence arising from individual complaints – and Ghandhi argued early on that "jurisprudence" was the appropriate term for the Committee's views in these cases – were also parsed in a series of articles spanning over three decades. Throughout his career he was simultaneously interested in the jurisprudence and procedures of domestic courts and regional human rights courts. He paid particular attention to the European Court of Human Rights and the relationship between Strasbourg and British courts. His early writing in this area was critical of British judges' failures to grapple with EctHR jurisprudence.[16] However, after the relevance of the Strasbourg Court's jurisprudence was more firmly entrenched in the UK, Ghandhi did not hesitate to criticise Strasbourg and defend the jurisprudence of the House of Lords where warranted. Most notably, in the comment on *Al Skeini*, mentioned above, Ghandhi departed from his usual understated language and, in decrying the lack of coherent guidance given to national courts on the subject of the extraterritorial reach of the European Convention, described the EctHR as speaking with a "forked tongue."[17]

In the last decade or so, Ghandhi has focused on the contributions to human rights protection made by the International Court of Justice (ICJ). He viewed the Court as having real potential to further individual and group rights protection, despite the Court's 1945 inter-State design. In arriving at this cautiously optimistic position he took the long view, as he so often did: why should the ICJ not make these contributions, he asked, when the Permanent Court of International Justice (PCIJ) had done so before it with respect to minority protections?[18] His optimism was also spurred by the presence on the bench of jurists with extensive human rights experience, including Thomas Buergenthal and Ghandhi's mentor, Dame Rosalyn Higgins.[19] He had studied Higgins'

---

16 See, for example, Sandy Ghandhi, "Judicial Review and Prison Governors," *The Modern Law Review* 48, 3 (1985): 348.

17 Ghandhi, *supra* note 4, at 590.

18 Ghandhi, *supra* note 10, at 527. Ghandhi's historical bent could also be seen in his extensive use of *travaux préparatoires.* Using the *travaux,* for instance, he argued that the intent of the drafters of the International Convention on the Elimination of All Forms of Racial Discrimination (CERD) was that the treaty be given only territorial application; see Sandy Ghandhi, "The International Court of Justice and the Provisional Measures Order in the *Georgia v. Russian Federation* Case," in *Conflict in the Caucasus: Implications For International Legal Order*, edited by James A. Green and Christopher P.M. Waters (Basingstoke: Palgrave Macmillan, 2010), 80–113.

19 See also Sandy Ghandhi, "Avena and Other Mexican Nationals (*Mexico v. United States of America*), Provisional Measures, Order of 5 February 2003," *International and Comparative Law Quarterly* 53, 3 (2004): 738, 745–746.

jurisprudence when she was a member of the Human Rights Committee and would now analyse her jurisprudence as a member, and then President, of the World Court.[20] Even in unattributed decisions he would see the trail and evolution of Higgins' contributions to human rights jurisprudence.[21] It is a nice piece of symmetry, therefore, as well as an honour, to have Dame Rosalyn write the Foreword to this book.

While not opposed to an International Human Rights Court or, more modestly, some standing amalgamation of the UN treaty bodies, Ghandhi is ultimately a pragmatist, happy to explore human rights adjudication wherever it has a reasonable prospect of furthering human protection. He wrote in 1978 that "the creation of such a court by the international community would represent an enormous achievement."[22] However, after pointing out the obstacles the creation of such a court faced, he continued: "[e]ven if it is thought that the establishment of such a court is both desirable and an attainable objective, it is suggested that until such a time arrived, the Committee is more than capable of protecting the rights of individuals at the international level."[23] Indeed, for Ghandhi and others, the Committee was already a quasi-judicial body adjudicating rights in a meaningful way (and, perhaps, although he did not say it explicitly, in a manner akin to an international human rights court).[24] Two

---

20 Indeed, in the Foreword to *The Human Rights Committee, supra* note 9 at xxiv, he writes that the "inspiration for this book came from an admiration of the contribution of Her Excellency Dame Rosalyn Higgins to the Human Rights Committee."

21 J. Craig Barker and Sandy Ghandhi, "International Court of Justice: *Application on the Elimination of All Forms of Racial Discrimination (Georgia v. Russian Federation)*, Provisional Measures Order of 15 October 2008," *International and Comparative Law Quarterly* 58, 3 (2009): 713.

22 *The Human Rights Committee, supra* note 9 at 409.

23 *Ibid.*, By contrast, for a damning assessment of the utility of UN Human Rights bodies, see M. Cherif Bassiouni, "A Critical Introduction Assessment of the UN Human Rights Mechanisms," in *New Challenges for the un Human Rights Machinery: What Future for the un Treaty Body System and the Human Rights Council Procedures?*, edited by M. Cherif Bassiouni and William A. Schabas (Cambridge: Intersentia, 2011).

24 See Sandy Ghandhi, "The Human Rights Committee and Interim Measures of Relief," *Canterbury Law Review* 13, 2 (2007): 203, at 219. See also Lord Millett's dicta in *Tangiora v. Wellington District Legal Services Committee*, 1 NZLR 17 (NZPC 2000), at 21, that the Judicial Committee of the Privy Council was "not wholly persuaded that the function of the Human Rights Committee is not adjudicative...Moreover, there is much force in the provisional view...that its functions are adjudicative...[W]hen it reaches a final view that a State party is in breach of its obligations under the Covenant, it makes a definitive and final ruling which is determinative of an issue that has been referred to it."

decades later, in an article on the individual petition mechanism under the Convention to Eliminate All Forms of Discrimination Against Women (CEDAW), he did not downplay the problems faced in the UN system but noted wryly that an International Human Rights Court still did not exist despite much discussion. Meanwhile, Ghandhi was content to commend the CEDAW Committee for incrementally developing "a congruent and unified jurisprudence" with the Human Rights Committee, the Committee on Enforced Disappearances and the Committee against Torture.[25] Given the lack of ambition shown by recent intergovernmental efforts to reform the UN treaty bodies, Ghandhi's praise for at least an organic congruence between the bodies seems prescient.[26]

Ghandhi was fond of quoting from a lecture of Sir Hersch Lauterpacht, given at Chatham House, London on 27 May 1941, that "the protection of human personality and of its fundamental rights is the ultimate purpose of all law, national and international."[27] Accordingly, it is fitting that the present volume includes chapters devoted to human rights protection in a number of different institutional contexts, ranging from the ICJ and the Human Rights Committee to truth commissions and NAFTA arbitration tribunals. If an international court of human rights is ever created, one suspects Ghandhi will celebrate for a moment before quickly asking whether the new court's jurisprudence will be logical, clear, and carefully build on the work of courts and human rights bodies which came before it.

3 The Content of This Volume

Sir Nigel Rodley's contribution follows this introduction. Sir Nigel, who currently chairs the Human Rights Committee, looks at the use by the ICJ of the UN human rights treaty bodies' jurisprudence. He suggests that on the limited number of occasions where the Court has dealt squarely with matters coming within the ambit of a human rights treaty, the relevant treaty body's views have

25 Sandy Ghandhi, "Practice and Procedure of Dispute Settlement in Individual Communication Cases within the Human Rights Committee and the Committee on Elimination of Discrimination against Women; Congruence or Conflict?," in *International Law and Dispute Settlement; New Problems and Techniques*, edited by Duncan French, Matthew Saul and Nigel White (Oxford: Hart Publishing, 2010), 111, at 142.

26 G.A. Res. 68/268, U.N. Doc. A/RES/68/268 (Apr. 9, 2014) ("Strengthening and enhancing the effective functioning of the human rights treaty body system").

27 Ghandhi, *supra* note 19, at 746.

been given due deference by the Court. Perhaps this is not surprising given the presence of human rights experts on the bench and the quality of the jurisprudence emanating from the treaty bodies (at least with respect to "views" on individual petitions and general comments – Rodley concedes frankly that concluding observations on State reports are sometimes hastily assembled). For Rodley, the deference shown by the ICJ – which of course retains ultimate authority to establish its own authoritative position on a matter – has helped maintain the coherence of global human rights jurisprudence.

If both Ghandhi and Rodley have suggested in passing that the presence on the ICJ of human rights experts has helped the Court taking human rights law seriously, Chapter 2 provides us with an analysis of the contributions of one such ICJ judge in particular. In a piece of what might be termed "critical appreciation," Robert P. Barnidge, Jr. examines the jurisprudence of Antônio Augusto Cançado Trindade at the World Court, with focused analysis of the judge's views on diplomatic protection. Barnidge suggests that this jurist's natural law orientation to give primacy to human rights protection over procedural, formalist or substantive State-centric doctrines is both inspiring and limited in terms of its practical significance and, ultimately, conceptual rigour.

As with the debate over the place of human rights vis à vis State-centric notions of diplomatic protection, some observers have portrayed substantive human rights as being in conflict with State immunities. Craig Barker tackles this alleged conflict in Chapter 3. He does this by revisiting the *Pinochet* litigation – and a joint article that he wrote with Ghandhi – a decade and a half later to ask whether the case was the "game changer" for the advancement of human rights that it was alleged by some to have been. Barker and Ghandhi argued in 2000 that, in fact, the *Pinochet* case was ultimately decided on a narrow point of English law and that attempts to use the case as precedent for the substantive triumph of human rights norms over immunities would fail.[28] Barker suggests that recent jurisprudence from the ICJ and national courts has indeed shown a reluctance to further scale back the notion of State immunity, a doctrine that continues to play a useful role in the ordering of international affairs. Barker goes on to suggest that upholding immunities does not mean downgrading the fight against impunity. His sympathy with the fight against impunity is clear – and he advocates for strengthened human rights mechanisms to aid in this fight – but human rights cannot automatically trump immunities.

28 Sandy Ghandhi and J. Craig Barker "The Pinochet Judgment: Analysis and Implications," *Indian Journal of International Law* 40, 4 (2000): 657.

Another area where human rights have not automatically trumped – despite overreaching claims to the contrary – is with respect to the UN Security Council's targeted sanctions regime. The regime has led to sanctions being imposed against individuals through a precautionary approach to terrorism. In practice, this means that individuals are sometimes listed without adequate procedural protection from arbitrariness and, therefore, it is hard to argue that the regime is human rights compliant. Nonetheless, suggests David Leary in Chapter 4, despite some judicial decisions imposing human rights obligations on governments implementing Security Council sanctions – and pointed *obiter* criticisms of the sanctions regime – no high level court has purported to judicially review the Security Council's actions. Despite the absence of a direct judicial challenge to the Security Council's authority, however, there remains a lack of coherence in terms of the obligations on States to both implement Security Council resolutions and maintain their international, regional and national human rights obligations.

Returning to the theme of dialogue between legal regimes – and the possibility of a lack of coherence in human rights protection that that entails – Tawhida Ahmed in Chapter 5 examines the relationship between the European Union and the ECHR. Building on her previous work in examining the extent to which the ECtHR has required the EU to respect ECHR standards of human rights protection, here she asks the inverse; to what extent has the European Court of Justice ensured the protection of ECHR standards? While recognising that a human rights protection gap between the two regimes is more than theoretically possible, she comes to the counter-intuitive conclusion that "at present, EU law and adjudication in the EU, better protects ECHR rights in situations involving EU law, than the ECtHR does itself for its own instrument."

One area where a global conversation on human rights appears to have broken down is with respect to the human rights of sexual minorities. As Javaid Rehman points out in Chapter 6, States with Muslim-majority populations have retained penal sanctions against homosexual activity despite gradually expanded protection for sexual minorities on the international human rights plane. With a focus on Pakistan, Rehman highlights the lack of judicial protection for sexual minorities domestically and the oppositional role Pakistan has played with respect to the advancement of sexual minority rights at the international level. At the same time, Rehman points out, one sexual minority in Pakistan, the transgendered *hijra* community, has received limited protection from Pakistan's Supreme Court, albeit that the protection has come through concern for a specific community of "disordered" individuals rather than protection for sexual minorities generally. Still, this jurisprudence with respect to *hijras* cautions against making definitive statements about the future of LGBT rights in the Muslim world.

Another group of vulnerable persons whose protection remains incomplete and contested on the international level is female refugees. Gender of course is not an enumerated ground of discrimination in the 1951 Refugee Convention but has gradually found recognition internationally and domestically. Even where this has happened, however, as Nora Honkala points out in Chapter 7, women's experiences have been given short shrift in the refugee determination process. With focus on the question of an internal relocation option for women refugees claiming status in the United Kingdom, Honkala argues that adjudicators have often ignored the fact that women refugees are more likely to be fleeing non-State actors than men and that what is a "reasonable" internal flight alternative has not been considered in a gender-sensitive manner.

While most of the chapters in this book are focused on treaty law, my co-editor James A. Green, in Chapter 8, examines customary international human rights in the context of the persistent objector rule. With a focus on US practice – including in the NAFTA context – Green argues that while it is clear that there can be no valid persistent objection to a *jus cogens* norm, overreaching attempts to expand the list of peremptory norms, or hold that no customary human rights norms can be subject to a persistent objection, are simply not borne out in law. Green concludes that, as a social fact, this state of the law is not as problematic as it may seem since States will generally not persistently object to "ordinary" customary international human rights law in the long run.

The last two chapters of the book look at alternatives (or, at least, co-existing parallel models) to decision-oriented human rights adjudication models. In Chapter 9, Alison Bisset considers the role of truth commissions in transitional States. She argues that these mechanisms are well situated to contribute to the transitional justice objectives of "truth, justice, reparation and non-repetition." Despite their frequent use since the early 1970s, however, truth mechanisms are being overshadowed by the current focus on criminal justice and the International Criminal Court (ICC) in particular. In light of the limited objectives of criminal trials – and the limited successes of the ICC – she argues for renewed focus on truth mechanisms as one important, victim-oriented way to address past human rights violations and prevent future violations.

In the final contribution to this book, Malcolm D. Evans continues with this theme of prevention in Chapter 10. Evans argues that the focus on remedial decision-making following human rights violations has overshadowed the preventative roles of human rights treaty bodies. Using the torture context, however, he argues that preventative human rights engagement with domestic actors – including through providing tailored, practical guidance for domestic officials rather than simply articulating standards – can lead to prevention of violations in the first instance, which is, after all, a key goal of all human rights protection regimes.

Ghandhi recently described a judgement of the late Lord Rodger of Earlsferry, his undergraduate tutor at New College, Oxford, as evidencing "an acute legal brain."[29] "It comprises," Ghandhi added, "a penetrating, carefully reasoned, and coherent analysis."[30] Ghandhi's writings share these qualities with the jurisprudence of Lord Rodger – an academic lawyer *par excellence* – and in the following chapters we aim modestly to honour that approach.

---

29 Ghandhi, *supra* note 4, at 587.

30 *Ibid.*

CHAPTER 1

The International Court of Justice and Human Rights Treaty Bodies

Sir Nigel Rodley

It is a matter of deep satisfaction to me to be invited to contribute this essay to honour the work of Sandy Ghandhi. The title of this book could not have been more apposite in the light of his consistent scholarship on the work of courts and quasi-judicial bodies mandated to adjudicate issues under international human rights law. As a member and current Chairperson of the UN Human Rights Committee (HRC), a body whose activity has been the subject of so much of Sandy's shrewd, authoritative analysis, it is a privilege to be able to acknowledge the value of his contribution in this way.

* * *

It is often forgotten that, as the preeminent judicial authority of general international law, the International Court of Justice (ICJ or World Court) is also a forum for the adjudication of international human rights law as much as any other area of international law. In fact, from its earliest days, the Court was called upon to address human rights issues, indeed consider the scope of applicability of the first post-World War II international human rights treaty: the Genocide Convention.[1] Equally rarely noted is the fact that the compromissory clauses of some human rights treaties, including a majority of the nine

1 Convention on the Prevention and Punishment of the Crime of Genocide, 9 December 1948, 78 U.N.T.S. 277; *Reservations to the Convention on Genocide*, advisory opinion, 1951 I.C.J. 15. See generally, Gentian Zyberi, *The Humanitarian Face of the International Court of Justice: Its Contribution to Interpreting and Developing International Human Rights and Humanitarian Rules and Principles* (Antwerp: Intersentia, 2008); Egon Schwelb, "The International Court of Justice and the Human Rights Clauses of the Charter," *American Journal of International Law* 66 (1972): 337; Nigel Rodley, "Human Rights and Humanitarian Intervention: The Case Law of the World Court," *International and Comparative Law Quarterly* 38 (1989): 321; Rosalyn Higgins, "Human Rights in the ICJ," *Leiden Journal of International Law* 20 (2007): 745; and Bruno Simma, "Mainstreaming Human Rights: The Contribution of the ICJ," *Journal of International Dispute Settlement* 3 (2012): 7.

 | DOI 10.1163/9789004261181_003

"core" human rights treaties, render the Court itself as a human rights treaty body,[2] although in only one case has it acted as such, namely *Belgium v. Senegal*.[3]

The International Human Rights Committee of the International Law Association has considered the relationship in a recent study prepared by its Co-Rapporteur, Dr Eva Rieter, that has been of considerable assistance for the preparation of the present chapter.[4] The decision of the Committee in 2008 to undertake that study was prophetic, as until then there had only been one case in which the ICJ had directly considered the practice of a treaty body, namely the *Wall* opinion in 2004.[5] Since then, there have been three others, two of them involving extensive consideration of UN treaty body practice: the *Diallo* case,[6] the *Belgium v. Senegal* (or *Hissène Habré*) case,[7] and the *IFAD* case.[8]

Two questions should be illuminated by our inquiry. One relates to the juridical status of the outputs of the treaty bodies. The other relates to concerns about the possible fragmentation of different fields of international law.

2 International Convention on the Elimination of All Forms of Racial Discrimination, 21 December 1965, 660 U.N.T.S. 195, Art. 22; Convention against Torture and Other Cruel, Inhuman or Degrading Treatment or Punishment, 10 December 1984, 1465 U.N.T.S. 85, Art. 30; Convention on the Elimination of All Forms of Discrimination against Women, 18 December 1979, 1249 U.N.T.S. 13, Art. 29; International Convention on the Protection of the Rights of All Migrant Workers and Members of their Families, 18 December 1990, 2220 U.N.T.S. 3, Art. 92; and International Convention for the Protection of All Persons from Enforced Disappearance, 20 December 2006, 2715 U.N.T.S. 1, Art. 42.

3 *Questions relating to the Obligation to Prosecute or Extradite* (*Belgium v. Senegal*) (*Hissène Habré*), judgment, 2012, I.C.J 422.

4 International Law Association, Washington DC Conference (2014), Draft International Human Rights Committee Final Report, available at http://www.ila-hq.org/en/committees/index.cfm/cid/1027.

5 *Legal Consequences of the Construction of a Wall in the Occupied Palestinian Territory*, advisory opinion, 2004, I.C.J 136.

6 *Diallo* (*Republic of Guinea v. Democratic Republic of the Congo*), preliminary objections, 2007, I.C.J 582; *Ahmadou Sadio Diallo* (*Republic of Guinea v. Democratic Republic of the Congo*), merits, judgment, 2010, I.C.J 639; *Ahmadou Sadio Diallo* (*Republic of Guinea v. Democratic Republic of the Congo*), compensation, judgment, 2012, I.C.J 324.

7 *Hissène Habré*, *supra* note 3.

8 *Judgment No 2867 of the Administrative Tribunal of the International Labour Organization upon a Complaint Filed against the International Fund for Agricultural Development*, advisory opinion, 2012, I.C.J 10.

1 The Juridical Status of Treaty Body Outputs

It is self-evident that the UN treaty bodies are not courts and, accordingly, that their outputs are not of themselves binding on States. The principal outputs of these bodies are concluding observations emitted as the outcome of the review of States' periodic reports,[9] "views" adopted by way of findings on the validity of otherwise of individual complaints,[10] and general comments or recommendations addressed to all States parties reflecting the treaty body's view of the latters' obligations under the treaty in question.

For a number of reasons, *concluding observations* need to be treated with caution. They are adopted under extreme time pressure. Covering the whole range of a State party's commitments under each treaty, the treaty body typically has only a matter of hours to agree a draft text produced by one of its members. Further, the language used may leave some elements of imprecision. Thus, the "concerns" expressed may not always be clear as to whether a violation is being found. Similarly, the recommendations flowing from these concerns may not always restrict themselves to those measures the treaty body considers to be obligatory: they may sometimes, for example, reflect "best practice" as a means of avoiding future violations. Moreover, the observations have to be adopted by consensus, with no means of permitting individual opinions of members to be placed on record. This limits the amount of specificity that can be framed in the resulting text. So, increasingly, do word limits imposed by the General Assembly.[11] Of course, this does not mean that the contents of concluding observations are simply ad hoc propositions. Typically, a number of countries will evince similar problems and, with the support of the Secretariat, Committees are able to mine previous approaches – and even language – so that like may be treated as like. So, there may still be genuine precedential value in concluding observations. It is this writer's sense that concluding observations produced by the HRC generally represent the highest common factor, rather than the lowest common denominator.

The *"views"* in individual cases are inevitably a more reliable and authoritative guide to the opinion of the Committee. This is because on all but the most

9 Typically, treaty bodies review reports of States parties to their treaties and issue evaluations (concluding observations) on the basis of the reviews.

10 Most treaty bodies now have an optional procedure, whereby a State party may, either by adhering to an optional protocol or depositing a special declaration, accept the right of individuals to communicate complaints to the relevant treaty bodies which may then adjudicate the complaint.

11 General Assembly resolution 68/268 (2014), ¶ 15.

straightforward issues, the Committee will generally take as much time as it needs to finalise a "view" that reflects a careful examination of the facts and a conscientiously arrived at application of the law.[12] As the HRC has put it in its General Comment No. 33:

> While the function of the Human Rights Committee in considering individual communications is not, as such, that of a judicial body, the views issued by the Committee under the Optional Protocol exhibit some important characteristics of a judicial decision. They are arrived at in a judicial spirit, including the impartiality and independence of Committee members, the considered interpretation of the language of the Covenant, and the determinative character of the decisions...The views of the Committee under the Optional Protocol represent an authoritative determination by the organ established under the Covenant itself charged with the interpretation of that instrument. These views derive their character, and the importance which attaches to them, from the integral role of the Committee under both the Covenant and the Optional Protocol.[13]

This language indicates the Committee's understanding that States parties are not free simply to dismiss its findings and the remedies that it indicates. Sometimes a State party may refuse to accept the views in a specific case, for example, because of disagreement on the facts or law. The disagreement may be the result of failure to participate in the process at all, or to participate sufficiently so as to clarify its analysis of the facts of the State party's view of the law. Here the Committee reminded States that they are obliged "to act in good faith, both in their participation in the procedures under the Optional Protocol and in relation to the Covenant itself."[14] Implicit here is the understanding that while States may have the right to disagree with the Committee's determination of the facts and interpretation of the law, the good faith principle requires them to have fully conveyed the relevant information and legal analysis during

12 1.3 hours has been established by the General Assembly, based on the average time taken by the Human Rights Committee; *ibid.*, ¶ 26 b; evidently the average takes account of routine cases, often dismissed as inadmissible, as well as discontinued cases; many take much longer.

13 UN Human Rights Committee, *General Comment No. 33: Obligations of States Parties under the Optional Protocol to the International Covenant on Civil and Political Rights*, 25 June 2009, U.N. Doc. CCPR/C/GC/33, at ¶¶ 11–13.

14 *Ibid.*, ¶ 15.

the deliberative process and subsequently to explain the basis for its refusal to comply with the Committee's "views."

Of course, this is not just a matter of the respect due to a body established under the treaty in question and elected by the States parties. For the Committee, it is a duty owed to the other States parties, so that they too may arrive at an appreciation of the well-foundedness or otherwise of the position advanced by the State party in question. Again, as the Committee has put it elsewhere, States' obligations under the Covenant apply *erga omnes* and, accordingly, "every State Party has a legal interest in the performance by every other State Party of its obligations."[15] In any event, the Committee will treat earlier cases as precedents to be invoked in subsequent ones, in the same manner as a judicial body. Certainly the UN Secretariat classifies the "views" as "jurisprudence," a word that has come to mean, not only legal theory (the traditional understanding), but is now internationally used in the Civil Law sense of what is still typically called "case law" in the Common Law system.[16]

The general comments of treaty bodies are also intended to provide authoritative guidance on the nature of States parties' obligations under specific provisions of the treaty (or protocols). Certainly the practice of the HRC has reflected an attempt to codify its accumulated practice, often over decades. Typically, HRC general comments will be the result of a careful drafting process: a rapporteur will prepare a draft that will be considered, paragraph by paragraph, by the plenary body. After a "first reading" the provisionally agreed text will be made available for "stakeholders" (notably States parties, other IGOs, other treaty bodies and civil society) to react to. A second reading will then take place to consider these contributions, as well as second thoughts of members, with a view to finalising the text of the new general comment. The overall drafting process may thus take some two years of deliberations.

The ensuing general comment will then constitute an important reference source for the Committee, capable of being invoked in the context of concluding observations and in the "views" arrived at in individual cases. The significance of the general comments is also attested to by the intense interest of

15 UN Human Rights Committee, *General Comment No. 31: The Nature of the General Legal Obligation Imposed on States Parties to the Covenant*, 26 May 2004, U.N. Doc. CCPR/C/21/Rev.1/Add.13, ¶ 2. Here the Committee is acknowledging a notion famously articulated in the ICJ's *Barcelona Traction Case* (*Belgium v. Spain*), 1970, I.C.J. 3, at ¶ 33.

16 See OHCHR treaty bodies website: http://www.ohchr.org/EN/HRBodies/Pages/TreatyBodies.aspx.

States and civil society in proposing what should be the subject of the Committee's next general comment.[17]

2 Fragmentation?

One of the debates that have in recent years engaged international lawyers is whether international law has somehow spawned a series of sub-fields that have developed according to sub-field-specific doctrines, rather than in accordance with the normal doctrines of general international law. This is known as the "fragmentation debate."[18] The various sub-fields of international law considered in this debate are mainly products of the post-World War II world. They include the law of outer space, environmental law and human rights. It is natural that human rights in particular would elicit fears of a kind of subject-specific secessionism. The very nature of human rights law required it to turn on its head fundamentally understood precepts relating to domestic jurisdiction.

The traditional mission of international law was to resolve disputes of a transnational nature. Avoidance of concern with what went on inside a State was seen as a condition *sine qua non* for such a project. For a State's system of governance to become a matter of "international concern" was to put grit in the oil that was designed to lubricate the issue of transnational tension. Yet this is the essence of the universal human rights project that the Charter of the United Nations instigated.[19] In recent years, the potential tension between

17 See, for example, the October 2013 interactive dialogue in in the Third Committee of the General Assembly with the Chairperson of the Human Rights Committee (the present writer), where delegations suggested a new Committee general comment on Art. 17 (right to privacy) and the Report to the Human Rights Council of the Special Rapporteur on Extrajudicial, Summary or Arbitrary Executions, U.N. Doc A/HRC/26/36 (2014), ¶ 119 (suggesting one on the right to life).

18 Martti Koskenniemi, "Fragmentation of International Law: Difficulties Arising from the Diversification and Expansion of International Law," Report of the Study Group of the International Law Commission, finalised by Martti Koskenniemi, A/CN.4/L.682. See also: James Crawford, "Chance, Order, Change: The Course of International Law," in 365 *Collected Courses of The Hague Academy of International Law* (Leiden: Martinus Nijhoff Publishers, 2013), 9, 205–229; Mads Andenas, "The Centre Reasserting Itself: From Fragmentation to Transformation of International Law," in *Volume in Honor of Pär Hallström*, edited by Mattias Derlén and Johan Lindholm (Uppsala: Iustus, 2012); and Philippa Webb, *International Judicial Integration and Fragmentation* (Oxford: Oxford University Press, 2013).

19 Nigel Rodley, "International Human Rights Law," in *International* Law, edited by Malcolm Evans (4th ed., Oxford: Oxford University Press, 2014), 783–820. See, in particular, Charter of the United Nations, 26 June 1945, 892 U.N.T.S. 119, Arts. 1(3), 55, 56, and 68.

universal international law and the perceived exceptionalism of human rights has been played out in a way that reconciles the two paradigms. This was the issue of reservations to treaties.

In 1994 the HRC adopted General Comment No. 24 on reservations to treaties.[20] Not only did the Committee "necessarily" claim the right to determine the validity of a reservation in terms of its compatibility with the Covenant: it could not discharge its functions of reviewing States' periodic reports and deciding cases under the Optional Protocol without doing so. It then controversially went on to pronounce on the legal consequences of a finding of invalidity:

> In order to know the scope of its duty to examine a State's compliance under article 40 or a communication under the first Optional Protocol, the Committee has necessarily to take a view on the compatibility of a reservation with the object and purpose of the Covenant and with general international law. Because of the special character of a human rights treaty, the compatibility of a reservation with the object and purpose of the Covenant must be established objectively, by reference to legal principles, and the Committee is particularly well placed to perform this task. The normal consequence of an unacceptable reservation is not that the Covenant will not be in effect at all for a reserving party. Rather, such a reservation will generally be severable, in the sense that the Covenant will be operative for the reserving party without benefit of the reservation.[21]

In fact, in 1993 the International Law Commission (ILC) had decided to draft guidelines on reservations to treaties. In 1997, its Rapporteur, Alain Pellet, produced draft conclusions on this issue, including draft conclusion 10:

> The Commission notes also that, in the event of incompatibility of a reservation with the object and purpose of a treaty, it is primarily the reserving State that has the responsibility of taking action. This action may consist, for example, in the State either foregoing becoming a party or withdrawing its reservation, or modifying the latter so as to eliminate the incompatibility.[22]

---

20 UN Human Rights Committee, *General Comment No. 24: Issues Relating to Reservations Made upon Ratification or Accession to the Covenant or the Optional Protocols thereto, or in Relation to Declarations under Article 41 of the Covenant*, 4 November 1994, U.N. Doc. CCPR/C/21/Rev.1/Add.6.

21 *Ibid.*, ¶ 18.

22 U.N. Doc A/CN.4/L.540 (1997).

This text was clearly intended as a refutation of the approach taken in HRC General Comment No. 24. The draft conclusion did not even refer to the possibility of severability being the result of invalidity.[23] The Special Rapporteur had taken the view that universal human rights treaty bodies (unlike regional courts) did not have the power to determine the consequences of invalidity.[24] Indeed he objected to the "excessive pretentions of the Human Rights Committee in seeking to act as the sole judge of the permissibility of reservations."[25]

There were a number of meetings between treaty bodies and the ILC[26] in which the treaty bodies clarified that they took the view that general principles of treaty interpretation applied, but that there should be a strong presumption in favour of severability in respect of human rights treaties. This was because of the non-synallagmatic nature of human rights obligations, that is, no other State suffers direct harm from one State's violation and so has no immediate interest in protesting such a violation. They did, however, accept that the presumption of severability was rebuttable and that, ultimately, it was the intention of the reserving State that determined the severability or otherwise of the reservation.[27] The ILC concluded in relation to invalid reservations that "[u]nless the author of the invalid reservation has expressed a contrary intention or such intention is otherwise established, it is considered a contracting State or a contracting organization *without the benefit of the reservation.*"[28]

Thus, the presumption in favour of severability argued for by the treaty bodies, at least as regards human rights treaties, was now accepted by the ILC in respect of *all* multilateral treaties. So, far from the treaty bodies promoting fragmentation of the normal understanding of the expected consequences of

---

23 "Severability" means that, despite the reservation, the State remains bound by the treaty in question without benefit of the reservation; the other possibility is that an invalid reservation prevents the State becoming party to the treaty.

24 U.N. Doc. A/52/10 (1997), ¶¶ 82–87.

25 *Ibid.*, ¶ 87; it may have been relevant that the word "generally" is absent from the French version of *General Comment No. 24, supra* note 20, ¶ 18.

26 For the last of which, see report of the meeting of the ILC with the treaty bodies inter-committee working group on reservations, 15–16 May 2007, U.N. Doc. A/CN.4/614 (2009); the present writer co-chaired the final segment as Chairperson/Rapporteur of the working group: *ibid.*, ¶ 2.

27 Report of the Working Group on Reservations, U.N. Doc. HRI/MC/2007/5: the State remains a party without benefit of the reservation, "unless its contrary intention is incontrovertibly established" (page 7, recommendation 70).

28 ILC, Guide to Practice on Reservations, U.N. Doc. A/66/10 (2011), ¶ 75, Guideline 4.5.3, ¶ 2, emphasis added.

invalid reservations, general international law seemed to have embraced for the whole corpus what had been perceived as a subject-specific approach.

3 The General Approach of the ICJ

The ICJ has expressed itself in terms that address both the juridical nature of treaty body outputs and the concern to avoid fragmentation. As will be seen below, the Court in the *Wall* advisory opinion referred with respect and approval to all the outputs of the treaty bodies: concluding observations of the HRC and of the Committee on Economic, Social and Cultural Rights, "views" of the HRC in individual cases under the Optional Protocol and a general comment of the HRC. It did this without indicating any general approach.

In the 2010 *Diallo* case, however, the ICJ gave the following exposition of its understanding of the HRC's general comments and decisions under the Optional Protocol:

> Since it was created, the HRC has built up a considerable body of interpretative case law, in particular through its findings in response to the individual communications which may be submitted to it in respect of States parties to the first Optional Protocol, and in the form of its 'General Comments'.
>
> Although the Court is in no way obliged, in the exercise of its judicial functions, to model its own interpretation of the Covenant on that of the Committee, it believes that it should ascribe great weight to the interpretation adopted by this independent body that was established specifically to supervise the application of that treaty. The point here is to achieve the necessary clarity and the essential consistency of international law, as well as legal security, to which both the individuals with guaranteed rights and the State obliged to comply with treaty obligations are entitled.[29]

This passage merits close attention. The language of the first of the quoted subparagraphs is particularly important. First, the Court's use of the term "case law" ("*jurisprudence*" in the French version) is noteworthy. This is a term that, as already indicated, would normally be reserved for judgments of a court.

29 *Ahmadou Sadio Diallo*, merits, *supra* note 6, at ¶ 66. See P.R. Ghandhi, "Human Rights and the International Court of Justice in the *Ahmadou Sadio Diallo* Case," *Human Rights Law Review* 11, 3 (2011): 536.

Evidently, the ICJ is treating HRC decisions in respect of communications under the Optional Protocol as if they were judicial decisions. It may seem unexpected that it uses the same terminology in respect of the Committee's "General Comments." This presumably reflects the Court's awareness of the careful drafting process that precedes adoption of General Comments, including its tendency to "codify" existing Optional Protocol decisions.[30] The use of the adjective "interpretative" also acknowledges the necessary Committee role of interpreting the Covenant: its function is not just to make factual conclusions or offer advice in the form of recommendations.

The second of the quoted sub-paragraphs of paragraph 66 of the *Diallo* judgment is similarly illuminating. While quite rightly maintaining its independent authority to interpret the Covenant, the Court then explains why it should not lightly depart from the interpretation arrived at by the Committee. First, it feels that it should "ascribe great weight" to the Committee's interpretation, precisely because it is the "independent body…established specifically to supervise the application of that treaty." Implicit is the acknowledgement of a special status inherent in the HRC's creation by the Covenant and its members' election by States parties.

Secondly, the need to achieve "clarity and the essential consistency of international law" suggests a concern to avoid the fragmentation that could arise from two conceivable interpretations: one, that suggested by a general international law approach and one suggested by a more human rights-centred approach. In fact, it is clear that the Court is aware that the requirement to interpret any treaty in the light of its object and purpose[31] will conduce to an outcome that could not be human rights neutral in respect of a human rights treaty. A third motivation of the Court is to vouchsafe the "legal security" to which the individual rights bearers and the State party duty bearers are entitled. While located in a passage dealing with the fragmentation issue, the underlying concern, then, is that the Committee needs to be understood as speaking with determinative authority, given the role assigned to it by the Covenant. Accordingly, in *Diallo*, the ICJ laid the basis for the respect it accorded both to decisions on individual communications and to General Comments. *Diallo* itself only involved these two outputs. The *IFAD* and *Hissène Habré* cases (the latter of the Committee against Torture) only involved individual cases, while the *Wall* case alone also made use of concluding

30 See Judge Cançado Trindade, address to the 100th session of the Human Rights Committee, U.N. Doc. CCPR/C/SR. 2772 (2010), ¶¶ 1–17.

31 Vienna Convention on the Law of Treaties, 23 May 1969, 1155 U.N.T.S. 331; (1969) 8 ILM 679, Art. 31.

observations. As will be seen below, the concluding observations in question played a central role in the Court's reasoning.

4 Human Rights Issues Addressed by the ICJ

The issues that have been of concern to the World Court when referring to treaty body outputs have been of both a procedural (jurisdictional) and substantive nature. These two categories will be dealt with separately.

4.1 *Procedural Issues*

a Extra-Territorial Jurisdiction

One question that was central to the Court's handling of the *Wall* case was that of whether the International Covenant on Civil and Political Rights (ICCPR) required States parties to apply the Covenant outside their territorial jurisdiction. The matter was one of interpretation of Covenant Article 2 (i) which reads:

> Each State Party to the present Covenant undertakes to respect and to ensure to all individuals within its territory and subject to its jurisdiction the rights recognized in the present Covenant, without distinction of any kind, such as race, colour, sex, language, religion, political or other opinion, national or social origin, property, birth or other status.

The issue was whether this language meant that human rights guarantees contained in the Covenant benefitted only those persons who were both under the legal jurisdiction of the State and were at the same time geographically located within the territory of the State. That is, did the Covenant have extra-territorial effect?[32] The position defended on behalf of Israel and traditionally upheld by

32 See Michael J. Dennis and Andre M. Surena, "Application of the International Covenant on Civil and Political Rights in Times of Armed Conflict and Military Occupation: The Gap between Legal Theory and State Practice," *European Human Rights Law Review* 6 (2008): 714; and Nigel Rodley, "The Extraterritorial Reach and Applicability in Armed Conflict of the International Covenant on Civil and Political Rights: A Rejoinder to Dennis and Surena," *European Human Rights Law Review* 6 (2009): 628. See generally, *Extraterritorial Application of Human Rights Treaties*, edited by Fons Coomans and Menno T. Kamminga (Antwerp: Intersentia, 2004); Marco Milanovic, *Extraterritorial Application of Human Rights Treaties: Law Principles, and Policy* (Oxford: Oxford University Press, 2011); Françoise Hampson, "The Scope of the Extra-Territorial Applicability of International Human Rights Law," in *The Delivery of Human Rights: Essays in Honour of Professor Sir Nigel Rodley*, edited by Geoff Gilbert, Françoise Hampson and Clara Sandoval

the United States of America was that this (conjunctive) reading was the correct understanding of this provision. The alternative (disjunctive) reading, consistently defended by the Committee, was that the Covenant guarantees extended to persons within the States' territories and to persons within the jurisdiction, but who may be outside the territory. The Court preferred the Committee's interpretation. Having looked to the object and purpose of the Covenant, from which it inferred that it would be "natural" for States to be bound even when acting outside its frontiers, it immediately noted that "the constant practice of the Human Rights Committee is consistent with this." It referred to cases of arrests effected by Uruguay in Brazil and Argentina, as well as a case of a confiscated passport involving the same State party in Germany.[33] Then, having sought corroboration of its purposive interpretation of Article 2(i) in this case law of the Committee, it then turned to the *travaux préparatoires* to corroborate the Committee's own approach. Having found the necessary corroboration, it referred to the Committee's concluding observations on Israel in 1998[34] and 2003, the latter specifically addressing the responsibility of the State party's "authorities or agents" in the occupied territories.[35] The Court unambiguously concluded that it considered that the Covenant "is applicable in respect of acts done by a State in the exercise of its jurisdiction outside its own territory."[36]

b Jurisdiction in Armed Conflict

In addition to the dimension of the extra-territorial applicability of the ICCPR, the case of Israel also raised the issue of its applicability in time of armed conflict. Israel has consistently maintained that international human rights law (IHRL) stops where international humanitarian law (IHL) begins. A variation on this is that, to the extent that IHRL applies, it is to be sought in the *lex specialis* of IHL.

(London: Routledge, 2011), 157; and Ralph Wilde, "Human Rights Beyond Borders at the World Court: The Significance of the International Court of Justice's Jurisprudence on the Extraterritorial Application of International Human Rights Treaties," *Chinese Journal of International Law* 12 (2013): 639.

33 *Lopez Burgos v. Uruguay*, Communication No. 52/79 (1981) U.N. Doc. CCPR/C/OP/1 at 88 (1984); *Celiberti de Casariego v. Uruguay*, Communication No. 56/79 (1981) U.N. Doc. CCPR/C/OP/1 at 92 (1984); *Montero v. Uruguay*, Communication No. 106/81, U.N. Doc. Supp. No. 40 (A/38/40 at 186 (1983).

34 U.N. Doc. CCPR/C/79/Add.93 (1998), ¶ 10.

35 U.N. Doc. CCPR/CO/78/ISR (2003), ¶ 11.

36 *Wall, supra* note 5, 180 at ¶ 111. The Court could have cited *General Comment No. 31, supra* note 15, ¶ 10, but this was only adopted and made public after proceedings in the *Wall* opinion had closed.

Some credence was given to this conception in the ICJ's *Nuclear Weapons* advisory opinion.[37] There the Court addressed the argument – not unconvincing given that the human rights paradigm is one where State power is stable and the individual is relatively weak and in need of protection from it – that "the Covenant was directed to the protection of human rights in peacetime, but that questions relating to unlawful loss of life in hostilities were governed by the law applicable in armed conflict."[38] The Court's response was "that the protection of the [Covenant] does not cease in times of war, except by operation of Article 4 of the Covenant whereby certain provisions may be derogated from in time of national emergency."[39] However, it then went on to say that the content of Article 6 fell to be determined by the applicable *lex specialis*, namely, the law applicable in armed conflict.[40]

It may be noted parenthetically that the HRC had twelve years earlier adopted General Comment No. 14 on the Right to Life and Nuclear Weapons.[41] The Court ignored it. This was perhaps to the benefit of the Committee which, with no substantiation, had gone as far as to opine that "[t]he production, testing, possession, deployment and use of nuclear weapons should be prohibited and recognized as crimes against humanity."[42] This was not the sort of Committee output that an international judicial body could be expected to treat with uncritical respect.[43]

In the *Wall* opinion the Court reiterated the words quoted above from the *Nuclear Weapons* opinion. It then made clear that IHL would not always be the *lex specialis* for IHRL:

> As regards the relationship between international humanitarian law and human rights law, there are thus three possible situations: some rights

37 *Legality of the Threat or Use of Nuclear Weapons*, advisory opinion, 1996, I.C.J. 226.

38 *Ibid.*, 239–240 at ¶ 24.

39 *Ibid.*, 240 at ¶ 25.

40 *Ibid.*

41 UN Human Rights Committee, *General Comment No. 14: Article 6 (Nuclear Weapons and the Right to Life)*, 9 November 1984, U.N. Doc. HRI/GEN/1/Rev.9 (Vol. I), 9 November 1984.

42 *Ibid.*, ¶ 6.

43 Yet Nauru and the Solomon Islands invoked the General Comment (Nauru, at 20; Solomon Islands, at ¶¶ 4.34–5). The United Kingdom, responding, pointed out that it was controversial and was evidently anyway clearly making a Statement *de lege feranda*. (¶ 3.107); note, the submission also supported the broader notion of IHL being the *lex specialis*, not only for the right to life, but "*a fortiori*, in respect of the protection of other human rights" (¶ 3.109), accessed from the Court's website 5 May 2014: http://www.icj-cij.org/docket/index.php?p1=3&p2=4&k=5a&case=131&code=mwp&p3=1.

> may be exclusively matters of international humanitarian law; others may be exclusively matters of human rights law; yet others may be matters of both these branches of international law.[44]

In addition to the previous approval of the position of the HRC, the Court also invoked the rejection by the Committee on Economic, Social and Cultural Rights of Israel's claim that the International Covenant on Economic, Social and Cultural Rights was inapplicable to the occupied territory "inasmuch as they are part and parcel of the context of armed conflict, as distinct from a relationship of human rights."[45]

4.2 *Substantive Issues*

a Freedom of Movement

Freedom of movement has been a central issue in two cases: the *Wall* opinion and *Diallo*. In the *Wall* opinion, the issue was whether the security barrier – that at some points took the form of a wall several metres high – was an unlawful interference with the freedom of Palestinians to move within their territory, according to the guarantee of ICCPR Article 12(1).[46] The Court noted that this was not an absolute right: it would, under sub-paragraph 3, be subject to restrictions for certain public purposes.[47] In determining the scope of the principle in the light of the permitted restriction, the Court specifically cited the approach of the HRC as contained in its General Comment No. 27, namely, that the restrictive measures "must conform to the principle of proportionality" and "must be the least intrusive instrument amongst those which might achieve the desired result."[48] The ICJ concluded on the facts that these conditions were not met.

In *Diallo*, the pertinent issue was whether the expulsion of a Guinean national from the Democratic Republic of the Congo (DRC) had been reached in accordance with the law in conformity with Covenant Article 13.[49] The Court

44 *Wall, supra* note 5, 180–181 at ¶ 106.

45 *Ibid.*, ¶ 112.

46 International Covenant on Civil and Political Rights, 16 December 1966, 999 U.N.T.S. 171, Art. 12 (1) reads: "Everyone lawfully within the territory of a State shall, within that territory, have the right to liberty of movement and freedom to choose his residence."

47 *Wall, supra* note 5, 192–193 at ¶ 136.

48 *Ibid.*

49 Art. 13 reads: "An alien lawfully in the territory of a State Party to the present Covenant may be expelled therefrom only in pursuance of a decision reached in accordance with law and shall, except where compelling reasons of national security otherwise require, be

interpreted the paragraph as both requiring an expulsion's consistency with national law (a necessary condition) and that it be consistent with other Covenant provisions and not be arbitrary (sufficient conditions).[50] It then found that this interpretation "fully corroborated by the jurisprudence of the Human Rights Committee," citing an Optional Protocol case (*Maroufidou v. Sweden*) and Committee General Comment No. 15 (on the position of aliens under the Covenant).[51] The reference to the *Maroufidou* case, in which the Committee did not find a violation, was to the paragraph (9.3) requiring consistency of the proposed measure with both the provisions of the Covenant and the procedural and substantive aspects of national law. Paragraph 10 of General Comment No. 15 stresses the goal of avoiding arbitrariness. On the facts, the Court held that the DRC had violated Article 13 by not ensuring a prior consultation by the body established by law before an expulsion measure may be undertaken and by failing to give substantial reasons for the expulsion.[52]

Two of the ICJ judges disagreed with the majority view that Article 13 contained an independent element of arbitrariness in addition to the need for lawfulness and the procedural protection it requires. They argued, not that the HRC, as quoted by the Court, had got it wrong, but that the Court had misread the HRC. They asserted, with some justice, that in General Comment No. 15, all the Committee was doing was citing the avoidance of arbitrariness as a purpose of the procedures (indicating the avoidance of mass expulsions), while in *Maroufidou* the Committee had not referred to arbitrariness as an independent element.[53] The issue then was merely one of how to interpret the Committee's outputs, not about the correctness of their content.

b Liberty and Security of Person

Guinea's complaints about Mr Diallo's arrests and detentions (there were two admissible phases of arrest and detention[54]) claimed that the detentions were unlawful under DRC law and that they were arbitrary, thus violating ICCPR

---

allowed to submit the reasons against his expulsion and to have his case reviewed by, and be represented for the purpose before, the competent authority or a person or persons especially designated by the competent authority."

50 *Ahmadou Sadio Diallo*, merits, *supra* note 6, at ¶ 65; see *Maroufidou v. Sweden*, Communication No. 58/1979 (1981), U.N. Doc. CCPR/C/OP/1 at 65 (1984).

51 *Ibid.*, 663–664 at ¶ 66.

52 *Ibid.*, 665–666 at ¶ 72.

53 Separate Opinion Judges Greenwood and Keith in *Ahmadou Sadio Diallo*, merits, *supra* note 6, 712.

54 An earlier one was inadmissible.

Article 9(1).[55] There was also a claim for failure to inform him of the reasons for the arrest as required by Article 9(2). On the facts, the Court would and did have no trouble in upholding the claims, as long as detention effected for the purpose of effecting a deportation fell under Article 9 at all. On this, the Court cited HRC General Comment No. 8 dealing with Article 9 in support of its view that Article 9 would "apply in principle to any form of arrest or detention decided upon and carried out by a public authority, whatever its legal basis and the objective being pursued."[56] Indeed, the first paragraph of the General Comment made clear that the Committee's view that Article 9 covered "all deprivations of liberty, whether in criminal cases or in other cases such as, for example...immigration control etc." In a separate opinion Judge Cançado Trindade examined, approvingly, the Committee's case law at length, albeit not apparently to disagree with the majority.[57]

c Reparation

In *Diallo* the Court decided, without reference to but consistent with the practice of the HRC, that reparation for the violations of Articles 9 and 13 of the ICCPR should take the form of compensation for non-material and material injury. The Court noted that the HRC refrained from awarding specific sums, but rather indicated the need for "adequate compensation."[58] Accordingly, the Court looked to the practice of those tribunals that had previously awarded specific sums by way of compensation (especially the European and Inter-American Courts of Human Rights). Judge Cançado Trindade also referred to other forms of reparation that the HRC considered appropriate according to the nature of the violation, including restitution, rehabilitation and satisfaction.[59]

d Ill-Treatment of Prisoners and Universal Jurisdiction Regarding Torture

International treaty body practice on treatment of prisoners played a minor role in the *Diallo* case. Here Guinea had argued that Mr Diallo had been

55 Art. 9(1) reads: "Everyone has the right to liberty and security of person. No one shall be subjected to arbitrary arrest or detention. No one shall be deprived of his liberty except on such grounds and in accordance with such procedure as are established by law."

56 *Ahmadou Sadio Diallo*, merits, *supra* note 6, at ¶ 77.

57 *Ibid.*, 678–679 at ¶¶ 112–116 and 687 at ¶¶ 145–147.

58 *Ahmadou Sadio Diallo*, compensation, *supra* note 6, at ¶ 24. The same was true for the African Commission on Human Rights, whose African Charter on Human and Peoples' Rights the Court, 17 June 1981, 1520 U.N.T.S. 323, was also applying: *ibid.*

59 Separate Opinion Judge Cançado Trindade in *Ahmadou Sadio Diallo*, merits, *supra* note 6, 800 at ¶¶ 208–209, but these would not be typical in Art. 9 cases.

ill-treated in detention. The Court dismissed the claim for want of evidence. It did not refer to treaty body practice. However, it made an *obiter dictum* apparently inconsistent with that practice. This pointed out that, contrary to the claim of Guinea, Mr Diallo was able to communicate with his lawyers and relatives "without any great difficulty." It continued: "even if this had not been the case, such constraints would not *per se* have constituted treatment prohibited by Article 10, paragraph 1 of the Covenant."[60] In fact, HRC General Comment No. 21 dealing with Article 10 refers to the relevance of contacts with the outside world (family, lawyer, social and medical services, non-governmental organisations).[61] Indeed, General Comment No. 21 on the prohibition of torture and ill-treatment noted that protection of the detainee "requires that prompt and regular access be given to doctors and lawyers."[62] Since the Court's observation was evidently speculative and may, as suggested by Judge Cançado Trinidade, "have taken a somewhat hurried decision on this particular point" (that is, the treatment issue),[63] the Court's dictum should not be accorded too much weight, either in respect of the substantive issue or as regards the position of the Committee.

The obligations of States under the UN Convention against Torture and Other Cruel, Inhuman or Degrading Treatment or Punishment (UNCAT) were, by contrast, central to the issues in the *Hissène Habré* case, in which two cases decided by the Committee against Torture played a significant role. The case was brought by Belgium, which was seeking extradition of former Chadean dictator Hissène Habré, in particular under the universal jurisdiction clauses ("prosecute or extradite") of UNCAT. Indeed, the failure of Senegal to submit the case to prosecution, after its *Cour de Cassation* had declared that there was no legislative basis for prosecuting Habré, and the finding by the Committee of a consequent violation in the *Guengueng* case were part of Belgium's case against Senegal.[64] The Court had no difficulty in following the *Guengueng* case in respect of the finding that the delays in adoption legislation permitting

60 *Ahmadou Sadio Diallo*, merits, *supra* note 6, 671 at ¶ 88; Art. 10(1) reads: "All persons deprived of their liberty shall be treated with humanity and with respect for the inherent dignity of the human person."

61 UN Human Rights Committee, *General Comment No. 21: Article 10 (Humane Treatment of Persons Deprived of Their Liberty)*, U.N. Doc. HRI/GEN/1/Rev.1 at 33, 10 April 1992, ¶ 12.

62 *Ibid.*, ¶ 11.

63 Separate Opinion Judge Cançado Trindade in *Ahmadou Sadio Diallo*, merits, *supra* note 6, 752 at ¶ 72, pointing out that the burden of proof in such cases should fall on the State.

64 *Suleymane Guengueng* et al. *v. Senegal*, Communication No. 181/2001, U.N. Doc. CAT/C/36/D/181/2001 (2006).

Senegalese jurisdiction violated Article 6 or UNCAT[65] and the finding that the failure to submit the case for prosecution violated Article 7.[66] There had been no extradition request at the time of *Guengueng*, but the Court found, like the Committee, that the obligation to prosecute did not depend on the existence of a prior request for extradition.[67]

However, it relied on the very first individual case of the Committee, *O.R., M.M. and M.S. v. Argentina*, to conclude that the Convention applied only to acts committed after Senegal became a party to the Convention. Judge Cançado Trindade was critical of this, given that *Guengueng* (and another case)[68] had established no such limitation.[69] On the other hand, except in respect of continuing offences, such as enforced disappearance,[70] the doctrine of non-retroactivity is traditional treaty law.[71] The Court dismissed the relevance of *Guengueng*, on the grounds that the question of the temporal scope of the obligations contained in the Convention had not been raised, nor had the Committee itself raised that question.[72] In fact, it might have been open to the Court to conclude *ratione temporis* that, even though Senegal's obligation to prosecute could not have arisen before 26 June 1987 when the Covenant entered into force for Senegal, that obligation, once established, could have extended to acts of torture committed before that date. The Court's basic predisposition was to follow the Committee's cautious approach in its very first cases.

e Fair Hearing

The *IFAD* case[73] concerned an "appeal" by the Director-General of the International Fund for Agricultural Development against a decision of the

65 *Hissène Habré, supra* note 3, 452–453 at ¶ 81. Art. 6 requires States parties to detain a person alleged to be responsible for torture, make a preliminary inquiry and inform other relevant States parties.

66 *Ibid.*, 460–461 at ¶ 117. Art. 7 requires States parties to try or extradite alleged torturers on their territory.

67 *Ibid.*, 456 at ¶ 94.

68 *Bouabdallah Ltaief v. Tunisia,* Communication No. 189/2001, U.N. Doc. CAT/C/31/D/189/2001 (2003).

69 Separate opinion Judge Cançado Trindade in *Hissène Habré, supra* note 3, 551–552 at ¶ 163.

70 In fact, that first case concerned, not the typical problem of torture of prisoners, but of persons whose disappearance was argued to be a form of torture.

71 *Hissène Habré, supra* note 3, 457 at ¶ 100.

72 *Ibid.*, 457–458 at ¶ 101.

73 *Judgment No 2867 of the Administrative Tribunal of the International Labour Organization upon a Complaint Filed against the International Fund for Agricultural Development* (*IFAD*), advisory opinion, 2012, I.C.J. 10.

Administrative Tribunal of the International Labour Organization (ILOAT) upholding a staff member's claim against dismissal. The question arose whether the Court should exercise its discretion not to respond to the request in view of the anachronistic inequality of status between the employer and the employee. Under the ILOAT statute only the employing organisation could refer a case to the ICJ if it disagreed with the Tribunal decision, not the employee if the case went against her. Moreover under the Statute of the ICJ, only States have standing for the Court's contentious jurisdiction and, in any event, even in advisory proceedings[74] only States and intergovernmental organisations have standing to appear personally in the proceedings. The Court decided that in the circumstances it could give the requested opinion while signalling that, if the inequality were maintained, it may not do so in future.[75] It did so having found a way at least to redress the imbalance in terms of participants in the proceedings. Since it could not permit the staff member to submit documentation or to appear personally before it, it required the IFAD Director-General to transmit all material that she wished to submit and it refused the IFAD oral proceedings, given that the staff member could not appear in person.

The cornerstone of, and so the authority for the ICJ's reasoning in favour of the need for equality of arms is found in paragraph 39:

> To turn to the general question of the concept of equality, the development of the principle of equality of access to courts and tribunals since 1946, when the review procedure was established, may be seen in the significant differences between the two General Comments by the Human Rights Committee on Article 14, paragraph 1, of the International Covenant on Civil and Political Rights of 1966. That provision requires that "[a]ll persons shall be equal before the courts and tribunals." The first Comment, adopted in 1984, just seven years after the Covenant came into force, did no more than repeat the terms of the provision and call on States to report more fully on steps taken to ensure equality before the courts, including equal access to the courts (HRC, General Comment No. 13: Article 14 (Administration of Justice), paras. 2–3). The later Comment, one adopted in 2007 on the basis of 30 years of experience in

74 "Appeals" from some administrative tribunals of the UN family can take place by reference to the Court for an advisory opinion, which the relevant secretariats are committed to accept.

75 *IFAD*, *supra* note 73, 31 at ¶ 48. See also Separate Opinion of Judge Greenwood, in *ibid.*, 94.

> the application of the above-mentioned Article 14, gives detailed attention to equality before domestic courts and tribunals. According to the Committee, that right to equality guarantees equal access and equality of arms. While in non-criminal matters the right of equal access does not address the issue of the right of appeal, if procedural rights are accorded they must be provided to all the parties unless distinctions can be justified on objective and reasonable grounds (Human Rights Committee, General Comment No. 32: Right to Equality before Courts and Tribunals and to a Fair Trial, paras. 8–9, 12 and 13). In the case of the ILOAT, the Court is unable to see any such justification for the provision for review of the Tribunal's decisions which favours the employer to the disadvantage of the staff member.[76]

The passage stresses both equality of access and procedural equality. The comparison between the earlier and later General Comments is presumably intended to imply that the scope of the idea of equality may not have been so clear in 1984, but it was unmistakable nearly a quarter of a century later. The reference to the fact that under Covenant Article 14 there is no automatic right of appeal in non-criminal matters, but that where there is appeal the parties should be equal – a point addressed clearly in the General Comment and reflecting the Committee's case law[77] – is presumably to offset any argument in favour of IFAD that Article 14 principles would not apply to an appeal in a non-criminal case.[78]

As it happens there were also delays in IFAD's cooperation with the procedure indicated by the Court to assist submissions by the staff member. One is tempted to conclude that, had it not been clear that its decision would be to uphold the ILOAT decision in her favour, which gave it the opportunity to deliver a withering demolition of the system and of the behaviour of IFAD before and during the ICJ proceedings, it would indeed have declined jurisdiction as requested by the staff member.[79] It was for all of this that the HRC's General Comment provided the authority.

76 *IFAD*, *supra* note 73, 31 at ¶ 39.

77 *Paul Perterer v. Austria*, Communication No. 1015/2001, U.N. Doc. CCPR/C/81/D/1015/2001 (2004).

78 The only area of law in which the Covenant expressly requires provision for review of a judgment by a higher court is in the case of convictions for crimes, in Art. 14(5).

79 *IFAD*, *supra* note 73, 27–28 at ¶ 40.

5 Conclusion

The stars may well have been aligned when the ICJ considered the first case (after the *Genocide Convention* case) in which it had to confront human rights issues head on, that is, the *Wall* case. In that case, several of the judges had had experience of human rights work in UN bodies. Judge Al-Khasawneh had been a member of the Sub-Commission on Promotion and Protection of Human Rights and Judge Kooijmans had been the first UN Special Rapporteur on the question of torture. Meanwhile, Judges Buergenthal and Higgins had been members of the Human Rights Committee, while Judge Simma had been a member of the Committee on Economic, Social and Cultural Rights. There can be little doubt that this group brought with them a predisposition in favour of the human rights project generally and its institutional guardians specifically. This can only have been helpful in a court that had traditionally been hyper-respectful of the sovereign prerogatives of States. As has been seen, international human rights law represents a substantial limitation on earlier notions of State sovereignty. These judges could educate their colleagues in both the subject-matter of IHRL and the seriousness of the institutions, especially what was perceived as the most senior treaty body, the Human Rights Committee.[80] Having been apprised of this, it would follow that the Court would treat the outputs of the treaty bodies with respect, not just because of their official provenance and functions, but also because they had demonstrated that such respect was due in fact.

Once it was established that the treaty bodies and their outputs had to be reckoned with, it followed that it was important that there be as much coherence as possible as regards the pronouncements of the Court and the treaty bodies. This perception was highlighted by the prevalent concern about the risks of "fragmentation" of public international law. Indeed, it is no accident that when the Court came to articulate the basis of its policy of presumptive deference to the Human Rights Committee (and other universal and regional treaty bodies) in the *Diallo* case, it particularly underlined the value of achieving "the necessary clarity and the essential consistency of international law," in other words the value of avoiding fragmentation.

---

80 Note CERD was adopted a year before the ICCPR, but the power of its Committee to deal with individual petitions under Article 12 came into force after the Optional Protocol to the Covenant that gave the Human Rights Committee the same power. The latter body soon built up a far more substantial body of case law. As to the relevance of the backgrounds of the judges, see Higgins, *supra* note 1, at 746.

There has been a limited number of cases in which the Court has had to adjudicate human rights issues, albeit that these cases have covered a substantial number of them, including the rights to life, to liberty and security of the person and to a fair hearing, as well as some economic and social rights. The importance of the procedural or jurisdictional dimension, especially as regards the extra-territorial application of the ICCPR and the relationship with IHL should also not be underestimated.

Nevertheless, the Court has wisely reserved its own independent power of appreciation. After all, just as no single court has a monopoly of wisdom, neither does any one quasi-judicial treaty body. Indeed, it may well be that even different human rights treaty bodies may strive but fail to reach the same view of the same facts.[81]

For example, on the one hand, the Human Rights Committee has changed its practice in respect of automatic deprivation of the voting rights of people with mental disability. It now follows the view of the Committee on the Rights of Persons with Disabilities (CRPD) that any such deprivation must not be status based, but may only be on the grounds of actual individual inability. On the other hand, the Committee is unable to follow what seems to be the practice of the CRPD in determining that no mental disability whatever can justify denial of direct autonomous decision-making.[82]

It remains important for all decision-making bodies applying IHRL to seek to avoid taking positions that would place States in a situation of conflicting obligations. Consistency and coherence are inescapable demands of the rule of law. As long as the application of IHRL is not a regular feature of the World Court's docket, it is appropriate that when it does have occasion to interpret human rights treaties, it continues to apply the (inevitably rebuttable) presumption that a treaty body's interpretation of its own treaty is the appropriate one.

---

81 See Using Other Treaty Bodies' Interpretations to Construe the Covenant, Draft note prepared by the Rapporteur Mr Gerald L Neuman, U.N. Doc. CCPR/C/109/R.4, discussed in public session at the 3066th meeting of the Human Rights Committee, 28 March 2014.

82 Compare UN Human Rights Committee, draft *General Comment No. 35: Liberty and Security of Person and Freedom from Arbitrary Arrest and Detention*, U.N. Doc. CCPR/C/GC/R.35/Rev.3, with amendment adopted at second (final) reading in July 2014, on file with the author: procedures for detention "should ensure respect for the views of the individual" (¶ 19) with Committee on the Rights of Persons with Disabilities *General Comment No. 1*, U.N. Doc. CRPD/C/GC/1 (2014): "detention [of persons with disabilities] in institutions against their will...constitutes arbitrary deprivation of liberty" (¶ 36).

CHAPTER 2

The Contribution of Judge Antônio Augusto Cançado Trindade to the Adjudication of International Human Rights at the International Court of Justice

*Robert P. Barnidge, Jr.**

1 Introduction

Christopher Waters, in the Introduction to this book, pays tribute to the considerable contribution that Professor Sandy Ghandhi made to legal scholarship, teaching and advocacy, particularly, though not exclusively, in the area of human rights law. The present author fully agrees with this assessment and has himself drawn upon Ghandhi's insights in his own writing.[1] He would be remiss, however, not to also express his personal gratitude to Ghandhi for mentoring him when he began his academic career as a lecturer in the School of Law at the University of Reading (2007–12). Intellectually, of course, Ghandhi was first class, but what most remains with the present author after over five years as one of Ghandhi's mentees is his modesty, as well as his gentle nature and kindness. Perhaps this was because Ghandhi sensed that a commitment to human rights, understood holistically, is not simply about challenging the powerful to "humanise" their rule, though it is surely this, but also extends to caring for specific men and women as one encounters them in one's daily life, at a personal level. It is a privilege to be able to contribute to this collection of essays in honour of Ghandhi.

In line with the theme of this *festschrift*, this chapter examines Brazilian Judge Antônio Augusto Cançado Trindade's contribution to the adjudication of international human rights at the International Court of Justice (ICJ). Since

* The author is grateful to Dr Reuven (Ruvi) Ziegler for his comments on an earlier draft of this chapter. All errors remain those of the author, as do the views expressed.

1 See, for example, Robert P. Barnidge, Jr., "The International Law of Negotiation as a Means of Dispute Settlement," *Fordham International Law Journal* 36, 3 (2013): 554, at note 46.

 | DOI 10.1163/9789004261181_004

beginning his term of office in February 2009, Judge Cançado Trindade has distinguished himself as one of the most progressive, indeed, radical, voices on the bench. Consistent with his previous work at the Inter-American Court of Human Rights, Judge Cançado Trindade's jurisprudence at the ICJ has shown a reflexive hostility to the *raison d'État* and an impatience with procedural and substantive norms and practices that reify anything other than what he describes as the "human conscience, the universal juridical conscience, [...] the ultimate material 'source' of all Law, and of the new *jus gentium* of our times."[2] His is a jurisprudence that critiques the idea of the State as international legal subject *par excellence*, a jurisprudence that seeks to "speak truth to power" on behalf of individuals often at their most vulnerable. This chapter focuses on two aspects of Judge Cançado Trindade's ICJ jurisprudence in particular, namely the manner in which it aims to reorient international law away from State consent to the service of universal values and Judge Cançado Trindade's understanding of the law of diplomatic protection.

2 Reorienting International Law away from State Consent to the Service of Universal Values

A consistent theme in Judge Cançado Trindade's jurisprudence at the ICJ has been its concern with the proper role of the State. Inevitably, this has led to questions of the State's legitimacy *as an institution* and, more specifically, the basis upon which it can legitimately wield its coercive authority and benefit from the rights and obligations that adhere to it as an international legal person. This jurisprudence instinctively sees in the State a historiography of hysteria, a history of oppression and misdeeds, and for this reason, it inclines toward ethical and moral justifications for law.[3] In the cosmic "opposition of natural law – emanating from the *recta ratio* – to positive law (*jus positum*), in

2 *Pulp Mills on the River Uruguay* (Argentina v. Uruguay), 2010 I.C.J. 14, 161 (20 Apr.) (Cançado Trindade, J., separate).

3 In particular, see Judge Cançado Trindade's thoughts on the role of the State in *Accordance with International Law of the Unilateral Declaration of Independence in Respect of Kosovo*, Advisory Opinion, 2010 I.C.J. 403 (22 July) (Cançado Trindade, J., separate).

the longing for justice,"[4] it is clear that Judge Cançado Trindade sides decidedly in favour of the former.[5]

For legal positivists, of course, the crux of any legitimacy that international law can command, and any concomitant obligation to obey, lies in the concept of "consent," the "metaprinciple of sovereign liberty."[6] The idea here is that States have consented to, and continue to consent to, international law as such, the *idea* of international law, *an* international law, and also that they have consented to, and continue to consent to, specific international legal obligations. Although never quite explaining why consent, once given, should somehow be irrevocable,[7] positivists contend that consent, once demonstrated, justifies fealty to particular legal norms. For them, the *tabula rasa* of law was swept

---

4 *Application of the International Convention on the Elimination of All Forms of Racial Discrimination* (Georgia v. Russia), Preliminary Objections, 2011 I.C.J. 70, 306 (1 Apr.) (Cançado Trindade, J., dissenting). For some of international law's other methodological possibilities, see Anne-Marie Slaughter and Steven R. Ratner, "Appraising the Methods of International Law: A Prospectus for Readers," *American Journal of International Law* 93, 2 (1999): 293–295 (relating, *inter alia*, the policy-oriented jurisprudence of the New Haven School, international legal process, critical legal studies, international law/international relations, feminist jurisprudence and law and economics).

5 Indeed, in his 2005 General Course on Public International Law at The Hague Academy of International Law, Judge Cançado Trindade, then Judge of the Inter-American Court of Human Rights and not yet at the International Court of Justice (ICJ), put forward one of the most sustained and cogent critiques of positivism in the context of international law. See Antônio Augusto Cançado Trindade, "International Law for Humankind: Towards a New *Jus Gentium* (I): General Course on Public International Law," in 316 *Collected Courses of The Hague Academy of International Law* (Leiden: Martinus Nijhoff Publishers, 2005), 9–440; Antônio Augusto Cançado Trindade, "International Law for Humankind: Towards a New *Jus Gentium* (II): General Course on Public International Law," in 317 *Collected Courses of The Hague Academy of International Law* (Leiden: Martinus Nijhoff Publishers, 2005), 9–312. A revised second edition of Judge Cançado Trindade's General Course was published as: Antônio Augusto Cançado Trindade, *International Law for Humankind: Towards a New* Jus Gentium (Leiden: Martinus Nijhoff Publishers, 2013).

6 Martti Koskenniemi, "The Politics of International Law," *European Journal of International Law* 1 (1990): 13. See Prosper Weil, "Towards Relative Normativity in International Law?," *American Journal of International Law* 77, 3 (1983): 420–421 (discussing this idea within the context of, as he describes them, voluntarism, neutrality and positivism). See Slaughter and Ratner, *supra* note 4, at 293.

7 See Robert P. Barnidge, Jr., "Neocolonialism and International Law, With Specific Reference to Customary Counterterrorism Obligations and the Principle of Self-Defence," *Indian Journal of International Law* 49, 1 (2009): 28–29.

clean at international law's inception. As the Permanent Court of International Justice (PCIJ) put it in the *Case of the ss Lotus* (*Lotus*), the presumption lies very much against restrictions on the freedom of States, with "[t]he rules of law binding upon States [...] emanat[ing] from their own free will as expressed in conventions or by usages generally accepted as expressing principles of law and established in order to regulate the relations between these co-existing independent communities or with a view to the achievement of common aims."[8]

Let us consider the two sources of law that the PCIJ referred to in *Lotus*, international treaty law and customary international law. The foundation of the modern law of treaties, the 1969 Vienna Convention on the Law of Treaties (VCLT), very much reflects positivist concerns and understandings of law.[9] According to it, not only do States possess an international legal personality sufficient to conclude treaties,[10] the principle of "free consent" is said to be "universally recognized."[11] Consent appears both positively, tying together States and obligations through the *pacta sunt servanda* principle,[12] and negatively, as a defence to such encumbrances.[13] Although treaties have no terminal date as such according to general international law, the VCLT preserves the centrality of consent through such provisions as those that govern a "fundamental change of circumstances"[14]: original intent is reinforced as a reference point for legal obligation. The VCLT's codification of the concept of peremptory norms of general international law, or *jus cogens*, also, at least in part, reflects a consent-centric notion of international legal obligation, though the focus here is not with determining consent as regards a single State but, rather, with assessing whether a particular norm enjoys sufficient acceptance and recognition "by the international community of States as a whole."[15] The will of States undergirds an understanding of international legal obligation.

---

8 *Case of the SS Lotus* (France v. Turkey), 1927 P.C.I.J., Ser. A, No. 10, at 18 (7 Sept.). For a critique of *Lotus*, see *Kosovo, supra* note 3 (Simma, J., declaration).

9 Compare Vienna Convention on the Law of Treaties Between States and International Organizations or Between International Organizations, Vienna, 21 Mar. 1986.

10 See Vienna Convention on the Law of Treaties, Vienna, 23 May 1969, art. 6.

11 *Ibid.* at pmbl.

12 See *ibid.* at art. 26.

13 See, for example, the VCLT's rules in articles 34–38 regarding rights and obligations for third States.

14 See *ibid.* at art. 62.

15 *Ibid.* at art. 53. Of course, there are also very clear natural law dimensions to *jus cogens*. Judge Cançado Trindade, for example, has argued that obligations *erga omnes*, and the

Customary international law, the second source of law that the PCIJ referred to in *Lotus*, appears in article 38(1)(b) of the Statute of the ICJ as "evidence of a general practice accepted as law."[16] As with international treaty law, here, too, notions of consent underlie the basis for legal obligation, with article 38(1)(b) stressing that the relevant practice must be "*accepted* as law." To be sustainable, a customary norm must satisfy both a State practice element and a psychological, mental element, the latter of these being the sense that States feel that they are acting or refraining from acting out of a sense of legal obligation. It is this second element that most clearly reflects the positivist streak, though this is reinforced by the need for "constant and uniform usage practised by the States in question."[17] As the ICJ put it in *North Sea Continental Shelf*, the acts at issue must "be such, or be carried out in such a way, as to be evidence of a belief that this practice is rendered obligatory by the existence of a rule of law requiring it. The need for such a belief, i.e., the existence of a subjective element, is implicit in the very notion of the *opinio juris sive necessitatis*."[18] It was precisely by engaging with this methodology of State practice and *opinio juris* that the ICJ, in methodological fashion, discerned the customary contours of Germany's immunity as a State in *Jurisdictional Immunities of the State (Jurisdictional Immunities)*.[19]

Where positivism places a premium on consent and presumes a State's freedom to act as it wishes absent a demonstration that it has agreed otherwise, natural law theorists such as Judge Cançado Trindade refuse to perceive of an

related concept of *jus cogens* norms, "clearly transcend the individual consent of States, heralding the advent of the international legal order of our times, committed to the prevalence of superior common values, in the ongoing construction of the international law for humankind." *Questions Relating to the Obligation to Prosecute or Extradite* (Belgium v. Senegal), Provisional Measures, Order, 2009 I.C.J. 139, 190 (28 May) (Cançado Trindade, J., dissenting).

16 Statute of the International Court of Justice, art. 38(1)(b).

17 *Colombian-Peruvian Asylum Case* (Colombia v. Peru), 1950 I.C.J. 266, 276 (20 Nov).

18 *North Sea Continental Shelf* (Federal Republic of Germany/Denmark) (Federal Republic of Germany/the Netherlands), 1969 I.C.J. 3, 44 (20 Feb.).

19 See *Jurisdictional Immunities of the State* (Germany v. Italy; Greece intervening), 2012 I.C.J., at ¶ 55 (3 Feb.) (putting forth the black letter law of the methodology of customary international law in this context). See also *Interlocutory Decision on the Applicable Law: Terrorism, Conspiracy, Homicide, Perpetration, Cumulative Charging*, 2011 STL-11-01/I, at ¶ 102 (16 Feb.). The International Law Commission (ILC), under the special rapporteurship of Sir Michael Wood, is currently studying the topic identification of customary international law. See First Report on Formation and Evidence of Customary International Law, International Law Commission, 65th Sess., 6 May-7 June and 8 July-9 August 2013, U.N. Doc. A/CN.4/663 (2013).

international legal order with purely voluntarist moorings. According to them, the new paradigm that the United Nations Charter ushered into being cannot sustain itself on a purely contractual basis. The fear here is that the "higher values" of the post-war era, the values of human rights, peace and security, sustainable development and economic concern, will inevitably have to be sacrificed in a world order understood in purely horizontal terms and that a vertical "reference point" is needed to "check" the "egoistic impulses" of States. Judge Cançado Trindade captured this idea well in the final passages of his dissenting opinion in the preliminary objections phase of *Application of the International Convention on the Elimination of All Forms of Racial Discrimination* (*Georgia*): "consent is not 'fundamental', it is not even a 'principle'";[20] furthermore, "*conscience stands above the will*."[21] In this vision, consent acts, or at least *can* act, as but an encumbrance to the great project of international law.

Judge Cançado Trindade's particular vision of natural law arose very clearly in *Jurisdictional Immunities* with respect to the "right of access to justice."[22] It will be recalled that the primary issue in that case was the customary contours of Germany's immunity as a State. After recognising that Germany and Italy had "basic and opposing positions,"[23] Judge Cançado Trindade found against Germany. He did so, however, not after having meticulously engaged with State practice and *opinio juris* on the matter, as the ICJ did, but, rather, by reaching his sought-after conclusion and then patching together an *ad hoc* methodological justification for it.[24] It seemed that established sources of law could be, indeed, *should* be, transcended and jettisoned,[25] which is to say, the sources of

20 *Georgia*, *supra* note 4, at 321 (Cançado Trindade, J., dissenting).

21 *Ibid.* at 322 (Cançado Trindade, J., dissenting).

22 *Jurisdictional Immunities*, *supra* note 19, at ¶ 221 (Cançado Trindade, J., dissenting) (stating that the "right of access to justice *lato sensu* comprises not only the formal access to justice (the right to institute legal proceedings), by means of an effective remedy, but also the guarantees of the due process of law (with equality of arms, conforming the *procès équitable*), up to the judgment (as the *prestation juridictionnelle*), with its faithful execution, with the provision of the reparation due"). See G.A. Res. 67/1, at ¶¶ 11, 14–16, U.N. Doc. A/RES/67/1 (2012) (also stressing the importance of the right of access to justice).

23 *Jurisdictional Immunities*, *supra* note 19, at ¶ 79 (Cançado Trindade, J., dissenting).

24 This is not altogether surprising given that, in an article published in the *Cambridge Journal of International and Comparative Law* in 2012, Judge Cançado Trindade claimed that the State-centric nature of customary international law was no longer controlling as a methodological framework. See Antônio Augusto Cançado Trindade, "The Historical Recovery of the Human Person as Subject of the Law of Nations," *Cambridge Journal of International and Comparative Law* 1, 3 (2012): 16–19.

25 See *Jurisdictional Immunities*, *supra* note 19, at ¶ 148 (Cançado Trindade, J., dissenting).

law that States had agreed to be bound by in litigation before the ICJ were seen as being in and of themselves neither dispositive nor controlling.[26] As Judge Cançado Trindade's dissenting opinion in *Georgia* put it, "issues of principle" are more important than "evidence,"[27] and State consent can act as an obstacle to the adjudication of international human rights.[28]

If, for Judge Cançado Trindade, the right of access to justice is to be the lodestar in the adjudication of international human rights, then certain obvious questions arise. Whose "justice" is to be preferred, and on what basis? If what is "just" is to replace (rigid) adherence to established sources of law, then how are States to know what the law *is?* Will this mean that the sought-after ends of law will have effectively replaced its means, that is, its methodological processes? If so, what will the effects of this be for the principle of legality? Koskenniemi has expressed the liberal scepticism that "[a]ppealing to principles which would pre-exist man and be discoverable only through faith or *recta ratio* was to appeal to abstract and unverifiable maximums which only camouflaged the subjective preferences of the speaker. It was premised on utopian ideals which were constantly used as apologies for tyranny."[29] If a vague recourse to "human conscience [that] stands above the will of States"[30] is to be determinative, if States are to be "civilised" by "taming" their consent, then how does this differ from a perhaps all too easy recourse to that "brooding omnipresence in the sky,"[31] the dictates of which would hardly seem to be justiciable? Cannot this concern with natural law be said to be but subterfuge, merely a "religion which has changed its supreme beings?"[32]

26 Methodological rigidity was also suspect. See *ibid.* at ¶¶ 288–299 (Cançado Trindade, J., dissenting).

27 *Georgia, supra* note 4, at 314 (Cançado Trindade, J., dissenting).

28 See *ibid.* at 316 (Cançado Trindade, J., dissenting).

29 Koskenniemi, *supra* note 6, at 5. Compare Michael J. Glennon, "The Blank-Prose Crime of Aggression," *Yale Journal of International Law* 35, 1 (2010): 114 (questioning how "reasonable, well-intentioned jurists from different societies [can] identify the content of natural law in any culturally neutral, objectively useful sense").

30 *Questions Relating to the Obligation to Prosecute or Extradite* (Belgium v. Senegal), 2012 I.C.J., at ¶ 166 (20 July) (Cançado Trindade, J., separate).

31 *Southern Pacific Company v. Jensen*, 244 U.S. 205, 222 (1917) (Holmes, J., dissenting).

32 Georgii Plekhanov, "Anarchist Doctrine," in *Communism: Basic Writings*, edited by Anne Jackson Freemantle (New York: Mentor, 1970), 227.

3 The Law of Diplomatic Protection and the Adjudication of International Human Rights

Although there are numerous examples from Judge Cançado Trindade's ICJ jurisprudence of natural law thinking informing the adjudication of international human rights,[33] it is only possible here to focus on the law of diplomatic protection. The law in this area, it is well-known, has not (yet) been codified in treaty form. This means, of course, that one must turn to customary international law to ascertain its normative content.[34] The PCIJ's 1924 statement in *Mavrommatis Palestine Concessions* (*Mavrommatis*) remains the classic one: "By taking up the case of one of its subjects and by resorting to diplomatic action or international judicial proceedings on his behalf, a State is in reality asserting its own rights – its right to ensure, in the person of its subjects, respect for the rules of international law."[35]

This language in *Mavrommatis* is striking in that it conceptualises a State's nationals as being its "subjects," a notion that clearly reinforces the idea of the State as being situated in a hierarchically superior position to its nationals. To be "in reality asserting its own rights" implies that the State's nationals have been stripped of their rights, if, indeed, international law recognised them as having had such rights in the first place. As traditionally understood, then, the law of diplomatic protection engages with the national as one might adjudicate a property dispute, and the rights and obligations that disputing parties might assert with respect to such property in an adversarial setting. It is certainly a dehumanising manoeuvre since it recognises no independent status as such for the individual.[36]

33 See, for example, *Ahmadou Sadio Diallo* (Guinea v. Democratic Republic of the Congo), 2010 I.C.J. 639, 755–759 (30 Nov.) (Cançado Trindade, J., separate) (articulating a "hermeneutics of human rights treaties"). For Ghandhi's thoughts on Judge Cançado Trindade's "hermeneutics of human rights treaties" in *Diallo*, see Sandy Ghandhi, "Human Rights and the International Court of Justice: The *Ahmadou Sadio Diallo* Case," *Human Rights Law Review* 11, 3 (2011): 549–551.

34 Article 44 of the ILC's 2001 Articles on Responsibility of States for Internationally Wrongful Acts codifies the two requirements of a claim for diplomatic protection, namely nationality and exhaustion of "available and effective" local remedies. See Articles on Responsibility of States for Internationally Wrongful Acts, With Commentaries, in 2(2) Yearbook of the International Law Commission 20, 120, art. 44, U.N. Doc. A/CN.4/SER.A/2001/Add.1 (Part 2) (2001).

35 *Mavrommatis Palestine Concessions* (Greece v. United Kingdom), 1924 P.C.I.J., Ser. A, No. 2, at 12 (30 Aug.). See Chittharanjan F. Amerasinghe, *Diplomatic Protection* (Oxford: Oxford University Press, 2008), 21–27; Ghandhi, *supra* note 33, at 553–555.

36 The ILC's 2006 Articles on Diplomatic Protection recognise various types of nationals, with natural persons being but one such type. Nationality is discussed in articles 3–13, in

In November 2010, the ICJ rendered its judgment in *Ahmadou Sadio Diallo* (*Diallo*).[37] Guinea had brought suit in this case against the Democratic Republic of the Congo (DRC), alleging that the DRC had violated its obligations with respect to the protection of Guinean national Ahmadou Sadio Diallo's rights as an individual and his direct rights as *associé* in Africom-Zaire and Africontainers-Zaire. The ICJ rejected Guinea's allegations with respect to his direct rights as *associé* in Africom-Zaire and Africontainers-Zaire.[38] With respect to his rights as an individual, it held that between 1995 and 1996 the DRC had violated its obligations under articles 9(1)-(2) and 13 of the 1966 International Covenant on Civil and Political Rights, articles 6 and 12(4) of the 1981 African Charter on Human and Peoples' Rights and article 36(1)(b) of the 1963 Vienna Convention on Consular Relations,[39] though the ICJ found Guinea's allegations with respect to arrest and detention measures that the DRC had taken between 1988 and 1989 to be inadmissible on procedural grounds.[40] The ICJ saw its judgment as a form of satisfaction and ordered Guinea and the DRC to negotiate a precise amount of compensation within six months that the DRC would then have to pay to Guinea as reparation for the injury suffered.[41] In the event, the two States were unable to do this, and the ICJ ended up ordering the DRC in June 2012 to pay US$95,000 to Guinea, with annual interest of 6 percent to accrue from 1 September 2012 for any amount left unpaid by then.[42]

Ghandhi described Judge Cançado Trindade's separate opinion in *Diallo* as a "breath-takingly wide-ranging opinion on a number of both specific and broad-ranging issues, even outwith the strict confines of that necessitated by the case."[43] Certainly, Judge Cançado Trindade viewed the case as having a

---

Part II: Nationality. See Articles on Diplomatic Protection, With Commentaries, in Report of the International Law Commission, 58th Sess., 1 May-9 June and 3 July-11 August 2006, at 22, 30–70, U.N. Doc. A/61/10 (2006).

37 For Ghandhi's commentary on the case, see Ghandhi, *supra* note 33, at 527–555.

38 See *Diallo*, *supra* note 33, at 673–691.

39 See *ibid.* at 659–673. The ICJ rejected Guinea's allegation with respect to the prohibition on subjecting Diallo to mistreatment on the grounds that Conakry had failed to meet its burden. See *ibid.* at 670–671.

40 See *ibid.* at 652–659.

41 See *ibid.* at 691–692. Ghandhi looked favourably on the ICJ's approach with respect to the negotiation of compensation. See Ghandhi, *supra* note 33, at 552–553.

42 See *Ahmadou Sadio Diallo* (Guinea v. Democratic Republic of the Congo), Compensation, 2012 I.C.J. (19 June). See also Geir Ulfstein, "Awarding Compensation in a Fragmented Legal System: The *Diallo* Case," *Journal of International Dispute Settlement* 4, 3 (2013): 477–485.

43 Ghandhi, *supra* note 33, at 549.

momentous constitutional significance, seeing it as spurring on a "new era of international adjudication of human rights cases by the ICJ."[44] Even though it was due to the fortuitousness of a State's decision to press a claim against another State that led to the finding against the DRC in *Diallo* and the uncontested fact that Diallo would clearly have had no standing before the ICJ had he attempted to make a case *proprio motu*, Judge Cançado Trindade hailed the "instrumental role"[45] that the "traditional instrument"[46] of diplomatic protection had played.[47] *Diallo* also seemed to be an "end of history" moment for Judge Cançado Trindade in that one could seemingly identify in it and previous ICJ jurisprudence the "irreversibility of the advance of humanization, in the present domain of international law [which...] leaves no room for steps backwards, or hesitations."[48] In effect, then, Judge Cançado Trindade saw in *Diallo* the upending of *Mavrommatis*, which, in any event, he dismissed as "not a principle, simply a largely surpassed fiction."[49] Diallo was the "ultimate beneficiary of the reparation[] due,"[50] the "*titulaire* of the right to reparation."[51]

While one can certainly admire Judge Cançado Trindade's optimism and idealism with respect to the law of diplomatic protection and the possibility that it might play a greater role in the adjudication of international human rights, there are a number of reasons for hesitation and caution. First, diplomatic protection, which the Commentaries to the International Law Commission's (ILC) 2006 Articles on Diplomatic Protection refer to as an "important remedy for the protection of persons whose human rights have been violated abroad"[52] and which might also be thought of as a process or procedure for the vindication of rights, remains entirely discretionary under international law.[53] This is clear from the language of article 2 of the Articles

44 *Diallo*, *supra* note 33, at 733 (Cançado Trindade, J., separate).

45 *Ibid.* at 736 (Cançado Trindade, J., separate) (italics omitted).

46 *Ibid.* at 807 (Cançado Trindade, J., separate).

47 Ghandhi correctly observed, if in somewhat understated fashion, that diplomatic protection's discretionary nature "rests uneasily with the principles underlying the international law of human rights, which create directly enforceable rights by the individual against his own State." Ghandhi, *supra* note 33, at 553.

48 *Diallo*, *supra* note 33, at 793 (Cançado Trindade, J., separate).

49 *Ibid.* at 798 (Cançado Trindade, J., separate).

50 *Ibid.* (Cançado Trindade, J., separate).

51 *Ibid.* (Cançado Trindade, J., separate).

52 Articles on Diplomatic Protection, With Commentaries, *supra* note 36, at 26.

53 See John Dugard, "Diplomatic Protection," in *Max Planck Encyclopedia of Public International Law*, at ¶¶ 13–16 (last updated May 2009). See also David J. Bederman, "State-to-State Espousal of Human Rights Claims," *Virginia Journal of International Law Online* 1

on Diplomatic Protection, which speaks of a State's "right," not obligation, to exercise diplomatic protection.[54] That Guinea used its discretion in *Diallo* and sought to exercise diplomatic protection does not in any way mean that it was required to do so as a matter of international law. As the ICJ put it in 1970, a State that may in principle be endowed with a right to exercise diplomatic protection remains the "sole judge to decide whether its protection will be granted, to what extent it is granted, and when it will cease,"[55] and "States have, with regard to their nationals, a discretionary power to grant diplomatic protection or to refuse it."[56]

The ILC could have articulated a clear obligation for States to exercise diplomatic protection when it adopted the Articles on Diplomatic Protection in 2006, either in particular situations or *tout court*, but it chose not to do so, which is significant.[57] In its Comments and Observations to the ILC, Italy had suggested that exceptional circumstances might justify requiring the State of nationality to exercise diplomatic protection, though since Rome seemed to have confused the matter by referring to its suggestion in various parts of its submission to the ILC as being both "progressive development"[58] and "legal duty,"[59] it is difficult to see how precisely this (rejected) suggestion would have related to the traditional discretionary nature of diplomatic protection.[60] Apart from Italy, however, the Comments and Observations of other States to the ILC reaffirmed the traditional view.[61] Uzbekistan was quite frank when,

(2011): 3–11. Note that Ziegler has identified the "potential emergence of a qualified state *duty* to protect its nationals abroad." See Reuven (Ruvi) Ziegler, "Protecting Recognized Geneva Convention Refugees Outside Their States of Asylum," *International Journal of Refugee Law* 25, 2 (2013): 247–252.

54 "A State has the right to exercise diplomatic protection in accordance with the present draft articles." Articles on Diplomatic Protection, With Commentaries, *supra* note 36, at 28, art. 2. See *ibid.* at 28–30.

55 *Barcelona Traction, Light and Power Company, Limited* (Belgium v. Spain), Second Phase, 1970 I.C.J. 3, 44 (5 Feb.).

56 *Ibid.* at 50.

57 On the ILC's work on the law of diplomatic protection, see Annemarieke Vermeer-Künzli, "As If: The Legal Fiction in Diplomatic Protection," *European Journal of International Law* 18, 1 (2007): 56–65.

58 U.N. GAOR, Diplomatic Protection: Comments and Observations Received from Governments: Addendum, at 3, U.N. Doc. A/CN.4/561/Add.2 (2006).

59 *Ibid.*

60 See *ibid.* at 2–3. See also Vermeer-Künzli, *supra* note 57, at 58–61.

61 See, for example, U.N. GAOR, Diplomatic Protection: Comments and Observations Received from Governments, at 10, U.N. Doc. A/CN.4/561 (2006) (Norway, on behalf of the

with no apparent sense of dissatisfaction or derision, it noted that the draft articles "legalize[d] the longstanding and rather widespread practice of 'political lobbying' for property and other interests under foreign jurisdiction."[62] This view corresponds with the ICJ's understanding of diplomatic protection in the second phase of *Barcelona Traction, Light and Power Company, Limited* (*Barcelona Traction*), in which the Court acknowledged that the State of nationality "retains in this respect a discretionary power the exercise of which may be determined by considerations of a political or other nature, unrelated to the particular case."[63]

If the very possibility of a State's decision to exercise diplomatic protection remains discretionary, so also does the State of nationality retain the power to distribute as it deems fit any reparation that it might receive from the respondent State. In this respect, it is rather surprising that Judge Cançado Trindade voted in favour of paragraphs 7 and 8 of the *dispositif* in *Diallo*, which gave Guinea and the DRC six months to negotiate a precise amount of compensation in light of the judgment that the DRC would then have to pay to Guinea as reparation for the injury suffered. His separate opinion did express a "concern that the provision of adequate reparation is still to wait further [...and noted that this] looks somewhat disquieting"[64] and "does not appear reasonable."[65] Still, the fact that Judge Cançado Trindade voted in favour of paragraphs

---

Nordic States (Denmark, Finland, Iceland, Norway and Sweden)) ("support[ing] the chosen approach, on the basis of the main premise that States have a right, not a duty, to exercise diplomatic protection"); *ibid.* at 16 (the Netherlands) (stressing the "discretionary authority of the State in respect of [the] exercise of diplomatic protection"); U.N. GAOR, Diplomatic Protection: Comments and Observations Received from Governments: Addendum, at 4–5, U.N. Doc. A/CN.4/561/Add.1 (2006) (United Kingdom) (stating that "[e]very State retains the discretion, subject to its internal laws, as to how this right of diplomatic protection is exercised, if at all").

62 U.N. GAOR, U.N. Doc. A/CN.4/561, *supra* note 61, at 11.

63 *Barcelona Traction*, Second Phase, *supra* note 55, at 44. Compare *Kaunda and Others v. President of the Republic of South Africa and Others*, 2004 S. Afr., at ¶¶ 23–29, Case CCT 23/04 (4 Aug.) (Chaskalson, J.), at ¶¶ 148–151 (Ngcobo, J., concurring), at ¶¶ 214–217, 236 (O'Regan, J., dissenting). Dugard suggests that relevant considerations include the gravity of the national's injury, the credibility of the respondent State's legal system, reputational concerns, the nature of the State of nationality's political and economic relationship with the respondent State and the degree of support that the injured national enjoys in the State of nationality. See Dugard, *supra* note 53, at ¶ 68.

64 *Diallo*, *supra* note 33, at 797 (Cançado Trindade, J., separate).

65 *Ibid.* at 798 (Cançado Trindade, J., separate).

7 and 8 effectively meant that he was, in a way, contributing to the solidification of a jurisprudence on diplomatic protection that deemphasised the temporal urgency of distributing reparation to the injured national, subjected the precise amount of reparation to the inter-State "horse trading" of negotiation and in no way required the State of nationality to distribute any reparation received to the injured national. Effectively, then, the traditional posture was reaffirmed and reinforced.[66]

The ICJ's unanimity on paragraphs 7 and 8 of the *dispositif* in *Diallo* and the absence of any suggestion, express or implied, that Guinea had an obligation to distribute reparation received to its injured national is somewhat at odds with the "Recommended Practice" in article 19 of the Articles on Diplomatic Protection,[67] though since the ILC itself acknowledged that this article does not reflect customary international law, this can be regarded as, at most, progressive development.[68] The Commentary to article 19(c), which notes that a State that is successful in a claim for diplomatic protection *should* "[t]ransfer to the injured person any compensation obtained for the injury from the responsible State subject to any reasonable deductions,"[69] is also, it should be said, rather imprecise and contradictory. Specifically, it asserts that limiting a State's right to withhold reparation to an injured national after a successful claim for diplomatic protection "does not constitute a settled practice,"[70] yet it

66 In his separate opinion appended to the Compensation phase of *Diallo*, which was handed down in June 2012, Judge Cançado Trindade admitted that the awarded compensation was "formally due [...] to Guinea" but stated that this was "determined by the Court to *his* [i.e., Diallo's] *benefit.* This is the proper meaning, as I perceive it, of resolutory points (1) and (2) of the *dispositif* of the present Judgment, in combination with paragraph 57 of the reasoning of the Court." *Diallo*, Compensation, *supra* note 42, at ¶ 100 (Cançado Trindade, J., separate). This seems to be a strained reading of what the ICJ actually stated in paragraph 57, which seems at most to but ambiguously point in Judge Cançado Trindade's direction: "The Court recalls that the sum awarded to Guinea in the exercise of diplomatic protection of Mr. Diallo is intended to provide reparation for the latter's injury."

67 "A State entitled to exercise diplomatic protection according to the present draft articles, should: (a) Give due consideration to the possibility of exercising diplomatic protection, especially when a significant injury has occurred; (b) Take into account, wherever feasible, the views of injured persons with regard to resort to diplomatic protection and the reparation to be sought; and (c) Transfer to the injured person any compensation obtained for the injury from the responsible State subject to any reasonable deductions." Articles on Diplomatic Protection, With Commentaries, *supra* note 36, at 94, art. 19.

68 See *ibid.* at 94–95. See also Vermeer-Künzli, *supra* note 57, at 61–62.

69 Articles on Diplomatic Protection, With Commentaries, *supra* note 36, at 94, art. 19(c).

70 *Ibid.* at 100.

continues in the same paragraph to suggest that this is "supported by State practice and equity."[71] Quite what the distinction is between "settled practice" and "State practice" is obviously unclear, and the suggestion that article 19(c) is supported by equitable considerations contradicts the ICJ's clear statement in *Barcelona Traction* that equity "cannot require more than the *possibility* for some protector State to intervene."[72] The ICJ in *Diallo* did nothing to challenge or in any way undermine this position.[73] Of course, it is difficult to see how a law of diplomatic protection that does not even require intervention might oblige the State of nationality to distribute any reparation received to the injured national.[74]

Judge Cançado Trindade's suggestion in *Diallo* that the "individual concerned is at the *beginning* and at the *end* of the present case"[75] is questionable given that the "beginning," the effective judicialisation of a claim for diplomatic protection, was predicated upon the fortuitous will of the State of nationality and that the "end" amounted to ordering the transfer of a particular sum of money as compensation to the same State, with no suggestion, much less obligation, that it had to distribute said sum to its injured national. Indeed, there is much in Judge Cançado Trindade's contribution in *Diallo* that seeks to *aspire* a new law of diplomatic protection into being without concerning itself with the actual methodology that is conventionally engaged with with respect to (putative) customary international law norms.[76]

For example, Judge Cançado Trindade's separate opinion in *Diallo* asserts that "we cannot at all remain in the strict and short-sighted confines of diplomatic protection, as a result of not only its ineluctable discretionary nature, but also its static inter-State dimension."[77] The law of diplomatic protection can, and will, does and should, indeed, *must*, remain so, however, if the State practice and *opinio juris* that undergird any change in the customary international law of diplomatic protection do not support a change, in whatever

71 *Ibid.*

72 *Barcelona Traction*, Second Phase, *supra* note 55, at 48 (emphasis added).

73 But see Annemarieke Vermeer-Künzli, "Diallo: Between Diplomatic Protection and Human Rights," *Journal of International Dispute Settlement* 4, 3 (2013): 497–498.

74 Compare Amerasinghe, *supra* note 35, at 79–90.

75 *Diallo*, *supra* note 33, at 798 (Cançado Trindade, J., separate).

76 See José A. Cabranes, "Customary International Law: What It Is and What It Is Not," *Duke Journal of Comparative and International Law* 22, 1 (2011): 143–152 (stressing the importance of methodological rigour when discerning the existence of (putative) customary international law norms). See also Anthony Clark Arend, *Legal Rules and International Society* (New York: Oxford University Press, 1999), 72–73.

77 *Diallo*, *supra* note 33, at 804 (Cançado Trindade, J., separate).

direction and to whatever degree. There is little evidence, and certainly not "evidence of a general practice accepted as law,"[78] to suggest that the requisite body of State practice and *opinio juris* has developed to overturn, or discernibly change, the traditional rule. Furthermore, as the ICJ put it in the second phase of *South West Africa*, interpretations of law that go beyond that which can be sustained as reasonable, even understanding reasonableness in its most generous sense, risk treading on revision or rectification, and "[r]ights cannot be presumed to exist merely because it might seem desirable that they should."[79]

Rather than *aspiring* into being a new law of diplomatic protection that seems to be insufficiently rooted in State practice and *opinio juris*, it would seem preferable to look *beyond* this body of law to alternative forms of human rights protection.[80] Indeed, the Articles on Diplomatic Protection contain a saving clause in article 16 that recognises that diplomatic protection and the law related to human rights protection are "complementary."[81] Diplomatic protection *can* be exercised in a way that furthers the protection of human rights, as, indeed, it was, at least to some extent, in *Diallo*, but as a process or procedure for the vindication of rights, it necessarily operates according to certain modalities that continue to privilege "inter-State optics."[82] As the ILC notes, alternative avenues for the protection of human rights exist when "the obligation breached is owed to the international community as a whole,"[83] as was the case in *Questions Relating to the Obligation to Prosecute or Extradite*,[84] and can include certain rights of recourse pursuant to treaty-based international

78 Statute of the International Court of Justice, art. 38(1)(b).

79 *South West Africa* (Ethiopia v. South Africa; Liberia v. South Africa), Second Phase, 1966 I.C.J. 6, 48 (18 July).

80 See Amerasinghe, *supra* note 35, at 32–36.

81 Articles on Diplomatic Protection, With Commentaries, *supra* note 36, at 86. "The rights of States, natural persons, legal persons or other entities to resort under international law to actions or procedures other than diplomatic protection to secure redress for injury suffered as a result of an internationally wrongful act, [sic] are not affected by the present draft articles." *Ibid.* at 86, art. 16.

82 *Diallo*, *supra* note 33, at 802 (Cançado Trindade, J., separate).

83 Articles on Responsibility of States for Internationally Wrongful Acts, With Commentaries, *supra* note 34, at 126, art. 48(1)(b). See Dugard, *supra* note 53, at ¶ 52. On obligations *erga omnes* generally, see Yoshifumi Tanaka, "Obligations and Liability of Sponsoring States Concerning Activities in the Area: Reflections on the ITLOS Advisory Opinion of 1 February 2011," *Netherlands International Law Review* 60, 2 (2013): 223–225.

84 See *Prosecute or Extradite*, *supra* note 30, at ¶¶ 64–70. The subject matter in *Prosecute or Extradite* is now being litigated before the Extraordinary African Chambers in the Senegalese Courts. See Sarah Williams, "The Extraordinary African Chambers in the

human rights law and customary international human rights law.[85] Although these alternative avenues may not always be as effective in protecting human rights as diplomatic protection,[86] they may sometimes be more effective.[87] In any case, they are more convincingly rooted in the *lex lata*.[88]

4 Conclusion

In the closing passages of his dissenting opinion in *Jurisdictional Immunities*, Judge Cançado Trindade lamented the place of evil in the world.[89] He soberly predicted the likely continuation of evil, though he did hold out some hope, however hesitant, for the future: "even in this grim horizon, endeavours towards the primacy of the *recta ratio* also seem never to vanish, as if suggesting that there is still always hope, in the perennial quest for justice, never reaching an end, like in the myth of Sisyphus."[90] For him, international lawyers have a sacred role to play in the world, and they must strive ever onward to expand the right of access to justice for all, in all possible situations, against all obstacles.

Judge Cançado Trindade's jurisprudence at the ICJ shows how natural law thinking can animate the adjudication of international human rights. It could be argued, however, that the legal positivists with whom Judge Cançado Trindade quarrels are no less committed, certainly not in an ethical or moral sense, to the eradication of evil in the world. Rather, they (simply) contend that the adjudication of law should be sufficiently sensitive to the needs of those actors, primarily States, that international law charges with the creation and implementation of law. What does seem incontrovertible is that the adjudication of international human rights will continue to suffer as long as States continue to see the "cheap talk" of "justice" and "consent" as shields to their compliance with international human rights law.

Senegalese Courts: An African Solution to an African Problem?," *Journal of International Criminal Justice* 11, 5 (2013): 1139–1160.

85 See Articles on Diplomatic Protection, With Commentaries, *supra* note 36, at 86–89.

86 See Dugard, *supra* note 53, at ¶¶ 80–83.

87 See Sean D. Murphy, "What a Difference a Year Makes: The International Court of Justice's 2012 Jurisprudence," *Journal of International Dispute Settlement* 4, 3 (2013): 547–548.

88 Purely from the point of view of efficacy, Amerasinghe suggests that "[t]he acid test for the recognition of diplomatic protection as a useful and viable institution may be whether, where a human rights remedial procedure is also available, an injured alien would rather appeal to his national State for diplomatic protection." Amerasinghe, *supra* note 35, at 78.

89 See *Jurisdictional Immunities*, *supra* note 19, at ¶¶ 227–229 (Cançado Trindade, J., dissenting).

90 *Ibid.* at ¶ 228 (Cançado Trindade, J., dissenting).

CHAPTER 3

The *Pinochet* Judgment Fifteen Years on

J. Craig Barker

1 Introduction

I am delighted to have been invited to contribute to this volume. As a colleague of Professor Sandy Ghandhi for just over ten years, and a friend for even longer, I have benefitted, through countless engaging and challenging discussions, from Sandy's wisdom, thoughtfulness and rigour. It is particularly his rigour that I believe sets Sandy apart as a human rights lawyer. Christopher Waters, in the Introduction to this volume, has highlighted Sandy's concern with "proper procedure" and his focus on the achievement of the furtherance of human protection "within the confines of the relevant treaty or legislation."[1] The work that Sandy and I did together on the *Pinochet* case, resulting in a co-authored piece published in the *Indian Journal of International Law* in 2000,[2] fully reflects Sandy's rigorous approach. The purpose of that article was to examine the House of Lord's judgment in *Ex Parte Pinochet No. 3*[3] and to highlight some of the potential implications of that judgment in terms of both domestic and international law, with a particular emphasis on the question of the protection of human rights.

For many leading scholars writing at the time, the *Pinochet* case was a game changer. According to Ruth Wedgewood, for example, the decision "changed the structure of international law."[4] William Aceves asserted that the *Pinochet* case represented an "emerging trend towards the development of a universal system of transnational law litigation,"[5] while Christine Chinkin spoke of a

1 See Introduction to this volume, text accompanying notes 8–10.

2 Sandy Ghandhi and J. Craig Barker, "The Pinochet Judgment: Analysis and Implications," *Indian Journal of International Law* (2000) 40, 4: 657.

3 *R v. Bow Street Metropolitan Stipendiary Magistrate, Ex Parte Pinochet Ugarte* (*No. 3*) [1999] 2 All E.R. 97 (hereinafter *Pinochet No. 3*).

4 Ruth Wedgewood, "International Criminal Law and Augusto Pinochet," *Virginia Journal of International Law* 40, 4 (2000): 829, 831. Wedgwood further noted that "the case has dramatically limited the immunity that State officials can claim for criminal activities conducted during their days in power."

5 William J. Aceves, "Liberalism and International Legal Scholarship: The *Pinochet* Case and the Move Toward a Universal System of Transnational Law Litigation," *Harvard International Law Journal* 41, 1 (2000): 129, 135.

 | DOI 10.1163/9789004261181_005

victory for the globalisation of human rights law over the horizontal vision of international law based upon the sovereign equality of States.[6] Furthermore, the "unprecedented character" of the case led Andrea Bianchi to assert that "neither jurisdictional immunities nor act of State and other doctrines of judicial self-restraint are consistent with the notion of crimes of international law."[7] Sandy and I were far more circumspect in our analysis, noting the very limited *ratio* of the decision in relation to the various different elements at issue in the case, concluding, ultimately, that "in spite of the many claims that the case against Senator Pinochet stands at the threshold of a new international legal order, the reality is that the case was dependent on a certain very narrow question of UK law."[8]

Fifteen years after the *Pinochet* judgment this chapter will identify the key arguments in our original article and test that analysis against the present day state of international and domestic law, particularly within the context of the highly controversial relationship between immunities and human rights. Additionally, this chapter will seek to further analyse the judgment against recent case law emanating from domestic courts, the European Court of Human Rights and the International Court of Justice (ICJ). The analysis will also briefly consider the alternatives to the constant challenges to immunity from jurisdiction that have the potential further to undermine what is an important procedural safeguard in the conduct of international relations.

2 The *Pinochet* Case: A Limited Precedent

It will be recalled, briefly, that Senator (then General) Augusto Pinochet had become Head of State in Chile after leading a *coup d'état* on 11 September 1973 and had remained in power in that country until 11 March 1990.[9] Pinochet's time in office was notable for the many appalling acts of brutality perpetrated by his forces against the civilian population of that country. In 1998, Senator Pinochet visited the United Kingdom to receive medical treatment. Judicial

6 Christine Chinkin, "United Kingdom House of Lords: *Regina v. Bow Street Stipendiary Magistrate*, ex parte *Pinochet Ugarte*," *American Journal of International Law* 93, 3 (1999): 703, 711.

7 Andrea Bianchi, "Immunity versus Human Rights: The *Pinochet* Case," *European Journal of International Law* 10, 2 (1999): 237, 237.

8 Ghandhi and Barker, *supra* note 2, 707–708.

9 *Pinochet No. 3*, *supra* note 3. This factual account is drawn largely from the speech of Lord Browne-Wilkinson.

authorities in Spain learned of his visit to the UK and sought his extradition in order that he might stand trial in Spain for conspiracy to commit the crimes of murder, torture and hostage-taking. As a result of this action, an international arrest warrant was issued on 16 October 1998 and a provisional arrest warrant was confirmed by a London Magistrate under Section 8 of the Extradition Act 1989. In pursuance of this warrant, Pinochet was arrested in a London hospital on 17 October 1998. On 22 October, a further arrest warrant was issued by Bow Street Magistrates accusing Senator Pinochet of a range of additional offences.

Senator Pinochet commenced proceedings for *habeas corpus* and sought leave for judicial review of the issuance of the two provisional arrest warrants. The matter was heard before a Divisional Court on 28 October 1998 which quashed both warrants, primarily on the basis of the immunity to which Senator Pinochet was entitled as a former Head of State.[10] The Crown Prosecution Service was given leave to pursue an expedited appeal to the House of Lords, which first heard the case between 4 and 12 November 1998. The House of Lords decision in *Pinochet No. 1* by a majority of 3 to 2 found that Senator Pinochet was not entitled to immunity in relation to crimes under international law.[11] Unfortunately for some, this decision was set aside by the House of Lords on 15 January 1999 on the ground that the Appellate Committee had not been properly constructed during the first hearing of the matter (*Pinochet No. 2*).[12] The matter was reheard before the House of Lords on 18 January 1999 which delivered its final opinion on 24 March 1999 (*Pinochet No. 3*).[13]

In order to facilitate the present discussion, it would seem apposite briefly to summarise the conclusions we reached in our *Indian Journal of International Law* article in relation to the decision of the House of Lords in *Pinochet No. 3*. In outlining the legal issues, we highlighted the two specific questions of law that had to be addressed by the Appellate Committee. First, the question had to be addressed as to whether the offences of which Pinochet was accused constituted extradition crimes within the meaning of the Extradition Act 1989. In other words, were the requirements of double criminality met? The second question concerned whether Senator Pinochet was entitled to any form of immunity in respect of those crimes. Naturally this second question would only need to be addressed if the answer to the first question was in the affirmative.[14] In relation to the first question, we concluded that:

10 *Augusto Pinochet Ugarte* [1999] ILM 38 (Q.B. Div'l Ct, 1998).

11 *Ex parte Pinochet Ugarte No. 1* [1998] 4 All E.R. 897; [1998] 3 W.L.R. 1456.

12 *Ex parte Pinochet Ugarte No. 2* [1999] 1 All E.R. 577; [1999] 2 W.L.R. 272.

13 *Pinochet No. 3, supra* note 3.

14 Ghandhi and Barker, *supra* note 2, 658–661.

> [T]here was a general lack of willingness among their lordships to pursue a policy-oriented analysis, with their choosing instead to adopt a strict black-letter approach to the question of statutory interpretation. Similarly…their lordships were generally slow to adopt arguments relating to the right to prosecute an individual accused of torture on the basis that the right existed in customary international law.[15]

Our analysis of the issue of immunity drew attention to the inconsistency of the approach of their lordships to the crucial question of whether Pinochet was acting in an official capacity when he was committing torture or conspiring to torture.[16] Crucially, Pinochet could not have committed the crime of torture as defined in the United Nations Convention Against Torture 1984 had he not been acting in an official capacity.[17] However, insofar as Pinochet was entitled to immunity as a former Head of State, that immunity was only available in relation to his official acts. Accordingly, the immunity was co-extensive with the crime.

Three of the six law lords who made up the majority in the case sought to avoid this difficulty by asserting that Pinochet was not acting in an official capacity when he was committing the alleged crimes.[18] However, if this were the case then no crime would have been committed by Pinochet. The other

15 *Ibid.*, 706.

16 Immunity from jurisdiction is available to individuals either *rationae personae*, if they have a particular status or fill a particular office, for example as a diplomatic agent or Head of State. Immunity *rationae personae* continues as long as they have that status or office. Immunity *rationae materiae* is an immunity available to individuals either in relation to a specific act or residually after termination of the status or office attracting immunity *rationae personae* but only in respect of an official act performed on behalf of a State. Effectively this immunity is the immunity of the State as applied to an individual. The issue of whether an individual is acting within his or her official capacity is accordingly crucial to the determination of whether that person is or is not entitled to immunity.

17 Article 1 of the United Nations Convention Against Torture 1984 defines torture in the following terms: "For the purposes of this Convention, the term 'torture' means any act by which severe pain or suffering, whether physical or mental, is intentionally inflicted on a person for such purposes as obtaining from him or a third person information or a confession, punishing him for an act he or a third person has committed or is suspected of having committed, or intimidating or coercing him or a third person, or for any reason based on discrimination of any kind, when such pain or suffering is inflicted by or at the instigation of or with the consent or acquiescence of a public official or other person acting in an official capacity. It does not include pain or suffering arising only from, inherent in or incidental to lawful sanctions."

18 Lords Browne-Wilkinson, Hutton and Phillips.

three Law Lords who made up the majority argued, on the contrary, that Pinochet had been acting in an official capacity.[19] Ordinarily this would have meant that he was entitled to immunity. However, insofar as the international crime of torture had been incorporated into English law by Section 134 of the Criminal Justice Act 1988 and that provision was enacted after the coming into force of the State Immunity Act 1978, which governed the question of State immunity, and, by analogy, Head of State immunity within English law, their lordships considered that Parliament could not have intended to create, or establish jurisdiction over, a crime that was co-extensive with an immunity from jurisdiction that would be available to anyone accused of committing that crime.

Ultimately, the decision of the majority in *Pinochet No.3*, although lengthy and, at times, rather confusing, correctly concluded that Pinochet could be extradited to Spain to stand trial in respect of acts of torture committed after 29 September 1988. As we know, Pinochet's extradition was eventually blocked by Jack Straw, the then Home Secretary, on medical grounds. However, this should not take away from the fact that, as a matter of law, the House of Lords found that a former Head of State was *not* entitled to immunity form the criminal jurisdiction of the United Kingdom for acts of torture committed by them after the entry into force of Section 134 of the Criminal Justice Act 1988. Accordingly, this was a highly significant and historic decision.

Nevertheless, given our analysis of the limited value of *Pinochet No. 3* as a precedent, it is important to note what the decision did not do. First, the decision did not support the assertion that torture was subject to universal jurisdiction by virtue of customary international law. Lord Millett argued forcibly that the prohibition of the crime of torture had been a peremptory norm (*jus cogens*) since at least 1973, the year in which Pinochet had taken power in Chile, and that Pinochet could be tried anywhere on the basis of universal jurisdiction for torture offences committed at any time during his regime. The rest of the majority were not persuaded by this analysis.[20] They preferred the

19 Lords Hope, Saville and Millett.

20 For a detailed analysis of the jurisdictional question see Ghandhi and Barker, *supra* note 2, 677–694. We concluded, at 689: "Lord Millett aside, none of their lordships were willing to find that there existed in customary international law…a right to prosecute alleged offenders wherever they are found. In other words, customary international law did not provide for universal jurisdiction against torturers. Accordingly, the only legal base for the exercise of universal jurisdiction against an individual accused of the crime of torture is provided by treaty, specifically the Torture Convention."

argument that the Torture Convention had conferred on the UK the right to assert jurisdiction in relation to allegations of torture as defined by the Torture Convention, and that that right had been exercised through the enactment and coming into force of the relevant provision of UK domestic law. Crucially, the status of torture as *jus cogens*, or a peremptory norm of international law, did not confer on States the right to claim universal jurisdiction. Furthermore, in relation to the question of jurisdiction, the decision in *Pinochet No. 3* dealt only with criminal jurisdiction.

Secondly, in relation to the question of immunity from jurisdiction, the decision did not remove immunity for all State officials, serving or former. Thus, insofar as the case dealt only with a former Head of State, whose position was analogous to that of a diplomatic agent,[21] it left open the question of the immunity of other State functionaries, as well as other individuals acting on behalf of the State, who may be entitled to immunity *rationae materiae* in respect of their official acts. It is worth noting that the question of the immunity of State officials from the criminal jurisdiction of foreign States remains highly controversial and is currently under consideration by the International Law Commission with a view to codification.[22]

Finally, the decision rejected the idea that the *jus cogens* character of the prohibition against torture "trumped" any form of immunity from jurisdiction. This is, perhaps, the most controversial aspect of the decision and is deserving of further comment, not least because it is an argument that keeps being put forward despite its essential invalidity. It is, accordingly, an issue to which this chapter will return in due course.

---

21 Section 20(1) of the State Immunity Act 1978 provides that the Diplomatic Privileges Act 1964 (and hence the Vienna Convention on Diplomatic Relations 1961, which was incorporated verbatim into UK law by the 1964 Act) "subject...to any necessary modifications... shall apply to (a) a sovereign or other Head of State...as it applies to a Head of a diplomatic mission." Article 39(2) of the Vienna Convention on Diplomatic Relations 1961 provides that diplomatic agents (and hence Heads of States) retain immunity after they have ceased to function as a diplomatic agent (or Head of State) but only in respect to "acts performed by such person in the course of his functions as a member of the mission." Accordingly, a diplomatic agent (or Head of State) has immunity *rationae personae* up until the point where he ceases his functions after which time he retains residual immunity *rationae material* in respect of his official acts.

22 Analytical Guide to the Work of the International Law Commission, "Immunity of State Officials from Foreign Criminal Jurisdiction," http://legal.un.org/ilc/guide/4_2.htm.

3 Challenging Immunity from Jurisdiction in Cases Involving Abuse of Human Rights

Although the *Pinochet* case was unprecedented insofar as it was the first time "a former Head of a foreign country had been held accountable…before a municipal court for acts of torture allegedly committed while he was in his post,"[23] the case was certainly not the first time that the immunity of a State or a State official had been challenged in a domestic court. Having once been considered as absolute,[24] the immunity of States and State officials from the domestic jurisdiction of foreign countries underwent a radical transformation during the latter half of the twentieth century in favour of the so-called restrictive doctrine of State immunity.

Under this doctrine, which sought to distinguish between official or sovereign acts (acts *jure imperii*) and non-sovereign acts (acts *jure gestionis*), a State or State official was entitled to immunity from the domestic courts of a foreign State only in respect of the former (i.e., acts *jure imperii*). The development of the restrictive doctrine occurred not as the result of formal international agreement but, rather, as a result of challenges to the absolute rule of State immunity by domestic legal authorities and within domestic courts leading, eventually, to the enactment of legislation crystalising the restrictive theory.[25]

---

23 Bianchi, *supra* note 7, 237.

24 The origins of the rule of absolute immunity are disputed and it is asserted that the rule was never part of the civil law tradition. The origins of the rule within the common law tradition are linked to established rules of diplomatic immunity, and based on notions of sovereignty, equality and dignity (see *The Schooner Exchange v. McFaddon* 7 Cranch 116, 31 L.Ed. 287 (1812)). On the theory of absolute immunity as applied in the United Kingdom, see the decisions of the Court of Appeal in *The Parlement Belge* (1880) 5 P.D. 197 and *The Porto Alexandre* [1920] P. 20 and the House of Lords in *The Christina* [1938] A.C. 483. On the application of the approach in the United States of America see the decision of the US Supreme Court in *Berizzi Bros. Co. v. S.S. Pesaro* [1926] 271 U.S. 362.

25 The move to the restrictive approach was commenced in the US by the so-called Tate Letter (Letter from Jack B. Tate, Acting Legal Adviser of the US Department of State to Acting Attorney General Phillip B. Perlmann (May 19 1952) reprinted in 26 *Department of State Bulletin* 984 (1952)). The process in the UK took significantly longer and was primarily facilitated by the judiciary through a series of cases culminating with the Court of Appeal decisions in *The Phillipine Admiral* [1976] 2 WLR 214 and *Trendtex Trading Corporation v. Central Bank of Nigeria* [1977] QB 529 and ultimately confirmed by the House of Lords in *I Congress Del Partido* [1981] 2 All ER 1064. The restrictive theory was enacted into legislation the Foreign Sovereign Immunities Act 1976 in the US and the State Immunity Act 1972 in the UK. See also the European Convention on State Immunity 1972.

This seems to beg the question that if such an approach had been successful in relation to the restricting of immunity in the case of commercial transactions, why should a similar approach not prove equally successful in the context of limiting immunity of States and State officials in respect of breaches of international criminal law and massive human rights abuses? However, as will be shown, the approach has failed.

In fact a number of challenges to State immunity in the context of human rights claims had already been made in domestic courts, primarily within the United States, before the case against Pinochet was brought before the British courts, with varying degrees of success. One of the earliest such cases was *Filartiga v. Pena-Irala*[26] in which the US Court of Appeals for the Second Circuit held that the Alien Tort Claims Act 1789, which provides for the exercise of jurisdiction by the courts of the United States in cases in which an alien sues for a tort "committed in violation of the law of nations or a treaty of the United States," allowed for the exercise of jurisdiction in the US in a case brought by a Paraguayan national against a Paraguayan police official for acts of torture perpetrated in Paraguay. However, the *Filartiga* case did not directly address the potential immunity of the Paraguayan official. In a subsequent case involving similar allegations of State-sanctioned torture, that of *Siderman de Blake v. Republic of Argentina*,[27] it was held that the Alien Tort Claims Act did not constitute an exception to the principle of sovereign (State) immunity albeit in relation to an action that directly impleaded a State, as opposed to an official of a State, as had been the case in *Filartiga*.

Given the jurisdictional complications of these US cases, a more important claim in the context of the *Pinochet* litigation, had previously been brought in the UK courts in the case of *Al-Adsani v. Government of Kuwait*. Sulaiman Al-Adsani was a dual British and Kuwaiti national who was allegedly tortured in Kuwait during May 1991 by various Kuwaiti officials directed by a relation ("the Sheikh") of the Emir of Kuwait, resulting in burns to over 25% of his body. On 29 August 1992, Al-Adsani brought a civil claim against the Sheikh and certain other individuals. He later brought further claims against the Government of Kuwait. Apparently influenced by the case of *Filartiga v. Pena-Irala*, the Court of Appeal, in 1994, refused to apply the State Immunity Act 1978 and granted Al-Adsani leave to serve proceedings abroad against the Government of Kuwait.[28] However, a request from the Government of Kuwait to strike out the claim on the ground of State immunity was granted by the High Court in

26 *Filartiga v. Pena-Irala* 630 F2d 876 (2d. Cir. 1980).

27 *Siderman de Blake v. Republic of Argentina* 965 F.2d 699 (1992).

28 *Al-Adsani v. Government of Kuwait and Others* [1994] P.I.Q.R. 236; 100 ILR 465.

1995,[29] and this was then unanimously upheld by the Court of Appeal in 1996.[30] Leave to appeal was denied by the House of Lords.[31]

Although the State Immunity Act 1978 confirmed the application of the restrictive doctrine of State immunity in the United Kingdom, the Act by no means removed the right of a foreign State to claim immunity from the jurisdiction of the British courts. Indeed, Section 1 of the State Immunity Act 1978 explicitly provides for such immunity except as specified in the Act. The exceptions to immunity are outlined in Sections 2–11 of the Act and deny immunity to foreign States only in a small range of situations, including, most importantly, in relation to commercial transactions.[32] Additionally, in Section 5, the Act denies immunity to a State in case of torts but only where those torts have been caused by an act or omission in the United Kingdom. Accordingly, in relation to the inflicting of torture occasioning injury committed in Kuwait, the right to claim immunity in the face of a tortious claim, according to the terms of the statute, remained with the foreign government. To this extent, the High Court and the Court of Appeal in *Al-Adsani* had merely applied the normal rules of statutory interpretation.

Having exhausted his available remedies in the United Kingdom, Mr. Al-Adsani, initiated a claim before the European Court of Human Rights. The basis of his claim was not the torture inflicted upon him under Article 3 but, rather, the denial of the right to a fair trial in terms of Article 6.[33] The decision of the Grand Chamber, by a very narrow majority of 9 votes to 8, was to the effect that State immunity "pursues the legitimate aim of complying with international law to promote comity and good relations between States through the respect of another State's sovereignty."[34] On the other hand, according to the joint dissenting opinion of six of the minority, "the prohibition of torture, being a rule of *jus cogens*, acts in the international sphere and deprives the rule of sovereign immunity of all of its legal effects in that sphere."[35]

---

29 *Al-Adsani v. Government of Kuwait and Others* [1993] 103 ILR 420.

30 *Al-Adsani v. Government of Kuwait and Others* [1996] 107 ILR 536.

31 For a more detailed survey of the various hearings in this case see Ed Bates, "The *Al-Adsani* Case, State Immunity and the International Legal Prohibition on Torture" *Human Rights Law Review* 3, 1 (2003): 193.

32 State Immunity Act 1978, s. 3.

33 The issue as to whether a successful claim to State immunity was in breach of Article 6 ECHR was considered in *Al-Adsani v. uk* 2001-XI 79; (2002) 34 EHRR 273, alongside two other cases: *Fogarty v. uk* (2001-XI 157; (2002) 34 EHRR 302) and *McElhinney v. Ireland* (2001-XI 37; (2002) 34 EHRR 322).

34 *Al-Adsani, supra* note 33, ¶ 54.

35 *Ibid.*, joint dissent of Judges Rozakis and Caflisch joined by Judges Wildhaber, Costa, Cabral Barreto and Vajid, at ¶ 4.

By the time the Grand Chamber sat to hear this case in 2001, the *Pinochet* decision had been delivered. Given that *Pinochet* concerned a matter of criminal law and *Al-Adsani* concerned a civil claim, the former was not a direct precedent for the latter. Indeed, although the *Pinochet* decision was referred to in the judgment of the Grand Chamber, the majority sought to distinguish that case as a criminal case that removed the immunity *rationae materiae* from criminal jurisdiction of a former Head of State and "did not in any way affect the immunity *rationae personae* of foreign sovereign States from civil jurisdiction in respect of such acts."[36] For the minority, that distinction was spurious. According to Judge Ferrari Bravo, the Court need only have applied the decision in *Pinochet No.3* "to the effect that the prohibition of torture is now *jus cogens*, so that torture is a crime under international law. It follows that every State has a duty to *contribute* to the punishment of torture and cannot hide behind formalist arguments to avoid having to give judgment."[37] The rest of the minority merely rejected the distinction between civil and criminal proceedings as "not consonant with the very essence of the operation of the *jus cogens* rules."[38]

A slightly different approach was taken by the applicants in *Jones v. Saudi Arabia*, which was another civil claim involving similar facts to those in *Al-Adsani*. In *Jones*, Mr. Jones and Mr. Mitchell, with others, alleged that they had been systematically tortured while imprisoned in Saudi Arabia and claimed damages for physical and mental injuries they suffered as a result. In the first action, Mr. Jones made claims against the Kingdom of Saudi Arabia and officials of the Ministry of the Interior led by Lieutenant-Colonel Abdul Aziz. His attempts to serve the claim against Aziz had failed and he sought permission to serve Aziz out of the jurisdiction.[39] In the second action, Mr. Mitchell and others made claims against four named individuals and sought permission to serve these individuals out of the jurisdiction.[40] In the case brought by Jones, the Kingdom of Saudi Arabia claimed immunity for itself and for its agent in terms of Section 1 and Section 14(1) of the State Immunity

36 *Al-Adsani, supra* note 33, ¶ 65.

37 *Ibid.*, dissenting opinion of Judge Ferrari Bravo.

38 *Al-Adsani, supra* note 33, joint dissent of Judges Rozakis and Caflisch joined by Judges Wildhaber, Costa, Cabral Barreto and Vajid, ¶ 4.

39 *Jones v. Ministry of Interior Al-Mamlaka Al-Arabiya as Saudiya* (*the Kingdom of Saudi Arabia*), unreported decision of Master Whitaker, 30 July 2003.

40 *Mitchell and others v. Al-Dali and others and Ministry of Interior Al-Mamlaka Al-Arabiya as Saudiya* (*the Kingdom of Saudi Arabia*), unreported decision of Master Whitaker, 30 July 2003.

Act 1978. In the *Mitchell* action, it claimed immunity for its agents in terms of Section 14(1) of the 1978 Act. In both actions, at first instance, the right to serve Aziz and the four other officials was refused on the grounds of Section 1 of the State Immunity Act 1978 and on the basis of the decision of the European Court of Human Rights in *Al-Adsani*. In relation to the individual defendants, the judge, Master Whitaker, found that the immunity of the Kingdom of Saudi Arabia attached also to them on the basis that, if this were not the case, the immunity of Saudi Arabia could be circumvented by impleading its officials.

The immunity of the Kingdom of Saudi Arabia was upheld at the Court of Appeal after a conjoined hearing.[41] However, the Court was willing to accept a different approach in relation to the immunity of the individual officials. The decision to remove the immunity of the State officials relied heavily on the *Pinochet* decision. Mance LJ, in delivering the leading judgment, undertook an extensive review of relevant case law (primarily from the UK and the US). He acknowledged, first, that three of their lordships in *Pinochet No. 3* had stated, in *obiter*, that immunity *rationae materiae* would continue in respect of a former Head of State or other State official in civil proceedings.[42] However, he then argued that at least some of their lordships in that case had concluded that Pinochet's alleged acts could not be regarded as a function of a Head of State. For Mance, that finding could be applied equally to other State officials as well as to both civil and criminal cases and would have the effect of removing immunity *rationae materiae* in all cases involving allegations of torture. He concluded:

> Once it has been firmly established (as it has been by *Ex p Pinochet* (*No. 3*)) that a State can claim no immunity in respect of an individual officer committing systematic torture in an official context, the issue whether there is or should be civil immunity seems to me to acquire a different complexion, and to start from a different point, to that which applied when the argument was proceeding the other way around.[43]

In the House of Lords, this attempt to distinguish between the immunity of the State and that of a State's officials in respect of the same acts was firmly rejected.[44] Lord Bingham noted that Section 1(1) of the State Immunity Act 1978,

---

41 *Jones v. Ministry of Interior Al-Mamlaka Al-Arabiya as Saudiya* (*the Kingdom of Saudi Arabia*) [2005] QB 699; [2005] 2WLR 808.

42 *Ibid.*, ¶ 57.

43 *Ibid.*, ¶ 74.

44 *Jones v. Ministry of Interior Al-Mamlaka Al-Arabiya as Saudiya* (*the Kingdom of Saudi Arabia*) [2007] 1AC 270; [2006] 2WLR 1424.

in line with the domestic law of other States, provides only for specified exceptions.[45] He did not consider that the present case was one in which any of the relevant exceptions applied.[46] Furthermore, he considered that there was ample authority to show that a foreign State is entitled to claim immunity for its servants in circumstances in which it can claim immunity for itself; to do otherwise would be to implead the State through the back door.[47] Lord Bingham followed the clear reasoning of the majority in *Pinochet*, in finding that torture is only a crime under international law if it is committed by an official or person acting in an official capacity.[48] Other than in that context, the *Pinochet* precedent was categorically different from the circumstances of the present case, particularly in relation the question of jurisdiction.[49] Lord Hoffmann developed the jurisdictional question by noting that a conflict between the prohibition of torture and State immunity would exist if the prohibition on torture were subject to a rule of international law entitling or requiring States to assume civil jurisdiction over other States in cases where torture is alleged.[50]

4 Normative Hierarchy and the Problem of Impunity

Needless to say, the European Court of Human Rights decision in *Al-Adsani* and the House of Lords decision in *Jones* were the subject of significant academic criticism. Two such criticisms are worthy of further comment at this point in the analysis. Alexander Orakhelashvili has repeatedly argued in favour of the importance of *jus cogens* and the normative hierarchy of international law.[51] In relation to *Jones*, in particular, he argued that the normatively higher status of the prohibition on torture should have the effect of overriding the hierarchically inferior norm providing for State immunity.[52] As has been seen, this argument reflects the views of the minority in the *Al-Adsani* case at the European Court of Human Rights. However, the argument was not persuasive

45 *Ibid.*, ¶ 7.

46 *Ibid.*, ¶ 9.

47 *Ibid.*, ¶¶ 11–13.

48 *Ibid.*, ¶ 19.

49 *Ibid.*, ¶34.

50 *Ibid.*, ¶¶ 43–46

51 Alexander Orakhelashvili, "State Immunity and Hierarchy of Norms: Why the House of Lords Got it Wrong," *European Journal of International Law*, 18, 5 (2007): 955.

52 *Ibid.*, 963–970.

to the majority in *Al-Adsani*. Furthermore, the issue of *jus cogens*, although referred to extensively in the various majority speeches in *Pinochet* in fact did not form the basis of any of their lordship's decisions. In *Jones*, Mance LJ appeared to steer clear of the concept of *jus cogens* in his analysis, as did Lord Phillips who delivered a concurring opinion.[53] In the House of Lords, once again, the issue of *jus cogens* was largely avoided essentially through the approved citation of the now famous words of Lady Hazel Fox to the effect that:

> State immunity is a procedural rule going to the jurisdiction of a national court. It does not go to substantive law; it does not contradict a prohibition contained in a jus cogens norm but merely diverts any breach of it to a different method of settlement. Arguably, then, there is no substantive content in the procedural plea of State immunity upon which a jus cogens mandate can bite.[54]

This procedural versus substantive differentiation is persuasive and has more recently been cited with approval by the ICJ in the *Jurisdictional Immunities of the State* case.[55] However, for this author, the rejection of the *jus cogens* argument has a more practical aspect to it. If the *jus cogens* argument were to prevail, it would not be limited merely to the immunity of a State official, or even to the immunity of a Head of State. It would necessarily apply to all forms of immunity from jurisdiction. Furthermore, and even more problematically, it would "trump" not only immunity *rationae materiae*, covering official acts after the termination of a particular function, but also immunity *rationae personae*, an immunity that applies, for example, in relation to diplomatic personnel, as well as to serving Heads of State and other high-ranking State officials. Immunity would be subject to removal even where such individuals had merely been accused of violations of *jus cogens* norms. The unintended consequences of this and the potential impact on long established and important rules providing for the efficacious and orderly conduct of foreign relations, as well as for the physical security of State officials living and working outside their home country, could be devastating.

---

53 *Jones, supra* note 41, ¶ 101 *et seq.*

54 Hazel Fox, *The Law of State Immunity* (Oxford: Oxford University Press, 2002), 525. Cited in *Jones, supra* note 44, ¶ 44.

55 *Jurisdictional Immunities of the State* (*Germany v. Italy*: *Greece* intervening), 2012 I.C.J 99 (3 Feb.), ¶¶ 92–97.

A separate criticism of the decision of the House of Lords in *Jones* was provided by Lorna McGregor who argued, perhaps in light of the Fox statement cited above, that "formalistic interpretive techniques are often employed to deny the impact of immunity on impunity."[56] Specifically, McGregor noted that the procedural immunity rule essentially trumps the substantive human rights norm, and does so more often than not where no other remedy exists for the applicant. This effectively results in the vast majority of cases in a denial of justice. Persuasive as this argument undoubtedly is, it is worth noting that many other procedural rules will have the same effect in situations where the procedural rules are often disparagingly described as legal technicalities. For example, in *Jones*, the torture of Jones and his fellow applicants is unlikely to have been isolated and probably occurred as part of a regime of mistreatment and torture of prisoners in gaols across Saudi Arabia. Nevertheless, Saudi nationals subjected to the same or similar appalling treatment would not be entitled to bring a claim before British courts on the basis of which might be described as a similarly formalistic procedural issue, specifically, the lack of jurisdiction. This might seem to be a rather extreme example. However, the point is that procedural matters should not simply be condemned as overly formalistic. As Sandy Ghandhi has long argued, they are an integral part of every legal process.[57]

5 Immunity and Human Rights in International Courts

Reference has already been made to the, admittedly rather narrow, decision of the European Court of Human Rights in *Al-Adsani v. United Kingdom*. That decision was effectively upheld by the same court on 14 January 2014 when it delivered its long awaited judgment in the *Jones and others v. United Kingdom*,[58] which was an application submitted as a result of the decision of the House of Lords in *Jones v. Saudi Arabia*. A Chamber of the ECtHR, by a majority of six to one, upheld the decision of the House of Lords to grant immunity to the Kingdom of Saudi Arabia and to certain of its officials in civil proceedings on the basis that immunity was a generally recognised rule of public international

56 Lorna McGregor, "Torture and State Immunity: Deflecting Impunity, Distorting Sovereignty" *European Journal of International Law* 18, 5 (2007): 903, 905.

57 See, for example, Sandy Ghandhi, "*Avena and other Mexican Nationals* (*Mexico v. United States of America*), Provisional Measures, order of 5 February 2003," *International and Comparative Law Quarterly* 53, 3 (2004): 738.

58 *Jones v. United Kingdom* (*Application 34356/06 and 40528/06*) decision of 14 January 2014.

law. Immunity therefore did not contravene Article 6(1) of the European Convention on Human Rights. Furthermore, according to the Court, the immunity of the State could not be circumvented by suing that State's officials.

Since *Pinochet*, in addition to the European Court of Human Rights, the issue of the extent of the immunity from jurisdiction of States and State officials from the domestic courts of foreign courts has been considered by the ICJ on at least two occasions. The *Arrest Warrant Case*[59] concerned the validity of an arrest warrant issued by Belgium against Abdoulave Yerodia Ndombasi, the serving Minister of Foreign Affairs for the Democratic Republic of the Congo. The arrest warrant sought Yerodia's detention and extradition to Belgium as a result of his alleged violations of international humanitarian law. The DRC claimed that Belgium had violated its sovereignty and that it was in breach of international law relating to immunity from jurisdiction. Most notably for present purposes, Belgium, in its argument before the ICJ, relied on the *Pinochet* case, asserting that that case had established that an exception to immunity existed in the case of serious crimes under international law.[60] Given the above analysis, it is clear that this assertion was quite simply wrong and it was rightly ignored by the ICJ which held that the arrest warrant was a violation of Yerodia's immunity from criminal jurisdiction and the inviolability of the incumbent Minister for Foreign Affairs of the DRC.

The separate concurring opinion of Judges Higgins, Kooijmans and Buergenthal in the *Arrest Warrant Case* suggested the possibility of an emerging rule of international law providing potentially for the removal of immunity in cases of serious international crimes insofar as such activities cannot be considered as official acts.[61] However, the evidence they provided for this

59 *Arrest Warrant of 11 April 2000 (Democratic Republic of the Congo v. Belgium)*, 2002 I.C.J. 3 (11 Apr.).

60 *Ibid.*, ¶ 56.

61 *Arrest Warrant Case, supra* note 59, joint separate opinion of Judges Higgins, Kooijmans and Buergenthal: "immunity prevails only as long as the Minister is in office and continues to shield him or her after that time only for 'official' acts. It is now increasingly claimed in the literature...that serious international crimes cannot be regarded as official acts because they are neither normal State functions nor functions that a State alone (in contrast to an individual) can perform: (Robert Goff J...and Lord Wilberforce articulated this test in *1 Congreso del Partido* [1978] QB 500, at 528 and [1983] 1 AC 244, 268 respectively). This view is underscored by the increasing realisation that State-related motives are not the proper test for determining what constitutes public State acts. The same view is gradually also finding expression in State practice, as evidenced in judicial decisions and opinions. (For an early example, see the judgment of the Israel Supreme Court in the *Eichmann* case: Supreme Court, 29 May 1962, 36 ILR 5, 312.) See also the speeches of Lords Hutton and

assertion was rather limited and was made up, to a large extent, by the speeches of only two of their lordships in *Pinochet No. 3* and two in *Pinochet No. 1*, the latter of which, of course, had been vacated and therefore was of no legal effect. The development of a rule of international law that serious international crimes cannot be regarded as official acts, were it to happen, would be welcome and would help significantly in clarifying the availability of immunities in cases of serious international crimes. However, the evidence that has emerged from the attempts by the International Law Commission to codify the question of the jurisdictional immunities of States and the resulting United Nations Convention on the Jurisdictional Immunities of States and Their Property 2004[62] suggests that State practice has, in fact, gone the other way. States are less and less willing to accept further restrictions on their immunity and that of their officials from the jurisdiction of foreign States.

This perspective has been made all the clearer by the most recent decision of the ICJ on the issue of immunity from jurisdiction in the *Jurisdictional Immunities of the State* case in 2012.[63] The case relates to an action initiated in the Italian courts by Mr. Luigi Ferrini, an Italian national who had been arrested and deported to Germany during the Second World War. Mr. Ferrini and many of his compatriots had been forced to work in munitions factories in Germany, had been subjected to gross violations of their human rights and were seeking compensation in respect of that treatment. The Italian courts, at first instance, and on appeal, dismissed Ferrini's case due to the jurisdictional immunity of Germany.[64] However, at the Italian Court of Cassation on 11 March 2004, in reliance to a significant degree on the decision of the English House of Lords in *Pinochet No. 3*,[65] it was held that the immunity of Germany did not apply as the act complained of constituted an international crime.[66] The case was returned to the original court, which held, nevertheless, that the claim was time barred. This decision was, however, reversed by the Court of Appeal of Florence, and Germany was held liable to pay damages.[67] After the initial Court of Cassation

Phillips of Worth Matravers in *R v. Bartle and the Commissioner of Police for the Metropolis and Others*, ex parte *Pinochet* ('*Pinochet III*'); and of Lords Steyn and Nicholls of Birkenhead in '*Pinochet I*', as well as the judgment of the Court of Appeal of Amsterdam in the *Bouterse* case (Gerechtshof Amsterdam, 20 November 2000, para. 4.2)."

62 U.N. Doc. A/59/508.

63 *Jurisdictional Immunities of the State*, *supra* note 55.

64 See *Ibid.*, ¶ 27.

65 *Ibid.*, ¶ 87.

66 *Ferrini v. Federal Republic of Germany*, Decision No. 5044/2004 (Rivista di diritto internazionale, vol. 87, 2004, 539); 128 ILR 658 (2004).

67 See *Jurisdictional Immunities of the State*, *supra* note 55, ¶ 27.

decision in Ferrini, subsequent cases were brought by further claimants in Turin and Sciacca. These led to the filing of an interlocutory appeal by Germany before the Italian Court of Cassation requesting a declaration of lack of jurisdiction. By two orders of 29 May 2008, "the Italian Court of Cassation confirmed that the Italian courts had jurisdiction over the claims against Germany."[68] Ultimately, Germany brought the case to the ICJ, alleging *inter alia* that by allowing civil claims to be brought against it, Italy had failed to respect the jurisdictional immunity that Germany enjoyed under international law.[69]

It is not intended here to provide a detailed analysis of the Court's decision, something that has been done elsewhere by the present author.[70] Nevertheless, given the reasoning outlined above, it should come as no surprise that the ICJ considered that the *Pinochet* decision was irrelevant to the present case on the grounds that "Pinochet concerned the immunity of a former Head of State from the criminal jurisdiction of another State, not the immunity of the State itself designed to establish its liability to damages."[71] The Court further noted that: "In its later judgment in *Jones v. Saudi Arabia*, the House of Lords further clarified this distinction, Lord Bingham describing the distinction between civil and criminal proceedings as 'fundamental to the decision' in *Pinochet*."[72] Ultimately, the ICJ found that there is no limitation of State immunity by virtue of "the gravity of the violation or the peremptory character of the rule breached."[73] It noted that none of the relevant State practice and none of the relevant multilateral treaties, including the European Convention on State Immunity, 1972, the United Nations Convention 2004 or the draft Inter-American Convention on Jurisdictional Immunity of States included such an exception to immunity. Although it has been criticised by some as being too

68 *Giovanni Mantelli and others* (Italian Court of Cassation, Order No. 14201 (Mantelli) *Foro italiano*, vol. 134, 2009, I, 1568); and *Liberato Maietta* (Order No. 14209 (Maietta) *revisita di dritto* internazionale, vol. 91, 2008, 86). *Jurisdictional Immunities of the State, supra* note 55, ¶ 28.

69 See further *Jurisdictional Immunities of the State, supra* note 55, ¶¶ 15, 16, 17 and 37.

70 For my own analysis of the case see J. Craig Barker, "*Jurisdictional Immunities of the State* (*Germany v. Italy*) Judgment of 3 February 2012," *International and Comparative Law Quarterly* 62, 3 (2013): 741; and J. Craig Barker, "Negotiating the Complex Interface between State Immunity and Human Rights: An Analysis of the International Court of Justice Decision in *Germany v. Italy*," *International Community Law Review* 15, 4 (2013): 415.

71 *Jurisdictional Immunities of the State, supra* note 55, ¶ 87.

72 *Ibid.*

73 *Ibid.*, ¶ 89.

State-centric,[74] the ICJ in *Jurisdictional Immunities of the State*, in much the same way as the House of Lords strove to do in its *Pinochet* judgment, sought to state the law as it stands not as other would like it to be.

6 Conclusions

The decision in *Pinochet No. 3* certainly brought the issue of the relationship between immunities and human rights to the forefront of academic debate in international law. However, the decision itself has proved to be of limited value to proponents of further limitation of immunities beyond those of former Heads of States in relation to the crime of torture. It seems that States – and the highest national and international courts – are reluctant further to limit State immunity. As has been noted above, the International Law Commission is currently examining the question of "Immunity of State Officials from Foreign Criminal Jurisdiction"[75] and it remains to be seen whether that work will result in a strengthening or diminution of the immunity of such individuals.

The decision in *Jurisdictional Immunities of the State* has likely ensured that it will be some time before domestic courts will feel able to challenge any form of jurisdictional immunities in the context of human rights violations. This may be seen as a bad thing. However, it should be taken as an opportunity to reconsider existing laws in order to better provide for the adjudication of human rights. One way forward might be to strengthen human rights bodies and international judicial processes. Pinochet was undoubtedly an evil man but it should not have been left to a Spanish judge to issue an arrest warrant to have him arrested in the United Kingdom. He could have been dealt with by other means, both judicial and political. Similarly, the judges of the ICJ should not be in a position to condemn the acts of the Nazi regime during the Second World War as they did in the *Jurisdictional Immunities of the State* case, and then not be able to test the appropriateness of the compensation paid by Germany to the entirety of its victims. Mr. Ferrini should not have been left having to sue the German government in the Italian courts but should have been fully compensated by his home government who could then have sought compensation from Germany.

---

74 The most damning criticism of the decision came from within the Court itself: see *ibid.*, dissenting opinion of Judge Cançado Trindade.

75 See *supra* note 22 and accompanying text.

Perhaps, given the failure to further develop the Pinochet precedent beyond its very narrow *ratio*, it is time to consider other approaches to the development of human rights adjudication and application other than through challenging jurisdictional immunity. After all, immunity from jurisdiction, in all of its various forms, serves an important purpose in international relations and its demise would likely cause more problems than it would solve.

CHAPTER 4

Balancing Liberty and the Security Council

Judicial Responses to the Conflict between Chapter VII Resolutions and Human Rights Law under the Council's Targeted Sanctions Regime

David Leary

1 Introduction

The obligations imposed by the Security Council under Chapter VII of the United Nations Charter have the potential to significantly impede the application by States of their duties under human rights law. This is particularly apparent in view of the capacity of Charter-based commitments to prevail over conflicting obligations under Article 103 of the Charter. The danger of such encroachment by the Council on the application of States' human rights commitments has become increasingly evident in recent years, most notably in the context to be addressed in this chapter – the regime of targeted sanctions against individuals "associated with" Al Qaeda, Usama bin Laden and the Taliban.[1] These individuals are designated and placed on the Consolidated List by the Sanctions Committee, a subsidiary organ of the Council, pursuant to information received from States and regional organisations. Under the terms of the regime, States are required to impose severe financial restrictions and travel bans against all individuals that have been designated in this way, without the possibility of recourse to any effective review procedure through which the individuals might confront the evidence against them or challenge their continued subjection to the measures imposed.

This regime has been widely criticised in terms of its implications for the protection of human rights, and for the capacity of States to adhere to their countervailing duties under human rights treaties and customary law.[2] The human rights standards most visibly threatened by the Council's requirements

1 Initially adopted in Resolution 1267 (S/Res/1267 (2001)), and subsequently developed through a number of further Chapter VII resolutions.

2 See, for example, Jessica Almqvist, "A Human Rights Critique of European Judicial Review: Counter-Terrorism Sanctions," *International and Comparative Law Quarterly* 57 (2008): 303, 318–319; Larissa van den Herik and Nico Schrijver, "Eroding the Primacy of the UN System of Collective Security: The Judgment of the European Court of Justice in the Cases of *Kadi and Al Barakaat*," *International Organizations Law Review* 5 (2008): 329, 331.

 | DOI 10.1163/9789004261181_006

and their implementation by States are the rights of individuals to access to a court and to an effective remedy.[3] A number of other important protections are also implicated, for example the rights to property,[4] freedom of movement[5] and private and family life.[6] Unsurprisingly, the regime has therefore given rise to litigation before a number of courts and human rights bodies, in which those affected by measures implementing the Council's requirements have sought to challenge these measures on the basis of their infringement of States' human rights commitments. In response to these challenges, States have argued that the measures were required by a binding obligation under Chapter VII of the Charter, which prevailed over the countervailing human rights duties and rendered them inapplicable. The judicial bodies concerned have thus been faced with the question as to whether, and to what extent, States' commitments under human rights law may be given effect in circumstances where such obligations appear to conflict with requirements imposed by the Council under Chapter VII.

The capacity of judges to effectively uphold the relevant human rights protections in these circumstances is far from certain in view of the absence of clarity surrounding the existence of legal constraints on the Council in relation to the protection of human rights.[7] Significant uncertainties persist in this context, notwithstanding the Council's duty under Article 24 of the Charter to "act in accordance with the Purposes and Principles of the United Nations" when discharging its primary responsibility for the maintenance of international peace and security, which under Article 1(3) include the achievement of

---

3 Articles 14 and 2 of the International Covenant on Civil and Political Rights (ICCPR) and Articles 6 and 13 of the European Convention on Human Rights (ECHR).

4 Article 1 of the First Protocol to the ECHR.

5 Article 8 ECHR.

6 Article 2, Protocol 4 ECHR. See also Council of Europe Parliamentary Assembly, Report of the Committee on Legal Affairs and Human Rights, "United Nations Security Council and European Union Blacklists," Doc. 11454 (2008): ¶ 10. The severity the consequences of the required measures for individuals designated by the Sanctions Committee has led the United Kingdom's Supreme Court to describe such individuals as "effectively, prisoners of the State," *HM Treasury v. Mohammed Jabar Ahmed and others* [2010] UKSC 2 (27 Jan., 2010) (*Ahmed*), ¶ 60.

7 See, for example, Anthony Aust, "The Role of Human Rights in Limiting the Enforcement Powers of the Security Council: A Practitioner's View," in *Review of the Security Council by Member States*, edited by Erika de Wet, André Nollkaemper and Petra Dijkstra (New York: Intersentia, 2003), 31; T.D. Gill, "Legal and Some Political Limitations of the UN Security Council to Exercise its Enforcement Powers under Chapter VII of the Charter," *Netherlands Yearbook of International Law* 26 (1995): 33; and Gabriël H. Oosthuizen, "Playing the Devil's Advocate: The United Nations Security Council is Unbound by Law," *Leiden Journal of International Law* 12 (1999): 549.

"international cooperation...in promoting and encouraging respect for human rights and...fundamental freedoms."[8] Moreover, it is far from certain whether any judicial body has the capacity to review the substance or overriding impact of the requirements imposed by the Council on the basis of any such constraints, so as to place limits on the body's encroachment of States' human rights commitments.[9] Thus it would appear that the application of States' long-established obligations under human rights law may be suspended by any conflicting requirement under binding Chapter VII resolutions, giving rise to a clear danger of "wide and indefinite lacunae in human rights protection."[10]

However, following an initially high degree of deference to the requirements imposed by the Council, and to the argument advanced by governments and regional bodies that these served to preclude the application of any inconsistent human rights rules,[11] the position appears to have evolved, at least to some degree, with more recent decisions by a number of international and domestic judicial bodies. These decisions – most notably *Kadi* before the European Court of Justice (ECJ),[12] *Ahmed*[13] and *Abdelrazik*[14] before the domestic courts of the United Kingdom and Canada, *Sayadi* before the Human Rights Committee[15] and *Nada* at the European Court of Human Rights

8 Erika de Wet, "The Chapter VII Powers of the United Nations Security Council" (Oxford: Hart Publishing, 2004), 344; and August Reinisch, "Securing the Accountability of International Organizations," *Global Governance* 7 (2001): 131, 136.

9 Marko Milanović, 'Norm Conflict in International Law: Whither Human Rights?' *Duke Journal of International and Comparative Law* 20 (2009): 69, 94.

10 Kathryn Smyth, "*R. (on the application of Al-Jedda) v. Secretary of State for Defence*: Human Rights and Accountability in International Military Operations," 6 *European Human Rights Law Review* 6 (2008): 606, 620. See also Vera Gowlland-Debbas, "The Security Council as Enforcer of Human Rights," in *Securing Human Rights: Achievements and Challenges of the UN Security Council*, edited by Bardo Fassbender (New York: Oxford University Press, 2011), 36, 69.

11 See in particular Case T–315/01 *Kadi v. Council and Commission* [2005] ECR II-03649 (*Kadi* CFI); *Nada v. State Secretariat for Economic Affairs*, Bundesgericht (Federal Court), 133 *Entscheidungen des Schweizerischen Bundesgerichts* II 450–467 (14 Nov., 2007) (Switz.) (*Nada* FC). See also *R. (on the application of Al-Jedda) v. Secretary of State for Defence* [2007] UKHL 58.

12 Joined Cases C-402/05 P and C-415/05, *Yassin Abdullah Kadi and Al Barakaat International Foundation v. Council of the European Union and Commission of the European Communities* [2008] ECR I-6351 (3 Sept., 2008) (*Kadi* ECJ).

13 *Supra* note 6.

14 *Abdelrazik v. Minister of Foreign Affairs* [2009] F.C. 580 (Can.) (*Abdelrazik*).

15 *Nabil Sayadi and Patricia Vinck v. Belgium*, Communication No. 1472/2006, U.N. Doc. CCPR/C/94/D/1472/2006 (29 Dec., 2008) (*Sayadi*).

(ECtHR)[16] – provide evidence of a growing willingness among judicial bodies to challenge States' arguments regarding the prevalence granted to the Council's requirements over human rights norms, and to insist on the continued enforcement of States' human rights commitments notwithstanding their coexisting obligation under binding Chapter VII resolutions.[17]

In this way courts are understood to have adopted a more critical approach to the Council's subordination of human rights law,[18] with the deference demonstrated in earlier jurisprudence – wherein the emphasis had been placed firmly on the "fundamental" importance of the Council's role in maintaining international peace and security[19] – giving way to more "robust" judicial responses,[20] and even a "wave of defiance" against the Council's encroachment on long-established human rights standards.[21] In this sense, the precedence

---

16 *Nada v. Switzerland*, App. No. 10593/08, ECtHR (Judgment, Grand Chamber) (12 Sept., 2012) (*Nada* ECtHR).

17 Antonios Tzanakopoulos, "Human Rights and United Nations Security Council Measures," in *Norm Conflicts in Public International Law: The Place of Human Rights*, edited by Erika de Wet and Jure Vidmar (Oxford: Oxford University Press, 2012), 42, 55; Joy Gordon, "The Sword of Damocles: Revisiting the Question of Whether the United Nations Security Council is Bound by International Law," *Chicago Journal of International Law* 12 (2011): 605, 643; and Allan Rosas, "Terrorist Listings and the Rule of Law: The Role of the EU Courts," 2011, http://cadmus.eui.eu/handle/1814/17894: 21, indicating a trend towards "greater scrutiny" of measures to implement such requirements.

18 Jared Genser and Kate Barth, "When Due Process Concerns Become Dangerous: The Security Council's 1267 Regime and the Need for Reform," *Boston College International and Comparative Law Review* 33 (2010): 3, asserting that "judicial discontent" in this context has been growing. Similarly, Tzanakopoulos highlights the apparent reluctance of courts to accept that Security Council measures have the power to "simply do away with human rights," Tzanakopoulos, *supra* note 17, 23.

19 *Kadi* CFI, *supra* note 11, ¶ 247. This had the result "the applicants' interest in having a court hear their case on its merits" was considered to be insufficient to "outweigh the essential public interest in the maintenance of international peace and security in the face of a threat clearly identified by the…Council," *Ibid.*, ¶ 289.

20 Antonios Tzanakopoulos, "United Nations Sanctions in Domestic Courts: From Interpretation to Defiance in *Abdelrazik v. Canada*" *Journal of International Criminal Justice* 8 (2010): 249, 263.

21 Antonios Tzanakopoulos, *Disobeying the Security Council: Countermeasures Against Wrongful Sanctions* (New York: Oxford University Press, 2011), 16. See also the reference by Eckes and Hollenberg to the emergence of an "increased power" on the part of the judiciary when "determining the applicable normative framework," Christina Eckes and Stephan Hollenberg, "Reconciling Different Legal Spheres in Theory and Practice: Pluralism and Constitutionalism in the Cases of *Al Jedda*, *Ahmed* and *Nada*," *Maastricht Journal of European and Comparative Law* 22 (2013): 218, 220.

previously afforded to States' duties under the targeted sanctions regime, and corresponding prioritisation of collective security over human rights norms, is seen to have represented a "choice" of values by the judicial bodies concerned,[22] and one which has since been reversed by the more recent jurisprudence. This perceived re-prioritisation of human rights standards at the expense of obligations imposed by the Council under Chapter VII has in turn been argued to demonstrate a more restrictive interpretation by judicial bodies of Article 103 of the Charter,[23] placing clear limits on the capacity of the Council to wholly dispense with the application of States' duties under human right law. It has also been contended that these developments in the case law may give rise to alterations in the hierarchy of norms under international law in favour of those geared towards the protection of human rights standards, where necessary at the expense of those dictated by the Council in the interests of international security.[24]

However, it is possible that the impact of the respective decisions, and scale of their prioritisation of human rights norms over requirements dictated by the Council, may have been overstated in the literature, with the analysis of the judgments by commentators informed to some degree by their own, understandable prioritisation of human rights rules over those formulated by the Council, in the face of the body's increasingly intrusive impact on the rights of individuals. Tzanakopoulos, for example, observes that the subjection of these protections to the "whim" of the Council members is "not a very satisfying… picture," in view of the "long and arduous struggle" to establish international standards for the protection of human rights.[25]

While the Council's capacity to "cast aside" human rights in this manner,[26] ostensibly in the interests of maintaining security, is indeed a cause for significant concern, it is unclear how far the judicial decisions examining this issue

22 Vera Gowlland-Debbas, "Accountability of the Security Council," in *United Nations Reform Through Practice: Report of the International Law Association Study Group on United Nations Reform*, edited by Ralph Wilde, 2011, http://www.ila-hq.org/download.cfm/docid/1021324F-035F-42EF-8CF50763169CA1F2: 34, 37; Pasquale De Sena and Maria Chiara Vitucci, "The European Courts and the Security Council: Between Dédoublement Fonctionnel and Balancing of Values," *European Journal of International Law* 20 (2009): 193, 210.

23 Tzanakopoulos, *supra* note 21, 21.

24 Erika de Wet and Jure Vidmar, "Introduction," in *Norm Conflicts in Public International Law: The Place of Human Rights*, edited by Erika de Wet and Jure Vidmar (Oxford: Oxford University Press, 2012), 1, 2–4; Tzanakopoulos, *supra* note 17, 65.

25 Tzanakopoulos, *supra* note 21, 7.

26 *Ibid.*

have reversed or altered this position as a matter of international law, or indeed ensured the effective application of human rights protections in the particular situations to which the judgments responded.[27] This chapter will therefore examine each of the decisions with a view to assessing how far they in fact serve to ensure the effective protection of international human rights standards in the face of inconsistent obligations as dictated by the Security Council, and will evaluate whether they may be seen to provide a coherent framework through which States' competing obligations under international law might be reconciled.

2 Decisions within the EU's "Autonomous Legal System" – *Kadi v. Council*

The *Kadi* case before the ECJ concerned a request for annulment of European Community Regulation No 881/200252, adopted by the Council of the EU in order to implement the Security Council's targeted sanctions requirements uniformly in all Member States. The appellants claimed that the Regulation infringed their fundamental rights as protected under Community law, specifically the rights to a hearing, to respect for property and to effective judicial review. The Court of First Instance (CFI) had decided that Article 103 of the Charter had the result that the obligations of States under the resolution "clearly prevail" over every other obligation of domestic or international law, including those relating to the protection of human rights under the ECHR and the EC Treaties,[28] such that it could not review the Community measures against such standards other than to the extent that these could be deemed to constitute norms of *jus cogens*.[29]

The ECJ reversed the CFI's decision and annulled the Regulation in so far as it concerned the appellants. In justifying this decision, and the finding of infringements of the rights protected within the EU notwithstanding the

---

27 Bardo Fassbender, "Introduction," in Securing *Human Rights: Achievements and Challenges of the UN Security Council*, edited by Bardo Fassbender (New York: Oxford University Press, 2011), 1, 7.

28 *Kadi* CFI, *supra* note 11, ¶ 181.

29 "[U]nderstood as a body of higher rules of public international law binding on all subjects of international law, including the bodies of the United Nations, and from which no derogation is possible"; *ibid.*, 226. The Court ultimately found that the resolutions had not led to a breach of any such peremptory norms. *Cf.* Michael Wood, "The Legal Framework of the Security Council," 2006, http://www.lcil.cam.ac.uk/Media/lectures/pdf/2006_hersch_lecture_1.pdf): 20.

existence of conflicting Charter-based obligations, the ECJ emphasised the autonomy of the Community legal order, and the integral character of fundamental rights within this system, as enshrined in Article 6(1) of the EU Treaty.[30] The provision of judicial review and the need for all Community acts to respect fundamental rights were thus stated to represent the "expression…of a constitutional guarantee stemming from the EC Treaty as an autonomous legal system," and one which could not "be prejudiced by an international agreement."[31] In light of this guarantee it was held that the Community judicature "must… ensure the review, in principle the full review, of the lawfulness of all Community acts in the light of…fundamental rights,"[32] and that this requirement continued to exist in the context of measures "designed to give effect to the resolutions adopted by the Security Council under Chapter VII of the Charter."[33]

The *Kadi* decision has given rise to widely positive responses in relation to its capacity to ensure the protection of human rights standards, enabling the review of legislation introduced to implement Security Council resolutions for consistency with "the full panoply of human rights standards."[34] Commentators have thus suggested that the decision has had a clear impact on the relationship between Chapter VII resolutions and human rights law, emphatically rebutting the idea that the former set of rules may justify "every derogation from fundamental rights standards."[35]

However, the *Kadi* judgment is subject to a number of criticisms which may serve to limit its potential impact, both as a practical matter (in terms of securing the application of human rights standards) and in connection with its role in developing the position under international law. First, there is no engagement in the decision with the implications that should be attached to Article 103

30 *Kadi* ECJ, *supra* note 12, ¶¶ 303–304.

31 *Ibid.*, ¶ 316.

32 See also the more recent decision of the ECJ in Joined Cases C-584/10 P, C-593/10 P and C-595/10 P, *European Commission and the Council of the European Union v. Yassin Abdullah Kadi* (18 July 2013), in connection with the standard of review that this "in principle…full review" will entail.

33 *Kadi* ECJ, *supra* note 12, ¶ 327.

34 Gráinne de Búrca, "The European Court of Justice and the International Legal Order After *Kadi*," *Harvard International Law Journal* 51 (2010): 1, 31; Katja S. Ziegler, "Strengthening the Rule of Law, but Fragmenting International Law: The *Kadi* Decision of the ECJ from the Perspective of Human Rights," *Human Rights Law Review* 9 (2009): 288, 303.

35 Siiri Aulik, "Judgment of the European Court of Justice in *Kadi*: Challenges to International Law, the United Nations Sanctions Regime and Fundamental Rights," *Acta Societatis Martensis* 4 (2010): 25, 50.

of the Charter, the Court having distinguished itself from the system of international law – including the central place afforded to the UN Charter within this legal order – by basing its decision solely on the autonomous nature of the EU system.[36] The judgment thus provides limited assistance in terms of the manner in which the Charter and Article 103 might influence the application of other legal commitments, particularly in view of the fact that the EU is, at least in the Court's judgment, not formally subject to this body of law.[37]

This disregard for international rules and emphasis on the autonomy of the EU legal order holds limited potential in terms of ensuring the protection of standards established under international human rights law. The argument could, for example, clearly not be applicable in the context of the European Convention of Human Rights (ECHR) or the International Covenant of Civil and Political Rights (ICCPR), which could by no means be considered to be independent and separate from the system of general international law.[38] Indeed, Article 46 of the latter treaty expressly stipulates that "nothing in the present Covenant shall be interpreted as impairing the provisions of the Charter of the United Nations." The *Kadi* judgment is therefore of limited utility in clarifying the position with regard to the application of these international conventions, or indeed customary human rights law.[39]

There was, moreover, a distinct lack of engagement in *Kadi* with the question as to the existence of human rights limits that might curtail the binding impact of Security Council resolutions more broadly, outside the confines of the EU as an autonomous legal order. This question, and the application of international rules such as Article 103 of the Charter, was evaded by the Court through the assumption that Security Council's targeted sanctions regime did not directly bind the Community, an assumption that has itself been questioned by many in the literature.[40] Indeed, the Court did not even mention

36 Ziegler, *supra* note 34, 295–296.

37 Nikolaos Lavranos, "UN Sanctions and Judicial Review" *Nordic Journal of International Law* 76 (2007): 1, 16.

38 David Feldman, "The Role of Constitutional Principles in Protecting International Peace and Security through International, Supranational and National Legal Institutions," *New Zealand Journal of Public and International Law* 6 (2008): 1, 18; Marko Milanović, "The Human Rights Committee's Views in *Sayadi v. Belgium*: A Missed Opportunity," *Goettingen Journal of International Law* 1 (2009): 519, 526.

39 de Búrca, *supra* note 34, 23.

40 Andrea Gattini, "Case Law: *Yassin Abdullah Kadi, Al Barakaat International Foundation v. Council and Commission*, Judgment of the Grand Chamber," *Common Market Law Review* (2009): 213, 230; Ziegler, *supra* note 34, 294–296; Luis Miguel Hinojosa Martínez, "Bad Law

Article 103 of the Charter in its reasoning, notwithstanding that this was raised both by the applicant and by the United Kingdom as an intervening government.[41] Accordingly, no further information is provided by the ECJ regarding the potential human rights limits on the Security Council under international law,[42] with the Court instead demonstrating a notable reluctance to engage in "any challenge" to the binding nature and primacy of Chapter VII resolutions under international law, even as concerns any possible infringement of *jus cogens* norms.[43]

Finally, the judgment provides limited assistance, and indeed raises significant practical difficulties, in the context of the conflicting obligations of States that are Contracting Parties to the EU. Thus the difficulties of reconciling obligations under the Charter with human rights norms, including those encapsulated within the Community legal order, are simply displaced to EU Member States, and to domestic courts in responding to the national implementation of the sanctions regime.[44] The judgment of the ECJ does not address the question of the opposing obligations under the Charter and EU law to which individual States would now find themselves subject, beyond an indication that, in line with the Union's institutions, States may not under any circumstances "avoid review of the conformity of their acts with the [EC's] basic constitutional charter."[45]

Yet the decision evidently does not entail the consequence that States are no longer subject to the obligations under the relevant Security Council resolutions as a matter of international law, such that by following the decision EU Member States would simply be held responsible as a matter of international law for breaching their Charter obligations.[46] Indeed at paragraph 291 of the judgment the Court expressly recognises the continuing impact of the obligation incumbent on States to respect such resolutions, without indicating how they might reconcile the conflict between these requirements and the judgment itself.

---

for Good Reasons: The Contradictions of the *Kadi* Judgment," *International Organizations Law Review* 5 (2008): 339, 346.

41 *Kadi* ECJ, *supra* note 12, ¶¶ 250, 276. Martínez, *supra* note 40, 343.

42 Gattini, *supra* note 40, 231; Fredrik Stenhammar, "United Nations Targeted Sanctions, the International Rule of Law and the European Court of Justice's Judgment in *Kadi and Al-Barakaat*," *Nordic Journal of International Law* 79 (2010): 113, 115.

43 *Kadi* ECJ, *supra* note 12, ¶¶ 287–288.

44 Stenhammar, *supra* note 42, 139.

45 *Kadi* ECJ, *supra* note 12, ¶¶ 281–282; Gattini, *supra* note 40, 226.

46 de Búrca, *supra* note 34, 29; Göran Lysen, "Targeted UN Sanctions: Application of Legal Sources and Procedural Matters" *Nordic Journal of International Law* 72 (2003): 291, 292.

A number of commentators have thus highlighted the "sweeping practical difficulties" to be encountered by States in complying with their obligations under international law as a result of the decision,[47] which is thus seen to bring about a dilemma for States in terms of the choice faced between their conflicting international commitments.[48] Yet, in view of the ongoing status of the EU Treaties as "international agreements" for the purposes of Article 103,[49] as a matter of international law this suggested "dilemma" would lead simply to the precedence of the Charter obligations over those arising from the ECJ's judgment[50] – at least in the absence of any more coherent elaboration of the substantive limits on the Security Council's capacity to override States' human rights commitments.

The ECJ appears to have recognised this consequence as a matter of international law, conceding that its review of measures of the EU Council intended to implement a resolution of the Security Council "would not entail any challenge to the primacy of that resolution in international law."[51] It thus remained unclear on the issuing of the Court's judgment if and to what extent this could be followed either by the governments of individual EU members,[52] or by national and supranational courts charged with assessing the conflict between Council-imposed duties and human rights obligations in connection with of measures taken in this context by these States. As a result, the decisions of judicial bodies regarding the implementation measures that have been adopted by individual States may be of greater utility than the ECJ's judgment in terms of clarifying the position under international law as concerns the application of Article 103 of the Charter to States' commitments under human rights law.

---

47 Jean d'Aspremont and Frédéric Dopagne, "*Kadi*: The ECJ's Reminder of the Elementary Divide Between Legal Orders," *International Organizations Law Review* 5 (2008): 371, 377; André Nollkaemper, "Rethinking the Supremacy of International Law," *Zeitschrift für Öffentliches Recht und Öffentliche Verwaltung* 65 (2010): 65, 81.

48 Stenhammar, *supra* note 42, 139; Aulik, *supra* note 35, 47.

49 Martin Holterman, response to Kristen Boon, "The ECJ's New Appeal Judgment on *Kadi*," 2013, http://opiniojuris.org/2013/07/25/the-ecjs-new-appeal-judgment-on-kadi/.

50 Lysen, *supra* note 46, 292. See *Military and Paramilitary Activities in and against Nicaragua* (*Nicaragua v. United States*), Provisional Measures, 1984 I.C.J. 169, ¶ 107, stipulating that "all regional...arrangements that the parties may have must be made always subject to the provisions of Article 103 of the UN Charter."

51 *Kadi* ECJ, *supra* note 12, ¶ 288. See also Opinion of Advocate General Maduro, ¶ 39.

52 de Wet and Vidmar, *supra* note 24, 38.

3 Decisions of Domestic Courts – *Ahmed* and *Abdelrazik*

The *Ahmed* decision, adopted by the United Kingdom Supreme Court in 2010, concerned the review of the legality of national measures giving effect to the targeted sanctions regime within the UK, in the form of the Al-Qaeda and Taliban (UN Measures) Order 2006 (AQO). Authority to adopt executive orders of this kind stems from the United Nations Act 1946,[53] according to which the government may give effect to international legal requirements as imposed by the UN through Orders in Council where this is "necessary or expedient" for enabling the relevant duties to be effectively upheld.[54] Following the claimants' challenge to the freezing measures imposed upon them, the Supreme Court annulled this executive order, holding that the applicants were "entitled to succeed on the point that the regime to which [they have]...been subjected has deprived [them] of access to an effective remedy."[55] The procedures available under the sanctions regime were themselves deemed to fail to provide a merits-based review or allow for basic procedural fairness.[56]

The case of *Abdelrazik* concerned a Sudanese-born Canadian citizen, who – having been detained without charge by Sudanese authorities – was prevented from entering Canada on the basis of his inclusion in the Consolidated List in 2006. The applicant brought a case before the Canadian Federal Court claiming a violation of his right to return to Canada under Article 6(1) of the Canadian Charter of Rights and Freedoms.[57] In response, the Canadian government argued that it could not permit his return without violating its obligations under Chapter VII, specifically the travel ban established under Resolution 1822.[58] Nonetheless, the Federal Court found that Canada had violated the applicant's right to enter Canada under the Canadian Charter,[59] and decided that the claimant was entitled to an effective remedy for this breach whereby the Canadian government was to allow his return to Canada. The judgment emphasised the human rights deficiencies inherent in the targeted sanctions regime, which is described in the decision as "a denial of basic legal remedies... untenable under the principles of international human rights."[60]

53 United Nations Act, 1946, 9 & 10 Geo. 6, c. 45 (UK).

54 *Ibid.*, Section 1(1).

55 *Ahmed, supra* note 6, ¶ 81.

56 See for example *ibid.*, ¶ 80.

57 *Abdelrazik, supra* note 14, ¶ 42.

58 S/Res/1822 (2008).

59 *Abdelrazik, supra* note 14, ¶ 156.

60 *Ibid.*, ¶ 51.

The *Ahmed* and *Abdelrazik* judgments would appear to provide promising indications in terms of the increased scrutiny of Chapter VII implementation measures for adherence to States' human rights commitments. Thus, the measures introduced by the UK government were annulled in the *Ahmed* case based in part on the absence of any effective remedy within the targeted sanctions regime, while in *Abdelrazik* the Court ordered a remedy for Canada's violation of rights protected under the Canadian Charter, emphasising that the sanctions regime and its implementation were inconsistent with established human rights principles.[61] In this respect, the overriding impact of Article 103 of the Charter appears to have been effectively avoided in both cases,[62] with the Council-imposed requirements in effect "yield[ing] to fundamental human rights considerations."[63]

3.1 *Focus on Domestic Human Rights Standards*

However, it is important to underscore a number of limitations with regard to the decisions in *Ahmed* and *Abdelrazik*, in terms of their substantive impact on the relationship between States' conflicting legal commitments as a matter of international law, and as concerns any assurance that the relevant human rights protections will in practical terms be upheld in the event of such a conflict. The first of these limitations is that the decisions were based entirely on human rights protections established under domestic law, with the precedence of Chapter VII resolutions over States' commitments under human rights law avoided primarily as a result of this emphasis on domestic or constitutional standards.[64] The *Ahmed* and *Abdelrazik* judgments may therefore have a limited impact on any evolving interpretation of Article 103 of the Charter or alteration to the prevailing hierarchy of norms under international law. Moreover, they may hold limited potential as concerns the effective protection of established *international* human rights standards.

With regard to the relationship between Security Council resolutions and human rights standards established under international law, the Supreme Court's decision in *Ahmed* provides explicit recognition of the ongoing

61 *Ibid.*, ¶ 51.

62 Tzanakopoulos, *supra* note 21, 16.

63 *Ibid.*, 23.

64 Tzanakopoulos, *supra* note 20, 15; de Wet and Vidmar, *supra* note 24, 35. This position may also be ascribed to the decisions of the EU courts in *Kadi*, with the ECJ in particular having equated the Community to a domestic legal order, hence distinguishing itself from general international law and focusing instead on internal constitutional protections; Ziegler, *supra* note 34, 295–296.

precedence of obligations imposed by the Council over States' human rights commitments.[65] The Court stated, however, that this established position "left open" the question regarding the relationship between Security Council resolutions and domestic law.[66] Similarly, in its *Kadi* judgment, the ECJ did not question the capacity of the Council to override human rights standards protected under the ECHR,[67] focusing wholly on the Court's competence to uphold the EU's internal, constitutional human rights principles. It thus reviewed the legality of the EC regulation solely in terms of its compatibility with the general principles of Community law,[68] without regard to the standards of international protection of those rights[69] and, as noted, expressed its reluctance to engage in any challenge to "the primacy of [the Council's] resolution in international law."[70]

Finally, the *Abdelrazik* decision was based entirely on provisions within the Canadian constitution, albeit due largely to the absence of any claims before it based on international law. The decision does refer to international as well as domestic human rights protections when criticising the Security Council measures. Thus the sanctions regime is found to be "untenable under…international human rights principles,"[71] and to contravene the presumption of innocence, "a fundamental principle of Canadian *and international* justice."[72] However, this perceived contravention of international standards was not the formal basis for the decision, and the judgment provides no reference to specific provisions of international human rights law which were deemed to have been infringed,[73] nor any indication as to whether – or how – such standards could be applied notwithstanding the existence of competing legal commitments under Chapter VII of the Charter.

Therefore, the decisions of the UK and Canadian domestic courts and the ECJ do not question the continuing primacy of Charter obligations as a matter of international law, or apply international human rights standards in the face

65 *Ahmed, supra* note 6, ¶ 74. See de Wet and Vidmar, *supra* note 24, 26. Notably this position was reached notwithstanding the Court's consideration of the position adopted in the ECJ's *Kadi* judgment.

66 *Ahmed, supra* note 6, ¶ 75.

67 The judgment may be contrasted with the decision of the CFI in this respect; Stenhammar, *supra* note 42, 137.

68 *Kadi* ECJ, *supra* note 12, ¶¶ 285, 288; d'Aspremont and Dopagne, *supra* note 47, 372–373.

69 Gattini, *supra* note 40, 214; Aulik, *supra* note 35, 41; Ziegler, *supra* note 34, 294–295.

70 *Kadi* ECJ, *supra* note 12, ¶ 288.

71 *Abdelrazik, supra* note 14, ¶ 51.

72 *Ibid.*, ¶ 53, emphasis added. Tzanakopoulos, *supra* note 20, 15–16.

73 de Wet and Vidmar, *supra* note 24, 29.

of competing requirements under Security Council resolutions, with the *Kadi* and *Ahmed* judgments instead demonstrating a visible deference to the primacy of such decisions as a matter of international law.[74] This emphasis on constitutional protections represents an understandable approach, in terms of avoiding any direct conflict with the Security Council's prescriptions and the apparently inevitable application of Article 103 that would be associated with such a conflict.[75]

However, it evidently does not lead to the effective, universal protection of *international* human rights standards, whether customary or conventional,[76] and may instead, in effect, contribute to the marginalisation of the standards established under international human rights law.[77] Contrary to the suggestion of some in the literature,[78] it is submitted that the frequent similarities in substance between domestic and international human rights standards is not sufficient to prevent such marginalisation, given the importance which must be attached to the enforcement of consistently applied, internationally recognised standards of human rights protection,[79] the need for which indeed gave rise to the "long and arduous struggle" to establish the various international and regional human rights conventions.[80]

Secondly, reliance on domestic standards does not lead to – and to some degree may inhibit – the development of greater clarity in the position concerning the interaction of international human rights law with inconsistent Security Council requirements,[81] limiting the potential of the decisions to aid

---

74 *Ibid.*, ¶ 26.

75 *Ibid.*, ¶ 38.

76 André Nollkaemper, "The European Courts and the Security Council: Three Replies," *European Journal of International Law* 20 (2009): 862, 863; Gattini, *supra* note 40, 214. *Cf.* Aulik, *supra* note 35, 50, noting the "residual benefits" at international level of ensuring the application of fundamental rights as protected within the EU framework.

77 de Wet and Vidmar, *supra* note 24, 38.

78 Dapo Akande, "Are There Limits to the Powers of the Security Council?" *Journal of International Law and Policy* 5 (2007): 1, 9; Enzo Cannizzaro, "A Machiavellian Moment? The Security Council and the Rule of Law," *International Organizations Law Review* 3 (2006): 189, 190; Nollkaemper, *supra* note 76, 865–866.

79 de Wet and Vidmar, *supra* note 24, 6; Elizabeth Abraham, "The Sins of the Savior: Holding the United Nations Accountable to International Human Rights Standards for Executive Order Detentions on Its Mission in Kosovo," *American University Law Review* 52 (2002): 1291, 1320–1321.

80 See note 25, *supra*.

81 Gowlland-Debbas, *supra* note 10, 68.

in attempts to reconcile these conflicting norms or contribute to the coherence of the legal position with respect to such a conflict.[82]

Furthermore, as a matter of international law, any challenge to the binding application of Security Council resolutions based solely on domestic standards will lead simply to a breach of international law, and thus engage the responsibility of the State in question for non-compliance with its duties under the Charter. Thus while it may be possible to claim that the domestic and international systems constitute "independent legal orders" for the purpose of avoiding the application of Article 103,[83] as far as a State's duties under international law are concerned domestic law cannot be employed as an excuse for failing to comply with these commitments.[84]

3.2 *Limited Prioritisation of Human Rights Commitments*

However, it remains arguable that any preference afforded to human rights over Security Council resolutions within court decisions, whether based on domestic or international standards, may have implications for the suggested developments in the "hierarchy" between the two sets of norms under international law.[85] It has thus been argued by many that regardless of the formal source of the human rights standards on which the respective decisions were based, they nonetheless reflect the importance attached by the judicial bodies concerned to human rights protections as part of the "international public order."[86] Thus the perceived normative superiority of human rights over inconsistent Security Council measures is said to represent the underlying justification for the decisions.[87] Given the "substantive overlap" between international and constitutional human rights guarantees in many cases,[88] these rights may

82 Gattini, *supra* note 40, 213–214.

83 Nollkaemper, *supra* note 76, 863.

84 Gowlland-Debbas, *supra* note 10, 71; Cannizzaro, *supra* note 78, 205; Tzanakopoulos, *supra* note 21, 22. Article 27 of the Vienna Convention on the Law of Treaties provides that "a party may not invoke the provisions of its internal law as justification for its failure to perform a treaty"; U.N. Doc. A/CONF.129/15 (1986). See also *Applicability of the Obligation to Arbitrate under Section 21 of the United Nations Headquarters Agreement of 26 June 1947*, Advisory Opinion, 1988 I.C.J. 12, ¶ 57.

85 de Wet and Vidmar, *supra* note 24, 8; Tzanakopoulos, *supra* note 21, 3.

86 *Cf.* Ian Brownlie, "The Decisions of Political Organs of the United Nations and the Rule of Law," in *Essays in Honour of Wang Tieya*, edited by Ronald St. John Macdonald (Dordrecht: Martinus Nijhoff, 1994), 91, 102.

87 Tzanakopoulos, *supra* note 17, 65; Nollkaemper, *supra* note 76, 866; Feldman, *supra* note 38, 33.

88 Tzanakopoulos, *supra* note 17, 61.

be "cast in internationalist terms" so as to create an impact on hierarchy under international as well as domestic law, thus "transcending" the domestic legal order.[89] Indeed, in many instances the decisions regarding the protection of domestic human rights standards were visibly "informed by" norms enshrined in international treaties.[90]

In order for such a development to be established, however, there must be evidence of a consistent pattern of judicial bodies recognising the superiority of human rights norms over those dictated by the Council under Chapter VII.[91] Yet the degree of prioritisation afforded to human rights principles in the decisions themselves appears to have been significantly exaggerated, with the judgments of the two national courts – *Ahmed* and *Abdelrazik* – not in fact questioning the capacity of Security Council resolutions to override human rights standards, even those based on domestic or constitutional principles.

Thus the *Ahmed* decision was not based directly on the application of the protections established under the Human Rights Act, notwithstanding its reference to the absence of any "effective remedy" under the targeted sanctions regime and the UK's implementation measures.[92] Instead, the Supreme Court quashed the AQO on the basis of the principles of separation of powers and parliamentary sovereignty under domestic law.[93] Thus the Court did not focus on *whether* sanctions not providing for effective independent review could legally be adopted when such measures were required under binding Chapter VII resolutions, but rather *by whom* these restrictions could be introduced. The primary question addressed by the Court was therefore whether the actions adopted by the UK in implementing the Council-imposed measures were *ultra vires* the United Nations Act, which as mentioned requires executive orders to be either "necessary" or "expedient" to enable those measures to be effectively applied.[94] In light of this requirement, which in effect is one of administrative law rather than human rights protection, the implementing regulations were quashed on the basis that they violated the 1946 Act.[95]

89 Nollkaemper, *supra* note 76, 866–867; Martínez, *supra* note 40, 346.

90 de Wet and Vidmar, *supra* note 24, 35. See for example *Abdelrazik*, *supra* note 14, ¶ 51; Case T/85/09, *Yassin Abdullah Kadi v. European Commission and Council of the European Union* (30 Sept., 2010) (*Kadi II* EGC), ¶¶ 150, 176.

91 de Wet and Vidmar, *supra* note 24, 7; Genser and Barth, *supra* note 18, 10–11.

92 *Ahmed*, *supra* note 6, ¶ 81.

93 *Ibid.*, ¶ 80, referring to the avoidance by the UK executive of 'parliamentary scrutiny' through its reliance on the UN Act.

94 United Nations Act, *supra* note 53, ¶ 1.

95 *Ahmed*, *supra* note 6, ¶¶ 83, 155, 186–187.

This ruling had the practical result that introduction of the restrictive measures required by the Council had to be carried out through Parliament rather than the executive. Thus the Court held that it remained open to the UK to comply with the Council's targeted sanctions requirements, but that in order to do so legislation would need to be adopted by Parliament, removing the fundamental right of access to a court through clear and unambiguous language. De Wet contends that this requirement itself leads to an improved position as concerns the effective protection of human rights standards, in view of the need for the relevant measures to "survive parliamentary scrutiny," and for any restriction on individual rights to be "couched in clear and unambiguous terms."[96] Yet, in view of continuing obligation incumbent on the State to fulfil the terms of the relevant resolutions, and thus to ensure the listing of specific, named individuals, the requirement that the implementation measures are adopted by Parliament rather than the executive is likely to be of limited practical benefit in terms of ensuring the protection of the right to a remedy of those designated by the Sanctions Committee.

As a result, not only *could* Parliament suspend "any and every aspect of a merits based judicial review" in order to give effect to the targeted sanctions regime,[97] but it would in fact be *required* to do so in order to fulfil the State's international obligations.[98] This serves to underscore the artificial nature of the protection afforded to the applicants through the Supreme Court's requirement that the freezing measures be introduced by Parliament. Indeed in subsequent proceedings before the court relating to the UK government's request that the annulment of the AQO be suspended to allow the adoption of replacement legislation, Lord Hope observed that there was "the possibility – indeed more than that, the likelihood" that the measures in question would be approved by Parliament.[99] In practice, such legislation was subsequently introduced by the UK, first on a temporary[100] and now more permanent

96 de Wet and Vidmar, *supra* note 24, 27.

97 *Ibid.*, 27.

98 Craig Forcese, "Hegemonic Federalism: The Democratic Implications of the UN Security Council's 'Legislative' Phase," *Victoria University of Wellington Law Review* 38 (2007): 175, 196.

99 *Her Majesty's Treasury v. Mohammed Jabar Ahmed and others (No.2)*, 2010 UKSC 5 (*Ahmed II*), ¶ 22, Lord Hope (dissent), noting in addition that the need for "respect for our international obligations," together with the "national interest" in maintaining the efficacy of the Council's sanctions regime, required the Court to do what it could in order to enable this result.

100 Terrorist Asset-Freezing (Temporary Provisions) Act 2010.

basis,[101] in line with the State's duties under the Charter, and without any evident improvement in terms of ensuring the fulfilment of the rights to a remedy or fair hearing of those affected.[102]

Meanwhile, the decision in *Abdelrazik* rests solely on the Court's interpretation of the relevant resolution, and its relatively permissive nature in connection with individuals' travel to their State of nationality, rather than any indication that the applicant's right to travel was to be given priority over the need to comply with the Council's requirements. Thus the travel ban under consideration incorporated an express exception, permitting States to allow entry into its territory of its own nationals while prohibiting their transit through any other territory.[103] The Canadian Supreme Court proceeded quite naturally to define the term "territory" in this context so as to exclude the airspace over other States, through which the applicant would evidently have to pass in order to return to his country of citizenship.[104] As a consequence the Court was able to hold that there was "no impediment from the UN Resolution to Mr. Abdelrazik being repatriated to Canada."[105]

Thus while the Canadian Supreme Court's judgment refers on several occasions to the perceived incompatibility of the sanctions regime with human rights standards, including those established at the international level,[106] it does not indicate at any stage that the Security Council *could not* override the State's human rights commitments, whether constitutional or arising under international law, if denial of the applicant's entry into Canada's territory were in fact to have been required by the terms of the resolution. In this sense the judgment of the Federal Court does not display a willingness to allow a departure from requirements imposed by the Security Council so as to ensure the protection of human rights, but rather is able to ensure the protection of these standards on the basis that this would not entail any infringement of the Council's prescriptions.[107] As such, there is again no questioning of the Council's capacity to override human rights norms, with the Federal Court having never reached the question of whether Canada's obligations under the

101 Terrorist Assets Freezing Act 2010.

102 de Wet and Vidmar, *supra* note 24, 27.

103 S/Res/1822 (2008), 1(b); *Abdelrazik, supra* note 14, ¶ 57.

104 *Abdelrazik, supra* note 14, ¶ 127.

105 *Ibid.*, ¶ 124.

106 *Ibid.*, ¶ 51.

107 Genser and Barth, *supra* note 18, 21.

Charter might be restricted so as to enable the effective application of its human rights commitments.[108]

4 Decisions before International and Regional Human Rights Bodies – *Sayadi* and *Nada*

The case of *Sayadi* before the UN Human Rights Committee (HRC) concerned a husband and wife who had been placed on the Consolidated List following the submission of their names to the Sanctions Committee by Belgium, their State of residence. Following unsuccessful requests for delisting, the applicants brought a complaint before the HRC challenging Belgium's infringement of their rights under the ICCPR. The Committee concluded that while it could not rule on the legality of the Security Council resolutions themselves, it was competent to consider whether a State party had violated the rights under the Convention through its implementation measures.[109]

In light of this position, the Court found Belgium to be in breach of Article 12 of the Covenant, protecting the right to travel,[110] and Article 17 regarding the right to reputation,[111] on the basis that Belgium was "responsible for the presence of [their]...names" on the List,[112] having submitted these to the Sanctions Committee. Notwithstanding Belgium's argument that it had been required to report the names of those suspected of association with Al-Qaeda, the Committee found that the listing was "premature" and therefore illegal,[113] highlighting in particular that Belgium had submitted the names of the individuals concerned without awaiting the outcome of a national criminal investigation.[114]

The *Nada* case related to the sanctions and travel restrictions imposed by Switzerland against an Italian national of Egyptian origin, who had been listed following submission of his name by the United States based on his involvement with a financial network suspected of supporting terrorist activities. The

108 Craig Forcese and Kent Roach, "Limping into the Future: The UN 1267 Terrorism Listing Process at the Crossroads," *George Washington International Law Review* 42 (2010): 217, 255.

109 *Sayadi*, *supra* note 15, ¶ 7.2.

110 *Ibid.*, ¶ 10.8.

111 *Ibid.*, ¶ 10.13.

112 *Ibid.*

113 *Ibid.*, ¶ 8.1.

114 *Ibid.*, ¶ 10.13.

applicant was resident in the small Italian enclave of Campione, surrounded by Swiss territory, and under the terms of the travel ban was denied permission to transit through Switzerland. As a result, due to the unique circumstances of the applicant, his subjection to the ban had the result that he was unable to travel outside of the 1.6 square kilometre area of this enclave, even to other parts of his State of nationality.[115] The applicant, who had remained on the List for several years notwithstanding that the Swiss criminal investigation against him had been discontinued, claimed that his subjection to the travel ban infringed his right to respect for private and family life under Article 8 of the ECHR, and further that his confinement within the enclave constituted an infringement of his right to liberty under Article 5 of the Convention. He claimed, in addition, that he had no effective procedure through which to challenge the restrictions, giving rise to an infringement of his right to a remedy under Article 13.

The Swiss Federal Tribunal had dismissed the applicant's claim on grounds analogous to those of the CFI in *Kadi*, as described above, notwithstanding its acknowledgment that the procedures available for challenging his inclusion on the List were not in conformity with the standards of review required under the Swiss constitution and international human rights treaties.[116] In his subsequent action before the ECtHR, the Grand Chamber held that it had the capacity to review actions taken by Switzerland in implementing the Council's targeted sanctions requirements against the applicant, who had by this stage in any event been delisted by the Sanctions Committee. The Court proceeded to find that the implementation measures adopted by Switzerland had infringed his rights to private and family life under Article 8 of the ECHR and to an effective remedy under Article 13.

These decisions have each been argued to demonstrate the capacity of judicial bodies to ensure the effective protection of international human rights standards in the face of conflicting Security Council requirements, thereby giving rise to constraints on the body's capacity to override human rights protections when responding to threats to international security. Indeed, in both cases the infringements of the States' human rights duties in connection with their implementing measures were identified notwithstanding the arguments

115 It was acknowledged by the Swiss Federal Tribunal that this resulted in a situation which "comes close to house arrest," *Nada* FC, *supra* note 11, ¶ 16.7. Johannes Reich, "Due Process and Sanctions Targeted Against Individuals Pursuant to Resolution 1267" *Yale Journal of International Law* 33 (2008): 505, 512.

116 *Nada* FC, *supra* note 11, ¶ 8.3.

advanced by the States concerned that these duties had been overridden as a result of their binding, Charter-based obligations.[117]

In response to such arguments in *Sayadi*, the HRC expressly held that it was able to review the implementing measures adopted by Belgium so as "to consider whether [it] had violated rights set forth in the Covenant," notwithstanding the Committee's lack of competence to judge the legality of the resolutions themselves, and, importantly, "regardless of the source of the obligations implemented."[118] Genser and Barth have therefore suggested that the decision demonstrates that the possibility of justifying measures with reference to duties imposed by the Security Council "does not entirely shield the State from its other international legal obligations,"[119] while Keller and Fischer note that the HRC "made it unambiguously clear" in the judgment that measures taken to give effect to such duties must fully respect human rights norms.[120]

Similarly, with regard to the ECtHR's decision in *Nada*, the Court held that it was able to find the respondent State "responsible…for all acts and omissions of its organs regardless of whether [these resulted from] the necessity to comply with international legal obligations."[121] It thus indicated that it would apply Article 8 of the Convention notwithstanding these obligations, so as to determine whether the restrictions imposed by Switzerland pursued one or more of the "legitimate aims" listed in paragraph 2 of that provision, and were "proportionate to the legitimate aim that they were supposed to pursue."[122] Guggisberg has observed that, by reviewing Switzerland's implementation of the targeted sanctions requirements against the terms of Article 8 in this manner, the ECtHR was able to "protec[t] human rights,"[123] and provided confirmation that the Court "is moving away…from total deference" to the Council.[124]

Both judgments, however, are subject to significant limitations in terms of how far they may be seen to develop legal limits on the Council's capacity to override States' human rights duties, or to bring about the full, effective application of these commitments in the face of conflicting Chapter VII

---

117 *Sayadi*, *supra* note 15, ¶ 8.1.

118 *Ibid.*, ¶ 7.2.

119 Genser and Barth, *supra* note 18, 18.

120 Helen Keller and Andreas Fischer, "The UN Anti-Terror Sanctions Regime Under Pressure" *Human Rights Law Review* 9 (2009): 257, 264.

121 *Nada* ECtHR, *supra* note 16, ¶ 168.

122 *Ibid.*, ¶¶ 167 and 185.

123 Solène Guggisberg. "The Nada Case Before the ECtHR: A New Milestone in the European Debate on Security Council Targeted Sanctions and Human Rights Obligations," *Croatian Yearbook of European Law and Policy* 8 (2012): 411, 411.

124 *Ibid.*, 413.

decisions. In relation to the *Sayadi* judgment, it is noteworthy that no coherent legal basis was provided by the Committee for its capacity to review measures argued to have been required by a binding Security Council resolution, with the application of Article 103 of the UN Charter not addressed at any stage in the decision. As a result, the decision has attracted criticism in relation to both the absence of any examination of the effects of Article 103 and the questionable application of Article 46 of the ICCPR.[125] The decision is indeed criticised on this basis in the dissenting opinions provided by members of the Committee, with Ruth Wedgwood emphasising that "the only actions taken by Belgium were in accordance with the binding mandate of the Security Council."[126] Similarly, Nigel Rodley, Ivan Shearer and Iulia Antoanella Motoc observe that it is unclear how an infringement of the applicant's rights under the ICCPR could be maintained "unless the Committee believes that the State party's mere compliance with the Security Council listing procedure…is capable of itself violating the Covenant."[127]

Nonetheless, these assertions would themselves appear to suggest that the judgment gives *priority* to the application of States' human rights commitments, where necessary at the expense of States' duties under the targeted sanctions regime, albeit without any convincing explanation as to how such a result is possible in light of Article 103 of the Charter. Yet, in fact, and in line with the decision of the Canadian Federal Court in *Abdelrazik*, the reasoning in *Sayadi* is based on the conclusion that Belgium was *not compelled* under the terms of the relevant Chapter VII requirements to propose the names of the applicants for designation.[128] As a result, the submission of their names to the Sanctions Committee could be deemed to constitute an infringement of the ICCPR without calling into question the precedence of binding Chapter VII obligations over human rights and other international norms.[129]

Notably, the Belgian government had itself argued that it did have a commitment to submit the names of those suspected to be associated with

---

125 As highlighted above, this provision states that "nothing in the present Covenant shall be interpreted as impairing the provisions of the Charter of the United Nations." Milanović, *supra* note 38, 524; Kirsten Schmalenbach, "The Constitutional Limits to Security at UN and EU Level," 2009, http://ssrn.com/abstract=1458974: 25, 38.

126 *Sayadi, supra* note 15, dissenting opinion of Ruth Wedgwood.

127 *Ibid.*, opinion of Nigel Rodley, Ivan Shearer, and Iulia Antoanella Motoc, dissenting in part. Notably, the judges observe in passing that an "overstepping of the Security Council's powers" may alter this position, but without any further elaboration.

128 *Sayadi, supra* note 15, ¶ 8.1. See also ¶ 10.7.

129 de Wet and Vidmar, *supra* note 24, 12.

Al Qaeda to the Sanctions Committee.[130] Yet in fact none of the resolutions within the Council's targeted sanctions regime imposes a binding obligation on States to submit the names of individuals and entities to the Sanctions Committee, with both Resolution 1267 and Resolution 1333 only "calling upon" States to cooperate with the Committee through the supply of relevant information,[131] and Resolution 1390 "urging" States merely to "cooperate fully with the Committee."[132] Thus Belgium's responsibility under the ICCPR was established only for actions that were not required by the binding aspects of the relevant resolutions.[133] Therefore the *Sayadi* judgment did not contradict the binding requirements that *were* imposed under the Security Council resolutions or call into question the precedence of these obligations over human rights norms in line with Article 103 of the Charter.

Similarly, the *Nada* decision, at least in connection with the infringement of Article 8, was based on Switzerland's failure to take sufficient steps that were judged by the ECtHR to have been possible *within* the terms of the Council's requirements. Thus the infringement was found to result in part from the failure to take sufficient steps to secure the applicant's removal from the list, either through encouraging Italy to pursue a delisting request or by more promptly informing the Sanctions Committee of the dismissal of the criminal investigation against the applicant.[134] The breach of Article 8 was also said to arise from the perceived inadequacy of measures taken by Switzerland to *mitigate* the impact of the implementation measures on the applicant's rights through applications for humanitarian exemptions, in light of his unique circumstances – namely the confinement to such a small area together with his age and state of health – and the State's suggested discretion in this context.[135]

The ECtHR's finding that Switzerland had violated its obligations under human rights law was therefore based on its failure to take measures "*within the scope* of the relevant...resolutions."[136] As a result, the applicant's right to private and family life under Article 8 of the Convention could be applied in relation to the limited aspects of the State's implementation measures over

130 *Sayadi*, *supra* note 15, ¶ 8.1.

131 At ¶¶ 9 and 19, respectively.

132 At ¶ 7.

133 *Contra* the indication of Wedgwood that the only actions taken by Belgium were "in accordance with the *binding mandate* of the Security Council," see *ibid.*, dissenting opinion of Ruth Wedgwood, emphasis added.

134 *Nada* ECtHR, *supra* note 16, ¶ 188.

135 *Ibid.*, ¶ 196.

136 Marko Milanović, "More on *Nada v. Switzerland*," 2010, http://www.ejiltalk.org/more-on-nada-v-switzerland/ (emphasis added).

which it had, or was considered to have, sufficient discretion to mitigate the infringement of this right while simultaneously *fully complying* with the Council's requirements.

In this respect, it is noteworthy that the ECtHR referred in the course of its judgment to its intention to balance the proportionality of the infringement of the applicant's right to private and family life against the "legitimate aims" that it had identified, namely those of "prevent[ing] crime" and "contribut[ing] to national security and public safety."[137] Yet it would appear that the Court in fact measured the scale of this infringement only against the content of the States' Chapter VII obligations, as dictated under the relevant resolutions – or at least that this act of balancing was directly and significantly confined by the substance of these decisions, such that any 'disproportionate' infringement could be found only in connection with acts or omissions that were wholly ancillary to the requirements imposed therein.[138]

In neither *Sayadi* nor *Nada* did the relevant court or treaty body suggest that the ICCPR or ECHR standards could be utilised to impugn State conduct that *was* necessary in order to fulfil the Council-imposed obligations. Indeed, there is every indication in the judgments that the substantive requirements in the resolutions would in fact preclude the application of human rights law. Thus the HRC implicitly accepted in *Sayadi* that "obligations imposed…by the Security Council resolutions *may justify* the infringement" of the applicant's rights as protected under the Covenant, leaving only the question of the "extent" to which such infringement was necessitated by the terms of the relevant decision.[139] Similarly, in *Nada*, the Court stated that the actions required of Switzerland in order to mitigate the effects of resolution on the individual applicant would have to be adopted "without…circumventing the binding nature of the relevant resolutions or compliance with the sanctions provided for therein."[140]

It is also significant that neither of the human rights bodies engaged with the possible existence and scope of any substantive limits that might serve to restrict the Council's capacity to override or suspend States' duties under human rights law. Thus in *Sayadi* the HRC did not examine whether the

137 As prescribed under Article 8(2) of the Convention. *Nada* ECtHR, *supra* note 16, ¶ 185.

138 Arman Sarvarian, "*Nada v. Switzerland*: The Continuing Problem of Attribution of Conduct Taken Pursuant to Security Council Resolutions," 2012, http://www.ejiltalk.org/nada-v-switzerland-the-continuing-problem-of-attribution-of-conduct-taken-pursuant-to-security-council-resolutions/#more-5687.

139 *Sayadi*, *supra* note 15, ¶ 10.6.

140 *Nada* ECtHR, *supra* note 16, ¶ 196.

requirements imposed by the Council could be considered to be *ultra vires* as contrary to the Charter, or a violation of either a norm of *jus cogens* or the non-derogable core of States' duties under customary law,[141] notwithstanding that the validity and binding effect of the resolutions had been challenged by the applicants on both of these grounds.[142] Along similar lines, the ECtHR in *Nada* did not address the relationship between the human rights obligations of States under the Convention and those arising from the binding Council resolution, instead stating that its finding that Switzerland had not taken adequate measures to mitigate the resolution's effects "*dispenses the Court* from determining the question" of this relationship.[143] It thus "deftly avoided" the apparent implications of Article 103 for any conflict between the two sets of obligations,[144] but by doing so also failed to examine the possible existence of any substantive limits on the Council's capacity to prevent the effective application of human rights law.[145]

Moreover, and as a result of this lack of engagement with the possible legal constraints on the Council's encroachment on human rights norms, the findings of human rights infringements by the States concerned were in both instances limited and somewhat artificial in substance, giving rise to significant limitations in connection with the remedies that could be provided, and how far these would ensure the meaningful protection of the rights of the individual applicants. Thus, as noted, a breach of the States' human rights duties could only be found in relation to measures taken, or not taken, that were wholly ancillary to the imposition of severe restrictions on travel and access to financial assets that were required by the Council.

Yet without addressing the possible existence of substantive legal limits on the Council's encroachment of human rights norms, no infringement of the relevant treaty standards was or could have been found in relation to the prolonged imposition of the severe travel restrictions themselves, notwithstanding the doubts raised in relation to the nature of these measures and absence of any effective means to challenge their application. Nor could the States' continuing duty to impose these restrictions be questioned, in view of the

141 *Ibid.*

142 *Sayadi*, *supra* note 15, ¶ 5.6.

143 *Nada* ECtHR, *supra* note 16, ¶ 197, emphasis added. Again this question had been formally raised in the proceedings, by both the respondent and intervening governments.

144 Tobias Thienel, "*Nada v Switzerland*: The ECtHR Does Not Pull a *Kadi* (But Mandates It for Domestic Law)," 2012, http://invisiblecollege.weblog.leidenuniv.nl/2012/09/12/nada-v-switzerland-the-ecthr-doesnot-pu/.

145 Schmalenbach, *supra* note 126, 29.

expressed reluctance of the judicial bodies to "circumven[t] the binding nature of the relevant resolutions or compliance with the sanctions provided for therein."[146] Thus neither of the human rights bodies calls into question the ongoing obligation of the States concerned to fulfil the requirements imposed by the Council by implementing the required financial and travel restrictions against the named individuals, or indicates that the continued imposition of these measures could *in itself* constitute an infringement of the State's duties under human rights law.

In connection with the case before the ECtHR, as noted above, the applicant had in fact been delisted by the Sanctions Committee prior to the Grand Chamber's decision, independently of these proceedings. However, had Mr Nada remained on the Consolidated List, the application of the Convention as interpreted by the ECtHR would not have served to preclude his ongoing subjection to the travel restrictions and ban on access to financial assets, albeit with access to marginally improved "exemptions" as regards the former requirement and more strenuous efforts by Switzerland at the diplomatic level to attempt to bring about his delisting.

In the latter context, the sole remedy that the HRC was able to afford to the applicants in *Sayadi* is particularly instructive as concerns the limitations of the human rights protection that may be provided by judicial bodies in the absence of any engagement with the substantive limits on the Council's subordination of human rights norms. Thus Belgium was advised by the HRC that it had "the duty to do all it can to have their names removed from the List as soon as possible,"[147] with the Committee acknowledging that the State was not "itself… competent to remove the authors' names" from this List.[148] Yet Belgium had already initiated a number of requests before that Committee that the applicants be delisted, in part as a result of the earlier rulings of its domestic court in this context,[149] each of which had been *refused* by the Sanctions Committee without justification.[150] It is thus evident that the remedy stipulated by the HRC would be of extremely limited utility as concerns the individuals' continued subjection to the infringements of their rights under the Convention.[151]

---

146 *Nada* ECtHR, *supra* note 16, ¶ 196.

147 *Sayadi*, *supra* note 15, ¶ 12.

148 *Ibid.*

149 *Ibid.*, ¶ 4.7.

150 *Ibid.*, ¶ 5.4. See also Milanović, *supra* note 38, 531.

151 Contrary to the indication of the ECtHR in *Nada* that a remedy, as required under Article 13 ECHR, "must in any event be 'effective' in practice as well as in law," *Nada* ECtHR, *supra* note 16, ¶ 207.

It is significant, moreover, that these requests for the applicants' removal from the List had been rejected by the Sanctions Committee despite the fact that they had been presented to the Committee based in part on the dismissal of a criminal investigation against the applicants, in 2005.[152] This refusal to delist the applicants notwithstanding this dismissal of criminal proceedings, together with repeated requests by the designating State for the individuals to be removed from the List,[153] highlights the artificial nature of the "infringement" of the applicant's right to private and family life that was subsequently found to exist in *Nada*, in connection with Switzerland's suggested failure to notify the Sanctions Committee of the result of the criminal investigation or to encourage Italy to pursue a delisting request.[154]

It also serves to underscore the extremely limited substantive protection of this right that would have been forthcoming had Switzerland in fact acted *in line with* its stated duties in these contexts. Thus any decision to in fact delist the applicant, and thereby bring an end to the uniquely severe restrictions on movement to which he was subject, would have remained entirely at the discretion of individual members of the Sanctions Committee, and most notably the United States which had proposed his initial inclusion in the List. Yet this body had demonstrated a visible reluctance to agree to delisting requests on the basis of the dismissal of criminal prosecutions against designated individuals, and indeed in its Guidelines and elsewhere has repeatedly emphasised that a "criminal charge or conviction is not a prerequisite for listing as the sanctions are intended to be preventive in nature."[155]

It must be recognised that the ECtHR also found an infringement by Switzerland of the applicant's right to a remedy, under Article 13 of the Convention, holding that "the applicant did not have any effective means of obtaining the removal of his name from the List annexed to the [implementing legislation] and therefore no remedy in respect of the Convention violations that he alleged."[156] However, this part of the ruling, which was questioned by a

---

152 *Sayadi*, *supra* note 15, ¶ 10.8; See also ¶ 4.4.

153 *Ibid.*, ¶ 10.13.

154 Indeed Italy's eventual request for Mr Nada's delisting in 2008 had itself been rejected by the Sanctions Committee, notwithstanding the accompanying notification of the dismissal of its own criminal investigation into the applicant's activities; *Nada* ECtHR, *supra* note 16, ¶ 56.

155 Guidelines of the Committee for the Conduct of its Work (26 January 2011), 6(c). See also Third Report of the 1526 Sanctions Monitoring Team, U.N. Doc. S/2005/572, 9 September 2005, ¶ 39; S/RES/1735 (2006), preamble.

156 *Nada* ECtHR, *supra* note 16, ¶ 213. The Court highlights in particular that while the applicant "was able to apply to the national authorities to have his name deleted from the list,"

number of dissenting judgments,[157] appears to be based on a clear misinterpretation of the requirements dictated under the resolution. As a result it gives rise to significant grounds for criticism in terms of both the coherence of the decision and the significant practical difficulties for States attempting to reconcile their countervailing international duties, in line with the decision of the ECJ in *Kadi*. Indeed, the ECtHR's decision in this context was based on the assertion in the *Kadi* judgment that:

> it is not a consequence of the principles governing the international legal order under the United Nations that any judicial review of the internal lawfulness of the contested regulation in the light of fundamental freedoms is excluded by virtue of the fact that that measure is intended to give effect to a resolution of the Security Council.[158]

Thus the ECtHR asserts that the "same reasoning must be applied…to the present case," indeed observing in addition that there was "nothing in the *Security Council resolutions* to prevent the Swiss authorities from introducing mechanisms to verify the measures taken."[159]

Yet, as highlighted by Tzanakopoulos, this position rests on a clear misunderstanding of the requirements imposed by the Council under its targeted sanctions regime, in view of its direct specification of the individuals who are to be subjected to the required measures. Thus no result other than the continued freezing of each individual's assets and prohibition of their travel would be consistent with the requirements dictated by the Council,[160] such that any "judicial review" of the measures at national level, or introduction of "mechanisms to verify" these restrictions, would entail a direct breach of the resolutions if they led to a decision that the measures should not be applied against the individual concerned. As a result, it is evident that no meaningful review of an individual's subjection to these measures could be forthcoming at the national level – at least in connection with the rights protected under the ECtHR – without contravening the assertion of the Court itself that its review

---

those authorities "did not examine on the merits his complaints" and "could not lift the sanctions…on the applicant," see 210.

157 *Ibid.*, joint concurring opinion of Judges Bratza, Nicolaou and Yudkivska, ¶ 8; and concurring opinion of Judge Malinverni, ¶ 10.

158 *Kadi* ECJ, *supra* note 12, ¶ 299.

159 *Nada* ECtHR, *supra* note 16, ¶ 212, emphasis added.

160 Tzanakopoulos, *supra* note 17, 58–59.

of Switzerland's actions could not circumvent "the binding nature of the relevant resolutions."[161]

Therefore, contrary to the assertion of the Court that review of the measures may bring about an "effective means of obtaining the removal of his name from the list,"[162] the "remedies" that could be provided by a domestic court are restricted to those that would be compatible with the State's ongoing commitments under Chapter VII – in line with the actions and omissions that were judged by the ECtHR itself to have represented an infringement of the applicant's right to private and family life.

Yet in light of the foregoing it is evident that these omissions were wholly incidental to the more substantial infringement of the applicant's rights – namely his subjection to the travel ban and asset freezing measures – that was inherent in the State's continuing adherence to its Chapter VII obligations. It is submitted that these more significant infringements of the applicant's rights under the Convention, and the absence of any effective remedy or right to challenge in this context, could not themselves convincingly be challenged on human rights grounds in the absence of a more coherent examination of the relationship between the two sets of international obligations.

5 Conclusion

In light of the foregoing, it is evident that the judicial decisions that have been examined in this chapter have done little to dispel the prevailing position whereby Council-imposed norms may displace those concerned with the protection of the rights of individuals, in the event of a conflict. Thus while the judgments demonstrate an increasing concern among courts and human rights bodies with the magnitude of the Council's impact on States' important, long-established duties under human rights law, they also provide evidence of the difficulties involved in substantially constraining any such encroachment. Moreover, an analysis of each of the decisions draws attention to the limitations inherent in any attempt to effectively apply States' human rights commitments in the face of inconsistent Chapter VII requirements in the absence of more significant engagement with the relationship between these two sets of obligations as a matter of international law.[163]

---

161 *Nada* ECtHR, *supra* note 16, ¶ 196.

162 *Ibid.*, ¶ 213.

163 *Cf.* Fabbrini and Larik, observing that the ECtHR in *Nada* was able to "uphold, *at least as a matter of principle*, human rights protection within its own legal order"; Federico Fabbrini

While significant criticism of the Council's increasing intrusion on human rights standards may be found in each of the decisions examined, none of the judgments in fact constrains the capacity of requirements imposed by the Council to displace States' commitments under human rights law – at least aside from the ECJ's *Kadi* decision, which may be considered to be inherently limited in terms of its development of the legal position for States under general international law, in view of the EU's non-membership of the UN and proclaimed operation as an "autonomous…system," outside of this legal order.[164]

It is therefore submitted that the "wave of defiance" that has been argued to characterise these judicial reactions to the Council's encroachment on human rights norms through its regime of targeted sanctions[165] has been significantly overstated in much of the literature, and that the "tendency to accept that the Security Council is omnipotent and may override human rights," as identified by Aulik in relation to the earlier case law in this context,[166] has yet to be meaningfully dispelled. As such, it remains of paramount importance that future decisions seek to establish a clear and conceptually coherent framework through which the limits on the Council's capacity to override human rights law in the name of maintaining international security may be more convincingly identified.

---

and Joris Larik, "The Accession of the EU to the ECHR and its Effects: *Nada v. Switzerland*, the Clash of Legal Orders and the Constitutionalization of the ECtHR," 2013, http://papers.ssrn.com/sol3/papers.cfm?abstract_id=2334905: 103, emphasis added.

164 See *Ahmed*, *supra* note 6, ¶ 71. *Cf.* de Búrca, *supra* note 34, 49.

165 Tzanakopoulos, *supra* note 21, 16.

166 Aulik, *supra* note 35, 41.

CHAPTER 5

The EU's Protection of ECHR Standards

More Protective than the Bosphorus *Legacy?*

Tawhida Ahmed

1 Introduction

The concern regarding overlapping international human rights adjudication is yet another sign of the position that human rights holds as an uncompromising principle of relations between States and within States in the international legal framework. In Europe, the issue has been at the forefront of European Union (EU) and European Convention on Human Rights and Fundamental Freedoms (ECHR) relations for over fifty years. This chapter examines the extent to which rights found within the ECHR can be upheld when the act allegedly breaching human rights is one arising from EU (secondary) law such as EU Regulations and Directives. In 2008, I addressed this topic from the perspective of the ECHR and the European Court of Human Rights (ECtHR)[1] – that is, how did the ECtHR resolve a case involving breaches of the ECHR by EU acts? Or, to what extent does the ECtHR require the EU to respect ECHR standards of human rights protection? In this chapter, I address the topic from the perspective of the EU and the Court of Justice of the European Union (CJEU) – that is, how does EU law and the CJEU purport to meet human rights standards of the ECtHR in cases involving EU acts? Or, to what extent does EU law require its own institutions and Member States to respect ECHR standards of human rights protection? The chapter is thus interested in "human rights adjudication as a part of a global conversation across legal institutions" – an inquiry seen also in the work of Professor Ghandhi.[2]

1 Tawhida Ahmed, "The EU, the ECHR and the Effective Protection of Human Rights for Individuals," in New Problems and Techniques in International Dispute Settlement by Legal Means, edited by Duncan French, Matthew Saul and Nigel White (Oxford: Hart Publishing, 2009), 345.

2 See Introduction to this volume, text accompanying note 10; and Sandy Ghandhi, "Human Rights and the International Court of Justice in the *Ahmadou Sadio Diallo* Case," *Human Rights Law Review* 11, 3 (2011): 536.

 | DOI 10.1163/9789004261181_007

Human rights protection in Europe consists of a complex web of EU and Council of Europe instruments.[3] There is no legal principle that provides for the primacy of the jurisdiction of one organisation over the other, and the EU is not (yet) a signatory member of the ECHR (and consequently is not itself subject to the adjudicatory mechanism of the ECtHR). This gives rise to the possibility of diverging human rights standards between the two organisations, which can result in the weakening of human rights protection for individuals. A non-uniform application of ECHR rights may materialise in circumstances where a case involves a breach of individual human rights as a result of a Member State's application of EU law. A solution to such conflicts of standards was promulgated by the ECtHR in the cases of, *inter alia*, *Matthews*[4] and *Bosphorus*.[5] The *Matthews* case held that in disputes brought by individuals against a Member State that involved legal obligations arising from EU Treaty law, the State remained liable for securing ECHR rights. The State would consequently be held liable in the event of a finding that an individual's human rights had been breached. However, for EU secondary legislation or judicial decisions, with respect to the implementation of which the Member State in question had no discretion, the *Bosphorus* test permits the ECtHR to take account of the fact that the State had acted pursuant to EU legal obligations. To "take account of" in this context means that the where the EU is found to provide a level of protection "equivalent" ("comparable" not identical) to that found in the ECHR system in both substance and procedure, a substantive examination of whether there is a breach of Convention standards in the case at hand will not be undertaken and, consequently, the State in question will be presumed to have complied with ECHR obligations. According to *Bosphorus*, this format will be followed unless a proposition is made that there is a manifest deficiency in the protection of Convention

3 For discussion, see Eve Chava Landau, "A New Regime of Human Rights in the EU," *European Journal of Law Reform* 4, (2008): 557; Olivier de Schutter, "The Two Europe's of Human Rights: The Emerging Division of Tasks between the Council of Europe and the European Union in the Promoting of Human Rights in Europe," 14 *Columbia Journal of European Law* (2008): 509; John L. Murray, "The Influence of the European Convention on Fundamental Rights on Community Law," *Fordham International Law Journal* 33, 5 (2011): 1388; Nuala Mole, "The Complex and Evolving Relationship between the European Union and the European Convention on Human Rights," *European Human Rights Law Review* 7 (2012): 363–368; and Wolfgang Weiss, "Rethinking the Role of the European Convention on Human Rights after Lisbon," *European Constitutional Law Review* 7 (2011): 64–95.

4 *Matthews v. UK* [1999] 28 EHRR 361.

5 *Bosphorus Airways v. Ireland* (2006) 42 EHRR 1.

rights.[6] *Matthews* and *Bosphorus* present differences in liability of Member States in cases involving EU law; the stricter accountability of Member States in *Matthews* is based on the fact that Treaty law cannot be challenged before EU courts in EU law, whereas there are EU law avenues to challenge secondary legislation and judicial decisions.

In 2006, at the time of the judgment, the *Bosphorus* position was regarded as problematic for the protection of the human rights of individuals in accordance with the standards afforded by the ECtHR, because ECHR standards were at risk of being significantly lowered by the ECHR in EU-related contexts.[7] The case gave rise to different degrees of accountability of States party to the ECHR. The solution provided by the ECtHR was thus incapable of preserving the standards of ECHR protection that Europeans would receive in cases unrelated to the EU.

This chapter will examine solutions in EU law and will argue that these require more stringent preservation of ECHR standards than required by the ECHR itself through the *Bosphorus* mechanism. In other words, EU law requires the EU to protect ECHR rights more stringently than the ECHR does. It will also be argued that, nonetheless, some gaps remain within the EU mechanisms through which respect for ECHR rights are to be ensured.

2 The EU, Human Rights Protection and the ECHR

The relationship between EU law and the ECHR has grown in strength over several decades. The EU, originally formed as an economic entity, did not provide for a human rights protection system.[8] Although there were already plans in the early 1950s of the European integration process to integrate the ECHR

6 In cases where Member States had no discretion, normal ECHR standards of review would apply, *Bosphorus*, *ibid.*, ¶ 157.

7 Christina Eckes, "Does the European Court of Human Rights Provide Protection from the European Community? The Case of *Bosphorus Airways*," *European Public Law* 13, 1 (2007): 47, 63. See also Cathryn Costello, "The *Bosphorus* Ruling of the European Court of Human Rights: Fundamental Rights and Blurred Boundaries in Europe," *Human Rights Law Review* 6, 1 (2006): 87, 102 (noting that "the standard to rebut the presumption is worryingly high"). Concurring opinions in *Bosphorus* also note that it is "difficult to accept that Community law could be authorised, in the name of 'equivalent protection', to apply standards that are less stringent than those of the European Convention on Human Rights," *Bosphorus*, *supra* note 5, joint concurring opinion of Judges Rozakis, Tulkens, Traja, Botoucharova, Zagrebelsky and Garlicki, ¶ 4.

8 Guy Harpaz, "The European Court of Justice and its Relations with the European Court of Human Rights: The Quest for Enhanced Reliance, Coherence and Legitimacy," *Common*

into the Community framework, including through accession talks, this ambition ultimately failed.[9]

It was the CJEU which played an important role in the recognition of human rights within the EU legal order.[10] Through its case law it recognised that "respect for fundamental rights forms an integral part of the general principles of law protected by the Court of Justice"[11] as inspired by the constitutional traditions common to the Member States, and the international treaties to which Member States are signatory.[12]

Developing international treaties as a source, in the 1975 case of *Rutili*, the CJEU for the first time expressly relied on the ECHR,[13] and soon after employed the ECHR almost exclusively as the EU's international benchmark for human rights protection.[14] The CJEU has frequently described the ECHR as being of particular significance to the EU legal order.[15] The CJEU did not, however, only rely on ECHR rights but also on ECtHR jurisprudence,[16] and at times revised its

---

Market Law Review 46 (2009): 105, 107; Joseph Weiler, "Eurocracy and Distrust: Some Questions Concerning the Role of the European Court of Justice in the Protection of Fundamental Human Rights within the Legal Order of the Communities," *Washington Law Review* 61 (2006): 1103, 1110–1113; and Andrew Williams, *EU Human Rights Policies: A Study in Irony* (Oxford University Press: Oxford, 2005).

9 Grainne de Búrca, "The Evolution of EU Human Rights Law," in *The Evolution of EU Law*, edited by Paul Craig and Grainne de Búrca (Oxford University Press: New York, 2011), 465, 468–469.

10 On the role of the CJEU, see, for example: Franics Jacobs, "Human Rights in the European Union: The Role of the Court of Justice," *European Law Review*, working paper (2000), http://denning.law.ox.ac.uk/iecl/pdfs/working2colneric.pdf; and Bruno De Witte, "The Past and Future Role of the European Court of Justice in the Protection of Human Rights," in *The EU and Human Rights*, edited by Philip Alston (Oxford University Press: New York, 1999), 859–898.

11 See Case C 11/70 *Internationale Handelsgesellschaft v. Einfuhr und Vorratsstelle für Getreide und Futtermittel* [1970] ECR 1125, ¶ 4; and Case C-29/69 *Stauder v. City of Ulm* [1969] ECR 419, ¶ 7.

12 Case C-4/73 *Nold v. Commission* [1974] ECR 491, ¶ 13.

13 Case C-36/75 *Rutili v. Minister for the Interior* [1975] ECR 1219, ¶ 32.

14 See, for example, Case C-396/95 *Familiapress v. Heinrich Bauer Verlag* [1997] ECR I-3689, ¶ 18; Case C-185/95 *Baustahlgewerbe European Communities* [1998] ECR I-8417, ¶ 20; and Case C-299/95 *Kremzow v. Austria* [1997] ECR I-2629, ¶ 14.

15 See, for example, Case C-540/03 *Parliament v. Council* [2006] ECR I-5769, ¶ 35; Case C-36/02 *Omega v. Oberbürgermeisterin der Bundesstadt Bonn* [2004] ECR I-9609, ¶ 33; and Case C-71/02 *Karner v. Troostwijk* [2004] ECR I-3025, ¶ 48.

16 See, for example, Case C-13/94 *P v. S* [1996] ECR I-2143, ¶ 16; Case C-7/98 *Krombach and Bamberski* [2000] ECR I-1935, ¶ 39; and Case C-249/96 *Grant v. South West Trains Ltd* [1998] ECR I-621, ¶ 34.

own case law in order to bring it into line with ECtHR case law.[17] Consequently it was argued that the CJEU treats the ECHR as if it was binding upon the EU and that the CJEU follows that case-law of the ECtHR scrupulously.[18] This judicial development was enshrined in the Treaties and again the ECHR acquired a special status, starting in the Single European Act 1986[19] and the Maastricht Treaty 1992.[20] Thus, for many decades, EU law has persistently required the EU to respect ECHR rights.

However, initially, despite positive rhetoric towards the ECHR, the EU jurisprudential practice arguably only paid lip service to the standards of the ECHR. Instead, the CJEU acted rather autonomously and did not consider itself as so much bound by the ECHR, as merely inspired by it.[21] The reliance by the EU on the ECHR, however, strengthened over the years and significant change has occurred since the *Bosphorus* ruling: the Treaty of Lisbon entered into force, which strengthens the EU's commitment to human rights and even requires the EU to accede to the ECHR;[22] the EU Charter on Fundamental Rights

17 See, for example, Case C-46/87 and 227/88 *Höchst ag v. Commission* [1989] ECR 2859; and Case C-94/00 *Roquettes Frères sa v. Commission* [2002] ECR I-9011.

18 Francis Jacobs, *The Sovereignty of Law: The European Way* (Cambridge: Cambridge University Press, 2007), 54–55.

19 The Single European Act Preamble reads: "[d]etermined to work together to promote democracy on the basis of the fundamental rights recognised in the constitutions and laws of the Member States, in the Convention for the Protection of Human Rights and Fundamental Freedoms."

20 Art. F (2) (now Art. 6 (3) TEU provides that: "The Union shall respect fundamental rights, as guaranteed by the European Convention for the Protection of Human Rights and Fundamental Freedoms and as they result from the constitutional traditions common to the Member States, as general principles of Community law."

21 Indeed, often seeming only taking this approach to "allow for the triumph of community will," Jason Coppel and Aidan O'Neill, "The European Court of Justice: Taking Rights Seriously?," *Common Market Law Review* 29 (1992): 669, 683.

22 Art. 6(2) TEU. This itself has already been a long debated topic within the EU: see S. O'Leary, "Accession by the European Community to the European Convention on Human Rights – the Opinion of the ECJ," *European Human Rights Law Review* 4 (1996): 362. It is argued that the EU must accede to the ECHR to enhance human rights protection within the EU: see Rick Lawson, "Confusion and Conflict? Diverging Interpretations of the European Convention on Human Rights in Strasbourg and Luxembourg," in *The Dynamics of the Protection of Human Rights in Europe: Essays in Honour of Henry G.S. Schermers*, edited by Rick Lawson and Matthijs de Blois (Dordrecht: Martinus Nijhoff Publishers, 1994). For recent commentary on the accession negotiations, see Jean Paul Jacque, "The Accession of the European Union to the European Convention on Human Rights and Fundamental Freedoms," *Common Market Law Review* 48 (2011): 995; Adam Weiss, "EU

(EUCFR) was given legally binding status, making it equivalent to EU primary law (and, as a result, EUCFR provisions on the relationship between the EUCFR and the ECHR also became legally binding). These developments improve the protection of human rights within the EU and have the potential to reduce (if not eliminate) the risk that EU standards of human rights will not meet those of the ECHR. CJEU case law has clarified the nature of the obligations imposed by these new changes. Until the accession of the EU to the ECHR, these obligations represent the current practice of EU law towards the ECHR. Later sections of this chapter examine the specific nature of the obligations in question, and how these have been fulfilled more successfully in the recent practice of the EU.

3 Universality of Human Rights: Uniform Protection of ECHR Rights

i *Protection of ECHR Rights: The ECHR Position*

The issue of universal protection of human rights is, broadly speaking, the idea that all human beings possess human rights and that they hold as against all other institutions and individuals.[23] With respect to EU-ECHR relations, the issue has a much narrower focus: it refers to the achievement of uniform or consistent application of ECHR rights in non-EU and EU contexts alike (and thereby the prevention of double standards in the application of the ECHR). This principle of the consistent application of human rights to all persons within the jurisdiction of States party to the ECHR is a fundamental foundational principle of the ECHR, and can be seen as reflected by the Convention in Article 1.[24]

However, in 2006 in *Bosphorus*, the ECtHR applied a test of equivalence in favour of the EU, in relation to EU secondary law: that is, it considered that the

---

Accession to the European Convention on Human Rights Process: the State of Play and the Assessed Value for Victims of Human Rights Violations in Europe," *European Human Rights Law Review* 4 (2012): 391; Tobias Lock, "EU Accession to the ECHR: Implications for the Judicial Review in Strasbourg," *European Law Review* 35, 6 (2010): 777; Jose Martin and Perez de Nanclares, "The Accession of the European Union to the ECHR: More than just a Legal Issue," working paper of the Instituto de Derecho Europeo e Integración Regional (IDEIR), WP IDEIR n° 15 (2013), https://www.ucm.es/data/cont/docs/595-2013-11-07-the%20accesion.pdf.

23 Jack Donnelly, *Universal Human Rights in Theory and Practice* (2nd ed., Ithaca: Cornell University Press, 2003), 1.

24 Art. 1 provides that: "[t]he High Contracting Parties shall secure to everyone within their jurisdiction the rights and freedoms defined in Section 1 of this Convention."

EU's mechanisms for the protection of human rights were – in the abstract (not in relation to the facts of the specific case) – equivalent to the standards of the ECHR. Accordingly, where Member States had no discretion in applying EU law, the ECtHR could presume that the Member State in question complied with its ECHR obligations; the presumption is rebuttable only if it can be shown that the protection of human rights in the case was manifestly deficient (which was not shown in this case). The EU mechanisms referred to at the time included the Treaty references to human rights, the EUCFR and CJEU case law, all of which give special importance to the application of the ECHR and/or ECtHR case law. The EU mechanisms of adequate human rights protection also included EU judicial review, and litigation opportunities available before national courts (and thereby application of principles such as direct effect, indirect effect and State liability – with an oversight through the preliminary rulings procedure), all of which enable individuals to engage their human rights within the EU system.[25]

As a result of the application of the above *Bosphorus* test, neither the EU (which, as noted above, is not a signatory to the ECHR) nor its Member States were held liable for claimed breaches of the Convention rights. Amongst the concerns this raises, are the double standards the test permits between non-EU and EU-related cases before the ECtHR, and the fact that the EU is, in effect, given power to breach human rights, so long as it does not amount to a "manifest deficiency" of those rights. *Bosphorus* weighed too greatly in favour of international cooperation to the detriment of adequate human rights supervision.[26]

Moreover, recent ECHR case law shows that the way the *Bosphorus* test has been applied by the ECtHR remains favourable to the EU, in that it involves a rather cursory assessment of EU law, before a declaration of "no breach of rights" is made. For instance, in *Bosphorus*, the ECtHR found the EU system to be equivalent in its protection of human rights, *inter alia*, because of the use of the CJEU's preliminary ruling procedure in the case. In the subsequent case of *Cooperative v. France*,[27] the ECtHR reached the same conclusion regarding the adequacy of the EU system, even though the preliminary ruling procedure was not used in the case. The ECtHR did not provide a reason for its decision.

25 See *Bosphorus*, *supra* note 5, ¶¶ 159–165 (in which the ECtHR also refers to earlier paragraphs where it also discussed EU mechanisms of human rights protection, at ¶¶ 73–81; 86–90; 85 and 91; 96–99).

26 See *supra* notes 5–6 and accompanying text.

27 *Coopérative des Agriculteurs de la Mayenne et la Cooperative Laitière Maine-Anjou v. France* (App no 16931/04) (Section II), 10 October 2006.

In *Kokkelsisserij*,[28] the applicant was denied the right to provide written observations in response to an Opinion of the Advocate General in proceedings relating to his case (which, *inter alia*, concerned the interpretation of EU secondary law – a Directive). The applicant took the case before the ECtHR and complained that his right to adversarial proceedings under Article 6(1) ECHR had been breached. The Court found that the intervention of the CJEU, through the preliminary ruling mechanism, was actively sought by the Member State (i.e., an act of the Member State could be found) but that the nature of preliminary ruling in EU law meant that States had no discretion as to whether to apply the CJEU's ruling. Thus, the *Bosphorus* test could be applied.[29]

The ECtHR then went on to note that the EU judicial mechanism provided the possibility of re-opening the oral procedure in certain circumstances (even though there was no re-opening of the actual case here). As such, it found that there was equivalent protection of human rights between the EU and ECHR. The fact that the applicant could not respond to the Opinion of the Advocate General was held not to be manifestly deficient of ECHR standards and thus the claims of the applicant were manifestly ill-founded.

In *Biret*,[30] the applicant company complained of the application of two EU Directives, which left the company insolvent. The company complained that (a) it was unable to challenge the Directives directly before EU courts and that this was a breach of Articles 6 and 13 ECHR, and (b) there was a breach of its property rights, because the company had been deprived of its business when France took action in line with the requirements of the Directive (which he failed to challenge successfully under domestic law). The Court concluded that the first claim related solely to an act of the EU and could not be regarded as an act of the EU Member States.[31] In relation to the second claim, however, France

28 *Kokkelsisserij v. The Netherlands* (App No. 13645/05) (Section III), 20 January 2009, decision as to admissibility.

29 Cf. *Connolly*, where the labour dispute of an employee of Eurocontrol did not in any way involve action by a Member State, *Connolly v. 15 Member States of the European Union* (App no 73274/01) (Section V), 9 December 2008.

30 *Biret v. 15 Member States* (App no 13762/04), 9 December 2008, decision as to admissibility.

31 *Behrami* and *Connelly* show that in order for liability to be placed on the State, it must be shown that either that (a) there was an act on the territory of the State or (b) there was presence of a decision by the State: *Behrami and Behrami v. France* (App no 71412/01) and *Saramati v France, Germany and Norway* (App no 78166/01), 2 May 2007; and *Connolly v 15 Member States of the European Union* (App no 73274/01) (Section V), 9 December 2008. This was applied in *Boivin and Gasparini*, where the ECtHR did not examine the substantive issues relating to the EU because there was no direct or indirect intervention from the

had exercised an "act" when it applied the embargo to the Company as required by the EU Directive. The Court nonetheless went on to apply the *Bosphorus* presumption, without undertaking a detailed examination of the case. It merely stated that there was no manifest deficiency in human rights protection, and supported this with a reference to the *Cooperative v. France* case.[32] As argued by Lock, however, the reference to *Cooperative v. France* cannot be a substitute for a proper examination of *Biret*; the facts of *Biret* and *Cooperative v. France* were too dissimilar to be comparable.[33]

Furthermore, in *Biret*, the Court did not scrutinise whether there was any discretion on EU Member States in applying EU law. A lack of discretion on the part of Member States is a prerequisite to the application of the *Bosphorus* notion of equivalence. In *Cooperative v. France*, the Court did very briefly look at an EU Regulation and conclude that the State had no discretion, but in *Biret*, the Court did not raise the issue of discretion at all[34] and nonetheless applied *Bosphorus*. Although the actual Directive in this case did not, in fact, leave Member States with any discretion in applying EU law, the ECtHR did not discuss this point: a significant failure of supervisory monitoring, because the idea that certain EU mechanisms automatically leave no discretion to Member States is not correct.[35]

The *M.S.S v. Belgium and Greece* case[36] is a good illustration of this. The case concerned the Dublin Regulation, which provides criteria upon which to determine which EU Member State will assess an asylum application.[37] Regulations in EU law supposedly leave no discretion to Member States. However, in its examination of the Regulation, the ECtHR concluded that in accordance with provisions within the Regulation itself, Belgium could have

Member States which resulted in the impact on the applicants. Thus, there was no relevant action which could be attributed to the State for the ECtHR to examine: *Boivin v. 34 Member States of the Court of Europe* (Admissibility) (73250/01) Unreported 9 September 2008 (ECHR); *Gasparini v. Italy* (Admissibility) (10750/03) Unreported 12 May 2009 (ECHR).

32 *Cooperative v. France*, *supra* note 27.

33 Tobias Lock, "Beyond *Bosphorus*: the European Court of Human Right's Case Law on the Responsibility of Member States of International Organisations under the European Convention on Human Rights," *Human Rights Law Review*, 10, 3 (2010): 529, 542.

34 *Ibid.*, 544.

35 EU Regulations and preliminary rulings from the CJEU can leave considerable discretion to States and thus should be assessed on a case by case basis. See Costello, *supra* note 7, 110–111.

36 *M.S.S v Belgium and Greece* (App No, 30696/09), 21 January 2011.

37 Regulation 343/2003 EC of 18 February 2003 establishing the criteria and mechanisms for determining the Member State responsible for examining an asylum application lodged in one of the Member States by a third-country national OJ L 50/1-50/10 25.3.2003.

refrained from sending the applicant back to Greece (i.e., Belgium had a level of discretion in applying the EU law) and therefore its actions did not strictly fall within the legal obligations of the Regulation. Accordingly, the *Bosphorus* presumption did not apply.[38] It is argued that this level of examination of EU law should take place in all cases before the ECtHR. However, as demonstrated, this has not always been the case.

Finally, in *Boivin*,[39] the ECtHR stated that "[t]he Court observes that it has not been established, or even alleged, that the protection of fundamental rights generally afforded by Eurocontrol is not 'Equivalent'…"[40] This places the burden on the applicant to raise an issue of manifest deficiency in EU mechanisms for the protection of human rights in order to trigger the ECtHR to examine that question. The ECtHR is therefore arguably displacing its responsibility here to adequately apply the *Bosphorus* test.

In summary, the case law discussed indicates that the ECHR has cemented its *Bosphorus* model and generally acts in favour of an abstract – as opposed to a more detailed – examination of EU law, before concluding that EU offers equivalence in its protection of human rights (and thus that the *Bosphorus* presumption applies to the State before it).

ii *The EU Position: More Protective than the* Bosphorus *Legacy?*

How does EU law approach the question of the uniform and consistent application of ECHR rights? The brief historical review of EU-ECHR relations undertaken in section 2 demonstrates the importance given to the ECHR in the EU sphere.

Today, Article 6(3) of the Treaty of the European Union (TEU) and several provisions of the EUCFR[41] contribute towards the elimination of differences in standards of protection between the EU and the ECHR. Article 6(3) TEU observes that fundamental rights as guaranteed by the ECHR constitute general principles of EU law.

In the EUCFR, Article 52(3) states that rights found within the EUCFR that correspond to those in the ECHR shall be given the same meaning as that given in the ECHR. The Explanations to the Charter[42] reveal that Article 52(3) "is intended to ensure the necessary consistency between the Charter and the ECHR."[43]

38 *Ibid.*, ¶ 340.

39 *Boivin*, *supra* note 31.

40 *Ibid.*

41 The EUCFR is legally binding, in accordance with Art. 6(1) TEU.

42 The Explanations to the Charter must be given due regard, as per Art. 52(7) of the Charter.

43 Explanations Relating to the Charter of Fundamental Rights, 2007 OJ C303/02, Explanation on Article 52.

Article 53 EUCFR also requires that the interpretation of the Charter does not "restrict" or "adversely affect" various standards of human rights, including those within the ECHR. These Charter provisions suggest that the fundamental rights within the Charter must set as their benchmark the standard of rights within the Convention and, whilst Article 52(3) also provides that the EU may offer protection that is higher than that of the ECHR,[44] this implies that it must not provide lower protection. Therefore, "[s]ince these ECHR provisions become legally binding, there is no leeway on the part of the EU institutions to fall short of the ECHR level of human rights protection."[45]

What does the case law add to this legislative commitment to maintaining ECHR benchmarks? The CJEU's application of ECHR standards involves detailed scrutiny of ECHR case law which the ECtHR's *Bosphorus* decision itself did not require. Peers notes that, in general, post-2009 EU case law pays due regard to ECtHR jurisprudence:

> Where the Court's case law is most developed, it has provided a convincing reply to those who were concerned that the Charter would lead to divergence between the EU and the Strasbourg Court as regards human rights protection, in particular clarifying the correspondence between the Charter and the ECHR, using the explanations of the Charter effectively, applying the limitations rules of the ECHR...and reaffirming the obligation to follow the case law of the Strasbourg Court.[46]

Some examples of cases decided within the EU can be given.[47] In the case of *McB*,[48] the father of three children wanted their return to Ireland from England, where the children were residing with their mother. The case involved Regulation 2201/2003, the interpretation of which would affect Article 7 EUCFR

44 "This provision shall not prevent Union law from providing more extensive protection."

45 Wolfgang Weiss, "EU Human Rights Protection after Lisbon," in *The Treaty of Lisbon and the Future of European Law and Policy*, edited by Martin Trybus and Luca. Rubini (Cheltenham: Edward Elgar, 2012), 220, 224.

46 Steve Peers, "The Rebirth of the EU's Charter of Fundamental Rights," *Cambridge Yearbook of European Legal Studies* 13 (2010–2011): 283, 308.

47 In addition to the cases that will be discussed in this chapter, see also: C-238/00P, C-244/99 P, C-245/99 P, C-247/99 P, C-250/99 P to C-252/99 P, *LimburgseVinyl Maatschappij* (*LVM*) *and Others v. Commission* [2002] ECR I-8375; C-117/01, *KB v. The National Health Service and the Secretary of State for Health* [2004] ECR I-541; C-127/08; *Metock and Others v. Minister for Justice, Equality and Law Reform* [2008] ECR I-6241; and C-34/09 *Gerardo Ruiz Zambrano v. Office de nationale d'emploi* [2011] ECR I-0000.

48 Case C-400/00 *McB v. LE* [2010], 5 October 2010.

and Article 8(1) ECHR. The CJEU – interpreting Article 52(3) EUCFR for the first time – indicated that Article 52(3) requires Charter provisions to be read in line with ECHR case law (even though Article 52(3) itself does not expressly mention case law).[49] The judgment goes on to cite and apply legal principles deriving from ECHR case law to the facts before it.[50] The CJEU's formulation of the EU's commitment to the ECHR here was firm. The Court held that the Charter must be given the same meaning and the same scope as Article 8(1) of the ECHR, as interpreted by the case law of the ECtHR.[51] *Volker*[52] illustrates an application of this, where an ECHR case is directly relied upon to conclude that data relating to the applicant's "private life" can also include data relating to their professional activities.[53]

In *DEB*,[54] a German energy company (DEB) sought reparation from Germany, because Germany failed to transpose two EU directives on time. Those directives were intended to make non-discriminatory access to the national gas networks possible. DEB claimed that because of this delay, it was unable to obtain access to these networks and therefore suffered a loss. It also did not fall within the necessary national criteria for access to legal aid to fund necessary court costs. The higher regional court agreed that the criteria were not fulfilled, but was concerned about the principle of effectiveness, because a refusal of legal aid made it almost impossible for DEB to claim State liability. The Court referred the question to the CJEU.

In answering, the CJEU indicated that EU law would be interpreted in light of the case law of the ECtHR, as well as other provisions of EU law and the law of the Member States.[55] In the case, the CJEU undertook a detailed analysis of ECHR case law in order to identify whether a legal person (a German energy company) was entitled to legal aid. It applied the case law very closely in its ruling that the grant of legal aid to legal persons is not in principle impossible,

---

49 *Ibid.*, ¶ 53. This was reiterated in C-279/09 *DEB Deutsche Energiehandels- und Beratungsgesellschaft mbH v. Bundesrepublik Deutschland* [2010], 22 December 2010, ¶ 35. See also C-92/09 and C-93/09 *Volker and Markus Schecke GbR, Harmut Eifert v. Land Hessen*, [2010], 9 November 2010, ¶ 51, which reiterates the applicability of Article 53(2) EUCFR. Respect for ECHR case law is also required by the Explanations Relating to the Charter, *supra* note 43, Explanation on Article 52.

50 *McB*, *supra* note 48, ¶ 54. *DEB*, *supra* note 49 and *Volker*, *supra* note 49 also undertake a thorough assessment of ECHR case law.

51 *McB*, *supra* note 48, ¶ 53.

52 *Volker*, *supra* note 49.

53 *Ibid.*, ¶ 59.

54 *DEB*, *supra* note 49.

55 *Ibid.*, ¶ 37.

but that not granting it does not undermine the very core of the right of access to court.[56] It also found that selection procedures for legal aid are possible, as long as they are non-arbitrary.[57] The national Court was left to decide the case in light of these principles.[58]

In the *NS* case,[59] the CJEU again relied on ECHR case law to determine that the application of EU law must take into account knowledge in the public domain about the procedural deficiencies in EU Member States relating to asylum applications. In *NS*, an Afghan national applied for asylum status in the UK. In line with Regulation 343/2003,[60] the UK sought to return the applicant to Greece, which the UK believed to be the State responsible for processing the application. This was in accordance with the "responsible State" principle in the Regulation, which enables asylum seekers to be returned to the "responsible State" on an assumption that all EU Member States comply with relevant EU law and fundamental rights. In its judgment, the CJEU held that this principle could be rebutted, where – as in this case – a Member State could not be unaware of the systematic deficiencies in the asylum procedure and reception conditions in the territory of the "responsible State."[61] In identifying that the conditions in Greece did not meet human rights standards, the CJEU made detailed reference to the *M.S.S* case of the ECtHR,[62] in which the ECtHR held that conditions in Greece fall below ECHR standards.

In summary, in the EU's formulation of its commitment to ECHR rights, there is no "doctrine of equivalence" and no "manifest deficiency" test. Instead, its own human rights instrument – the EUCFR – requires the EU to provide the same level of protection as the ECHR, and the CJEU accordingly conducts a comprehensive analysis and application of ECHR case law. The level of scrutiny goes far beyond the requirements of the *Bosphorus* test at the ECHR and

---

56 *Ibid.*, ¶ 51, referring to *CMVMC O'Limov v. Spain*, ECtHR [2009] 24 November 2009, ¶ 26.

57 *Ibid.*, ¶ 49, referring to *Tolstoy-Miloslavsky v. the United Kingdom*, 13 July 1995, Series A No 316-B.

58 *Ibid.*, ¶ 42.

59 C-411/10 and C 493/10 *NS* [2011] ECR I-0000.

60 Regulation 343/2003 takes into account a variety of factors to determine which State is responsible for processing asylum applications in the EU, Regulation 343/2003, Article 31(1), 17 and 18(7): Council Regulation (EC) No 343/2003 of 18 February 2003 establishing the criteria and mechanisms for determining the Member State responsible for examining an asylum application lodged in one of the Member States by a third-country national OJ L 50/1 25.2.2003.

61 *NS*, *supra* note 59, ¶ 94.

62 *Ibid.*, ¶¶ 88–91, referencing *M.S.S. v. Belgium and Greece* (App No. 30696/09), 21 January 2011.

allows greater scope for adhering to ECHR standards (and consequently for avoiding double standards of human rights protection). This is in stark contrast to the more abstract – and therefore less stringent – analysis of EU-related cases by the ECtHR, which, contrarily, permits wider scope for double standards.

iii *The Question of the Continuing Autonomy of the EU Legal Order*

Whilst EU legislation and the CJEU have demonstrated resounding commitment to the ECHR above and beyond the call of *Bosphorus*, that question of commitment may still be unresolved on the basis of what appears to be contradictory EU legislative pronouncements: that is, those concerning the loyalty of the EU to the autonomy of its own legal order *vis-à-vis* the ECHR.

Several legal and institutional acts support this view, or at least obstruct the reaching of a clear-cut conclusion. Article 6 TEU presents three different roles for the ECHR.[63] Thus, by making the EUCFR legally binding, Article 6(1) arguably makes the references to the ECHR within the Charter also legally binding. However, Article 6(2) views the ECHR as an international instrument to which the EU must accede, and Article 6(3) presents the ECHR as a source of general principles of EU law. In addition, Protocol 8 to the Treaty of Lisbon guards against the EU's complete submission to the ECHR in the context of the EU's accession to the ECHR. It declares that "[s]such accession shall not affect the Union's competences as defined in the Treaties."

Further, EU accession negotiations have as a focal point the reconciling of the EU's accession to the ECHR with the task of preserving the autonomy of the EU.[64] This in itself follows the requirement of Declaration 2 to the Treaty of Lisbon to the effect that accession to the ECHR "should be arranged in such a way as to preserve the specific features of Union law." Similarly, the Explanations to the EUCFR stress that although there is to be consistency between the EU and the ECHR, this must not adversely affect the autonomy of EU law and the CJEU.[65] The European Parliament has also expressly maintained that the CJEU will not become subordinate to the ECtHR.[66] Perhaps all of this is reminiscent of the wider approach that the EU takes *vis-à-vis* its autonomy to the rest of the

63 This point is made by Weiss, *supra* note 45, 221.

64 Tobias Lock, "Walking on a Tightrope: The Draft ECHR Accession Agreement and the Autonomy of the EU Legal Order," *Common Market Law Review* 48 (2011): 1025.

65 Explanations Relating to the Charter, *supra* note 43, Explanation on Article 52.

66 Draft Report of the Committee on Constitutional Affairs of the European Parliament on "Institutional Aspects of Accession of the EU to the European Convention on Human Rights," 2009/2241(INI), cited in de Búrca, *supra* note 9, at fn85.

world: the ruling in *Kadi*[67] sent a strong message that not even the UN Charter could have primacy over the fundamental rights that were part of EU law – firmly and expressly maintaining the independent role of the EU in the world.

Furthermore, recent *obiter* remarks also indicate that the universality of ECHR rights might not be secure in the future as EU case law evolves. In *Scarlet Extended*,[68] the Advocate General opined that, where there are divergences between the Charter and the ECHR as to derogations from rights,[69] the Charter will need to adopt an autonomous interpretation. The idea of differences is again taken up by an Advocate General in the *NS* case:[70]

> It should be borne in mind in this connection that the judgments of the European Court of Human Rights essentially always constitute case-specific judicial decisions and not the rules of the ECHR themselves, and it would therefore be wrong to regard the case-law of the European Court of Human Rights as a source of interpretation with full validity in connection with the application of the Charter. This finding, admittedly, may not hide the fact that particular significance and high importance are to be attached to the case-law of the European Court of Human Rights with the result that it must be taken into consideration in interpreting the Charter.

So what does this all mean? It seems to place doubt on the clarity of the message of the legal developments presented earlier (i.e., Article 6(1) TEU and Articles 52(3) and 53 of the EUCFR, as applied in the cited CJEU case law), which impose a legal obligation on the EU to be consistent with ECHR standards of human rights protection. The expressions of EU autonomy leave open the possibility for the EU to diverge from ECHR standards. Another view, however, is that these points merely serve to distinguish the question of the EU's adherence to the ECHR from the question of the primacy of the EU and the CJEU.[71] In this regard, it has been argued that the most plausible interpretation

67 C–402/05 P and C–415/05 P, *Kadi and Al Barakaat International Foundation v. Council and Commission* [2008] ECR I–6351.

68 C-70/10 *Scarlet Extended* [2011] ECR I-11959.

69 For example in the wording of Art. 52(1) and the wording of paragraph 2 of most ECHR rights.

70 *NS*, *supra* note 59, ¶ 146.

71 de Búrca, *supra* note 9, 486–490; Laurent Scheek, "The Supranational Diplomacy of the European Courts: A Mutually Reinforcing Relationship?," in *The ECJ Under Seige: New Constitutional Challenges for the ECJ*, edited by Guiseppe Martinico and Filippo Fontanelli

of the references to the EU's autonomy is that they reflect the jurisdictional separation and autonomy between the two European courts: i.e., that until accession, the EU institutions are not directly subject to the jurisdiction of the ECtHR,[72] which means that the ECtHR "is not to be conceived as a 'superior' but rather a complementary and specialised court."[73]

The preservation of the principle of primacy does not, however, enable the EU and the CJEU to adopt levels of human rights protection that are lower than that which is provided by the ECHR, because – given Article 52(3) – doing so would be "violating a domestic obligation to ensure that the EHCR rights are guaranteed within the EU legal order."[74] The Explanations to the Charter also indicate that a lower level is not permissible[75] and this is also the view expressed by other scholars: the EU may only adopt higher standards.[76]

Thus, in light of all this and taking to account current practices, the present EU legal position, despite its loyalty to EU autonomy, still offers opportunities for better maintenance of ECHR standards than the ECHR's *Bosphorus* test does – a position well illustrated by the CJEU cases discussed above.

4 Gaps in the EU's Enforcement of ECHR Rights

Participation by individuals in the enforcement of their rights is an important aspect of the holding of human rights. Within the ECHR, all individuals possess the right to bring an action before the ECtHR.[77] However, the refusal by

(Hyderabad: Icfai University Press, 2009), 172–193; Guy Harpaz, "The European Court of Justice and its Relations with the European Court of Human Rights: The Quest for Enhanced Reliance, Coherence and Legitimacy," *Common Market Law Review* 46 (2009): 105.

72 Steve Peers, "Taking Rights Away: Limitations and Derogations," in Trybus and Rubini, *supra* note 45, 141, 170.

73 Peter Van Elsuwege, "New Challenges for Pluralist Adjudication after Lisbon," *Netherlands Quarterly of Human Rights* 30, 2 (2012): 195.

74 Peers, *supra* note 72, 171.

75 Explanations Relating to the Charter, *supra* note 43 ("In any event, the level of protection afforded by the Charter may never be lower than that guaranteed by the ECHR").

76 Weiss, *supra* note 45, 231 ("Even though the ECJ is bound by Strasbourg case law on corresponding ECHR provisions, the ECJ still enjoys considerable autonomy due to its leeway to identify higher standards of human rights protection than that in the ECHR or to introduce novel human rights").

77 Subject to *locus standi* criteria.

the ECtHR in *Bosphorus* to adjudicate on the specific facts of the case before it denies to individual applicants the right to a full litigious process before the ECtHR itself. How does the EU fare in providing individuals themselves with rights to challenge breaches of ECHR rights in the EU context?

The mechanisms in the EU that enable individuals to play a role in challenging EU law have improved somewhat since the introduction of the Treaty of Lisbon, which came after the *Bosphorus* ruling. However, gaps remain that do not enable individuals to effectively challenge some elements of EU law – and therefore by extension, breaches of the ECHR rights that may arise in those instances.

The most significant gap is that individuals have restrictive standing to challenge measures of EU law through EU judicial review. According to Article 263(1), paragraph 4, natural and legal persons can bring action in three types of cases. They may challenge acts addressed to them. They may also challenge acts not addressed to them but which are of direct and individual concern to them. *Direct* concern requires individuals to show an effect on their legal situation, which resulted directly from the EU law and not from an intervening measure of implementation.[78] However, if the measure affects the human rights of a large group, then it will not be regarded as being of *individual* concern.[79] Under Article 263(1) paragraph 4, individuals may also ask for the review of "regulatory acts" that are of direct concern to them, but only if these acts do not entail implementing measures. Such 'regulatory acts' cannot, however, be legislative measures.[80]

Thus, there are potentially a whole host of measures (which may breach ECHR rights) that cannot be challenged by an individual directly before the CJEU. These include measures not addressed to the individual and which affect the human rights of a large group. It also includes measures that originate from an EU regulatory act, but that are perhaps implemented by another act or actor. Furthermore, Article 263 TEU also does not enable EU primary law to be challenged, even if this affects the human rights of individuals.

These circumstances are not only a breach of Articles 6 and 13 ECHR relating to adjudication rights and the provision of adequate remedies, but are also

78 C 41-44/70 *International Fruit Company v. Commission* [1971] ECR 411; and C386/96 *Dreyfus v. Commission* [1996] ECR II-1101.

79 C 25/62 *Plaumann and Co v. Commission* [1963] ECR 95.

80 C 583/11 *P Inuit Tapiriit Kantami and Others v. Commission*, Judgment of 3 October 2013, ¶¶ 59-61.

contradictory to EU Law on effective judicial protection. In *UPA*,[81] the CJEU accepted that the EU's general principle of effective judicial protection (which is now enshrined in Art 47 EUCFR) applied to the remedies in the EU Treaties. Arnull points out that this was one of the reasons for the Court's decision in *Kadi*:[82]

> [T]he manner in which the contested regulation was adopted – which failed to respect the claimants' right to be heard – lead to an infringement of the principle of effective judicial protection, because it prevented the Court from reviewing the substantive lawfulness of the regulation.[83]

However, Arnull goes on to note that, when assessing the exercise of its own powers, the CJEU is not as forthright in protecting the right to effective judicial protection.[84] In *UPA*, the Court found that the gaps in judicial review (now Article 263 of the Treaty on the Functioning of the European Union (TFEU)) were filled by the plea of illegality (now Article 277 TFEU) and, most importantly, by the preliminary ruling procedure (now Article 267 TFEU): "[t]hus, it is for the Member States to establish a system of legal remedies and procedures which ensure respect for the right to effective judicial protection."[85]

In *Bosphorus*, the ECtHR took these mechanisms into account when considering that the EU provides equivalent protection to the ECHR.[86] These mechanisms do not, however, provide for effective protection, given the indirect nature of preliminary ruling proceedings in the EU and the splitting of powers between the national Court and the CJEU in both the assessment of the case, and the power to provide final interpretations and applications of the law.

Another shortfall in EU judicial review that can affect the ECHR rights of individuals is that the CJEU cannot review the validity or proportionality of operations by the police or law enforcement agencies, or the exercise of responsibilities of Member States with regard to the maintenance of law and order, and the safeguarding of internal security (Article 276 TFEU). Whilst these acts may be inspired by EU arrangements, they are not however subject

81 C 50/00 *UPA v. Council of the European Union* [2002] ECR I-6677 ¶ 39.

82 *Kadi, supra* note 67.

83 A. Arnull, "The Principle of Effective Judicial Protection in EU Law: an Unruly Horse?," *European Law Review* 36, 1 (2011): 51, 69.

84 *Ibid.*

85 *UPA*, supra note ?, ¶ 42, followed in C-263/02 P *Commission v.* Jégo Quéré [2004] ECR I-3425.

86 See *supra* note 25.

to judicial review. The area of CFSP is also not wholly satisfactory. The CJEU can only review measures of the CFSP that provide for restrictive measures against natural or legal persons adopted by the Council under Article 275 TFEU. This appears to fill the gap of measures that can be challenged under EU law. There are two caveats to this: (a) the clarity of the extent to which Article 275 does indeed fill a gap requires confirmation by the CJEU in future cases[87] and (b) the provisions assume that other CFSP measures cannot affect the rights of individuals.[88] Leczykiewicz argues that the measures can affect individual rights and that the wording of Article 275 TFEU favours a limited approach in those cases, in that individual standing cannot cover all of those acts.[89]

It is clear then that the EU does not provide adequate standing for individuals to challenge potential breaches of their ECHR rights before the CJEU, and thus may not provide human rights protection of a standard required by the ECHR. Instances such as those highlighted in this section ought to provoke the ECtHR to examine cases substantively, rather than to apply the doctrine of equivalence and the presumption of compliance. However, as seen in the manner in which *Bosphorus* has already been applied, the ECtHR is arguably too much in favour of the presumption. This also of course means that individuals are deprived both through EU mechanisms and ECHR mechanisms of having judicial declarations on their claims.[90] Moreover, and quite significant to the foundations of human rights, is that it deprives individuals of the safeguard of external supervision of their human rights – supervision which is independent from the State or entity (i.e., the EU) which has allegedly committed the breach.[91]

5 Conclusion

This chapter has analysed the extent to which ECHR standards of human rights protection are guaranteed in situations intertwined with EU law. It has argued

87 Dorota Leczykiewicz, "'Effective Judicial Protection' of Human Rights after Lisbon: Should National Courts be Empowered to Review EU Secondary Law?," *European Law Review* 35,3 (2010): 326, 326.

88 *Ibid.*, 327.

89 *Ibid.*

90 The sole aim of the ECHR is to provide individuals with the right to bring their own claims.

91 The ECHR system was intended to act as an external supervisor of States' respect for human rights.

that the ECtHR unduly limits its scrutiny of human rights cases involving the EU. As a result, the standard of protection for individuals by the Convention system itself suffers. This creates, *inter alia*, double standards of protection between EU and non-EU States and uncertainty for individuals in the protection they can expect from the ECHR.

Of course, one of the purposes of the ECtHR's equivalent protection doctrine in the way it was formulated in *Bosphorus* – with the component of "manifest deficiency" – was to maintain respectful political relations between international organisations. However, this doctrine, and especially the requirement that deficiencies must be manifest before the presumption of compliance with human rights can be rebutted, would have made more sense were there to be a politically charged relationship between the EU and the ECHR mechanisms. However, as shown by EU legislation and CJEU case law (which adhere to ECtHR case law closely), there has been, in fact, for a number of years, limited political urgency or conflict of standards of the kind which requires recourse to the equivalent protection doctrine in the lax way in which it was enunciated in *Bosphorus*, and applied in later ECHR cases. Rather, since the time of the *Bosphorus* ruling, (but also prior to that time), the CJEU has demonstrated that it is content to apply a strict scrutiny of ECHR protection in cases that come before it. Moreover, EU Treaty law enunciates its close respect for the ECHR in Article 6 TEU, and the EUCFR illustrates its strength of commitment, by ensuring that respect for the ECHR as a minimum threshold is a legal obligation under EU law. All of this certainly goes beyond the *Bosphorus* test of protection.

Thus, while it is acknowledged that pluralism in the European sphere of relationships between international organisations is a legal reality, that pluralism must be handled cautiously. It is argued that the EU-ECHR relationship is not an appropriate example of a case in point requiring the enunciation and application of the doctrine of equivalent protection in the form that the ECtHR has done so to date. As has been illustrated in this chapter, EU law and the CJEU have done much to ensure that EU law is respectful of ECHR rights, to a point where there is very limited tension for the *Bosphorus* test to diffuse. On the contrary, EU law is formulated for better levels of scrutiny of ECHR rights in cases involving the EU than the *Bosphorus* standard provides. Of course, gaps do remain regarding the extent of access to judicial scrutiny at the EU level (and therefore means of judicial declaration of human rights for individuals) and concern can be raised that the EU does not currently permit the ECHR to externally supervise its acts (until accession takes place). However, this chapter nonetheless indicates that, at present, EU law and adjudication in the EU, offers better opportunities for the protection of ECHR rights in situations involving EU law, than the ECtHR does itself for its own instrument.

CHAPTER 6

Adjudicating on the Rights of Sexual Minorities in the Muslim World

Javaid Rehman

> I want to talk about the work we have left to do to protect one group of people whose human rights are still denied in too many parts of the world today. In many ways, they are an invisible minority. They are arrested, beaten, terrorized, and even executed. Many are treated with contempt and violence by their fellow citizens while authorities empowered to protect them look the other way or, too often, even join in the abuse. They are denied opportunities to work and learn, driven from their homes and countries, and forced to suppress or deny who they are to protect themselves from harm.[1]

1 Introduction

Alongside the Jews and other vulnerable groups, sexual minorities were victims of incarceration, torture and genocide during the Second World War. It is estimated that as many as 100,000 gay men may have been sent to concentration camps; thousands perished or were executed by the Nazi machinery of hatred and oppression.[2] However, after the establishment of the United Nations, and amidst the tall claims of promoting individual human rights in the new world order, the plight of sexual minorities was ignored. While the focus of the Universal Declaration of Human Rights (UDHR, 1948) was upon individual human rights and non-discrimination, references to minorities – including

1 Hilary Rodham Clinton, "Free and Equal in Dignity and Rights," Palais des Nations, Geneva, Switzerland, 6 December 2011, http://www.humanrights.gov/2011/12/06/remarks-in-recognition-of-international-human-rights-day.

2 See Heinz Heger, *Men with the Pink Triangle: The True Life and Death Story of Homosexuals in the Nazi Death Camps* (Boston: Alyson Publications, 1994); Pierre Steel, *Liberation Was for Others: Memoirs of a Gay Survivor of the Nazi Holocaust* (New York: Perseus Book Group, 1997); and Pratima Narayan, "Somewhere over the Rainbow…International Human Rights Protection for Sexual Minorities in the New Millennium," *Boston University International Law Journal* 24 (2006): 313, 313.

 | DOI 10.1163/9789004261181_008

sexual minorities – or Lesbian, Gay, Bisexual and Transgender (LGBT) rights were omitted.[3] The UDHR is a conservative document. The *travaux préparatoires* reveal a conscious effort not to fracture the superficial consensus constructed over sensitive rights. The right to marry and found a family was initially perceived as a less significant right, and was therefore not envisaged as forming part of the Declaration.[4] Although incorporated in the Declaration, neither the drafting history nor the final text supports the extension of this right to marriage for same-sex partners.[5] Similarly, during the drafting of the International Covenant on Civil and Political Rights, (ICCPR, 1966)[6] the insistence on the phrase "husband and wife,"[7] was conducted in a manner which ensured that the Covenant would not cover homosexuality.[8] Subsequent to the adoption of the international bill of rights and notwithstanding the rapid growth and mushrooming of international human rights instruments in the last quarter of the twentieth century, there were very limited initiatives to promote sexual minorities, sexual orientation and gender identity.

As this chapter will examine, international adjudicating bodies, in particular the European Court of Human Rights (ECtHR) and the United Nations Human Rights Committee (HRCttee), have only in the recent past started considering claims for non-discrimination based on sexual orientation, and for *de facto* equality based on sexual orientation and gender identity. The stance of the Muslim world towards sexual orientation and gender identity continues to be a matter of considerable concern. Almost all Muslim majority States attach

3 G.A. Res. 217A (III), U.N. Doc A/810 at 71 (1948).

4 See Stéphanie Lagoutte and Ágúst T. Árnason, "Article 16," in *The Universal Declaration of Human Rights: A Common Standard of Achievement*, edited by Gudmundur Alfredsson and Asbjørn Eide (Dordrecht: Martinus Nijhoff Publishers, 1999), 325, 328; and William A. Schabas, *The Universal Declaration of Human Rights: The Travaux Préparatoires* (Cambridge: Cambridge University Press, 2013).

5 Art. 16(1) of the UDHR provides that "[m]en and women of full age, without any limitation due to race, nationality or religion, have the right to marry and to found a family. They are entitled to equal rights as to marriage, during marriage and at its dissolution." According to art. 16(3), "[t]he family is the natural and fundamental group unit of society and is entitled to protection by society and the State."

6 New York, 16 December 1966 United Nations, 999 U.N.T.S. 171; 6 I.L.M. (1967) 368.

7 Commission on Human Rights, ninth session (1953), A2929, Chap. VI, ¶¶ 155 and 159; Third Committee, Ninth Session (1954), A/5000, ¶ 1.

8 An intention to incorporate LGBT as sexual minorities in the Covenant cannot be deducted from the *travaux préparatoires*. See Marc J. Bossuyt, *Guide to the "Travaux Préparatoires" of the International Covenant on Civil and Political Rights* (Dordrecht: Martinus Nijhoff, 1987), 405–406 and 494.

penal sanctions to consensual same-sex activity, with some States retaining and enforcing serious punishments for homosexuality. The rights of transgender communities are similarly circumscribed. With its focus on Pakistan, this chapter examines the political implications arising out of the UN Human Rights Council Resolution 17/19 on "Human Rights, sexual orientation and gender identity" (17 June 2011)[9] and the constitutional and legislative provisions on sexuality minorities of Pakistan. It presents a critical assessment of the approaches adopted by Pakistan's judiciary and, in so doing, critiques the recent decisions of the Supreme Court of Pakistan as regards the *Hijra* community of Pakistan. The *Hijras* of Pakistan are usually identified as "eunuchs" or "castrated" men or people with genetic physical and hormonal disorders. Having said that, and as this chapter elaborates, there are substantial disagreements over *Hijra* identity within the Pakistani social, political and legal framework. Notwithstanding these ambiguities and disagreements, this study provides an important demonstration that the western binary classifications of gay, lesbian, bisexual and transgender are not universally applicable in all societies and communities – in the current debate on the rights of sexual minorities, it is of crucial importance to acknowledge that societal, cultural, anthropological and ideological influences have substantial bearings on human self-identification of sexual orientation as well as gender identity.

This chapter is divided into seven sections. After these introductory comments, section II presents an overview of adjudication on issues of sexual orientation and gender identity before the ECtHR and HRCttee. Sections III to VI shift the focus to adjudication within the Muslim world and examine the position within the State practice of Pakistan. Section III presents an overview of the position of sexual minorities in the Muslim world. More specifically, while section IV looks at the role played by Pakistan prior to, during and subsequent to the adoption of HRC Resolution 17/19 (2011), section V examines the constitutional and legislative provisions concerning sexual orientation and gender identity. Section VI presents a focused case-study of the *Hijras* of Pakistan. Finally, section VII sets out a number of concluding reflections on the subject.

In the development of human rights law, jurists, human rights activists and international human rights lawyers have played a substantial role. Professor Sandy Ghandhi is universally recognised as one of the leading human rights lawyer who has played a pioneering role in the growth of human rights law. He is probably the most influential academic scholar in advancing understanding of the operations and jurisprudence of the United Nations treaty bodies and in

9 Human Rights Council Res.17/19 of the Human Rights Council, 17th Sess., May 31–June 17, 2011, (A/HRC/RES/17/19) U.N. Doc.A/HRC/17/L.9/Rev.1 (17 June 2011).

particular the Human Rights Committee. It has been my great honour and privilege to be one of his students at the University of Reading and it was his inspirational teaching and command of the subject that led me towards specialising in human rights law. As this chapter confirms, Professor Ghandhi's excellent scholarship continues to influence the advancement and reshaping of international law and in particular modern human rights law.

2 Adjudication of the Rights of Sexual Minorities before the European Court of Human Rights and the Human Rights Committee

In 1981, the ECtHR handed down a powerful judgement advancing the equality regime for homosexual couples. In *Dudgeon v. UK*, Mr Dudgeon had challenged the continued criminalisation of acts of buggery (and attempted buggery) and acts of gross indecency committed between consenting men within Northern Ireland as violating Article 8(1) of the European Convention on Human Rights. In upholding the applicant's claim, the ECtHR found that the continuation of the aforementioned anti-sodomy laws constituted violation of the right to respect for private life of the claimant as provided by Article 8.[10] The Court treated a homosexual relationship between adult men as a "most intimate aspect of private life."[11] In *Norris v. Ireland*, the ECtHR adopted a similar approach to find a violation of the right to respect for private life under Article 8 of the Convention.[12] Since that time, the Strasbourg Court has delivered several key judgments related to same-sex couples, and transgendered individuals. In *Rees v. United Kingdom*, the applicant (a female to male transsexual) had undergone gender reassignment surgery during 1974, changed their name, had a new driving licence and was able to obtain a gender reassigned passport in 1984. However, Rees was unable to change sex (on his birth certificate) and was unable to marry as, in English law, marriage was only permitted between a "man and a woman."[13] Rees argued that claiming to be a man when the birth

10 *Dudgeon v. UK* A 45 (1981) 4 EHRR (1982) 149, http://hudoc.echr.coe.int/sites/eng/pages/search.aspx?i=001-57473.

11 *Ibid.*, ¶ 52.

12 *Norris v. Ireland* A 142 (1988) 13 EHRR (1991) 186, http://hudoc.echr.coe.int/sites/fra/pages/search.aspx?i=001-57547.

13 *Rees v. United Kingdom*, judgment of 17 October 1986, A 106 (1986) 9 EHHR (1987) 56. The Marriage (Same Sex Couples) Act 2013 (c.30) has legalised same sex marriage in England and Wales. Most of the provisions of the Act came into force on 13 March, 2014. For the

certificate states otherwise is perjury under section 3(1) of the Perjury Act 1911. The ECtHR found no violations of Articles 8 and 12, as the Court took the position that States are afforded a "margin of appreciation" in their failure to change a person's birth certificate after gender reassignment and to determine the nature of the right of marriage as the union of two people of the opposite biological sex under Article 12.[14]

By contrast, in *B v. France*, Miss B, who was born and registered as a male, had undergone a surgical sex change operation in 1972.[15] The French authorities refused to rectify her civil status certificate, which included her sex on her birth-certificate under French law and her name on all identity documents including identity card, passport and voting card. The ECtHR considered various factors: the purpose of French Civil registers, according to the Court, is to be "updated throughout the life of the person concerned," in contrast to English birth certificates which simply "record a historic fact."[16] The case was therefore distinguishable from *Rees*. The Court determined that there had been a violation of Article 8, since a fair balance had not been struck between the general public interest and the interest of the individual.[17]

Goodwin v. United Kingdom and I v. United Kingdom concerned applicants who were both post-operative male to female transsexuals. Christine Goodwin claimed that she had been the object of sexual harassment since her gender

---

text of the Marriage (Same Sex Couple) Act 2013, see http://www.legislation.gov.uk/ukpga/2013/30/contents/enacted/data.htm.

14 *Rees v United Kingdom*, *supra* note 13, ¶¶ 27–29; *Cossey v. UK* A 184 (1990) 13 EHRR (1991) 622, http://hudoc.echr.coe.int/sites/eng/pages/search.aspx?i=001-57641 (sex change from male to female though the issues were similar to *Rees*: the Court again found no violations of arts. 8 and 12). In *Sheffield and Horsham v. United Kingdom* 1998-v (1998) 27 EHRR 163, http://hudoc.echr.coe.int/sites/eng/pages/search.aspx?i=001-58212, the ECtHR, following *Rees* and *Cossey*, decided that there had been no violation of arts. 8 or 12. In *X, Y and Z v. United Kingdom*, X (a female to male transsexual) had been in a long-term relationship (13 years) with Y and the couple had a child Z through the procedure of artificial insemination. While Z was allowed to take X's name, X's application to be registered as Z's father was refused. The ECtHR, while recognising that family life was broader than marriage and marital relationships, found no violations of arts. 8, since according to the Court the provisions of art. 8 could not be taken to mean placing an obligation on a State party to accord formal recognition as the father of a child who was in fact not the child's biological father. *X, Y and Z v. United Kingdom* 1997-II (1997) 24 EHRR 143, http://hudoc.echr.coe.int/sites/eng/pages/search.aspx?i=001-58032.

15 *B v. France*, judgment of 25 March 1992, A 232-c (1992);16 EHRR (1992) 1, http://hudoc.echr.coe.int/sites/eng/pages/search.aspx?i=001-57770.

16 *Ibid.*, ¶ 52.

17 *Ibid.*, ¶ 63.

reassignment and had suffered from discrimination as regards the payment of her national insurance contributions. Goodwin also complained that (as she was legally a male) she was required to make payments until she was 65 and further alleged that her inability to change her national insurance number allowed her employer to identify her previous gender details. I, the complainant in the second case, alleged, *inter alia*, discrimination and inability to be admitted on a nursing course since she refused to present her birth certificate. In a reversal of previous judgments and demonstrating a change of attitude, the Court held violations of the right to privacy (Article 8) and violations of the right to marry (Article 12).[18] *Lustig-Prean and Beckett v. United Kingdom*[19] and *Smith and Grady v. United Kingdom*[20] were cases about investigation and subsequent discharge of lesbians and gay men from the military. The Court held that violations of the right to privacy were committed through invasive investigations into homosexual conduct interfering with the right to respect for privacy as well as discharge from the military because of sexual orientation. Such invasions into the right of privacy could not be justified under Article 8(2).[21]

In more recent times, the ECtHR has extended its scope of protection for LGBT communities in a diverse range of areas. The Strasbourg Court has found violations of the Convention in cases, *inter alia*, of denial of custody of children (violations of Article 8 in conjunction with Article 14),[22] denial of the right to family benefits such as occupation of the flat subsequent to the death of a homosexual partner,[23] differing ages of consenting homosexual and

18 See *Goodwin v. United Kingdom and I v. United Kingdom* 2000-vi (2002) 35 EHRR 18, http://hudoc.echr.coe.int/sites/eng/pages/search.aspx?i=001-57974. Following this decision, the UK government brought in the Gender Recognition Act 2004, which *inter alia* accords the right of transsexuals to marry. It also provides them the right to be treated as having the sex that they have adopted as their acquired gender.

19 *Lustig-Prean and Beckett v. United Kingdom* (2000) 29 EHRR 548, http://hudoc.echr.coe.int/sites/eng/pages/search.aspx?i=001-58407.

20 *Smith and Grady v. United Kingdom* 1999-vi (2000) 29 EHRR 493, http://hudoc.echr.coe.int/sites/eng/pages/search.aspx?i=001-58408.

21 See Kristen Walker, "Moving Gaily Forward? Lesbian, Gay and Transgender Human Rights in Europe," *Melbourne Journal of International Law* 2 (2001): 127.

22 *Salgueiro da Silva Mouta v. Portugal*, 1999-IX 31 EHRR (2001) 1055, http://hudoc.echr.coe.int/sites/eng/pages/search.aspx?i=001-58404.

23 *Karner v. Austria*, 2003-IX 38 EHRR (2003) 24, http://hudoc.echr.coe.int/sites/eng/pages/search.aspx?i=001-61263.

heterosexual relations,[24] refusal of adoption rights as a lesbian[25] and failure to grant permission to organise a pro-homosexual assembly.[26]

In comparing the ECtHR to the HRCttee, the approach of the latter appears to have been more conservative and is possibly more influenced by the global and societal dissensions on this subject.[27] Indeed, for a considerable period, the role of the HRCttee remained unsupportive towards the rights of sexual minorities. A significant opportunity to provide a positive response was missed in a communication lodged against Finland in 1979. In *Hertzberg v. Finland*, the authors of the communication alleged violation of their rights of freedom of expression and opinion by the State-controlled broadcasting company (FBC).[28] Their claim was that Article 19 rights were breached in relation to the sanctions imposed on expression and information through censorship of radio and TV programmes on homosexuality. In its defence, Finland relied *inter alia* upon the protection of public morals and claimed that these actions were fully supported by public opinion. Furthermore, the State also argued that the decision on sanctions represented the internal ruling of the autonomous broadcasting company. The HRCttee took account of the Finnish argument pertaining to the defence of public morals. It came to the conclusion that "since a certain 'margin of discretion' must be accorded to the responsible national authorities"[29] in issues concerning public morals, the application of Article 19(3) meant that no violation had taken place of the right to freedom of opinion and expression. It was equally the case that neither the UN Economic and Social Council, nor the UN Sub-Commission on Prevention of Discrimination and Protection of Minorities in the 1980s and the 1990s, considered sexual orientation and gender identity on their agendas.[30]

---

24 *L. and V. v. Austria*, 2003-I (2003) 36 EHRR 55, http://hudoc.echr.coe.int/sites/eng/pages/search.aspx?i=001-60876. According to the Court there was "an ever growing European consensus to apply equal ages of consent for heterosexual, lesbian and homosexual relations," *ibid.*, ¶ 50.

25 *EB v. France*, (2008) 47 EHRR 21, http://hudoc.echr.coe.int/sites/eng/pages/search.aspx?i=001-84571.

26 *Baczkowski and others v. Poland*, 2007-VI (2009) 48 EHRR 19, http://hudoc.echr.coe.int/sites/eng/pages/search.aspx?i=001-80464.

27 For an excellent analysis of the work of the HRCttee, see P.R. Ghandhi, *The Human Rights Committee and the Right of Individual Communication: Law and Practice* (Aldershot: Ashgate, 1998).

28 *Leo Hertzberg et al. v. Finland*, communication No. 61/1979, 2 April 1982, CCPR/C/15/D/61/1979).

29 *Ibid.*, ¶ 10(3).

30 Ignacio Saiz, "Bracketing Sexuality: Human Rights and Sexual Orientation – A Decade of Development and Denial at the United Nations," in *Routledge Handbook of Sexuality,*

Probably the most significant change at the UN level occurred with the "views" of the HRCttee in *Toonen v. Australia.*[31] In *Toonen*, a claim that the Tasmanian Criminal Code making private homosexual conduct a criminal offense was upheld by the HRCttee to be in breach of Article 17 (the right to privacy) in conjunction with Article 2(1) (the right to non-discrimination) of the ICCPR. Although the law criminalising private homosexual activity had not been invoked for the past 10 years, the existence of risk was deemed sufficient by the HRCttee for practising homosexuals to be categorised as "victims." Justifying its views, the Committee noted that "[t]he threat of enforcement and the pervasive impact of the continued existence of these provisions on administrative practices and public opinion had affected [the author] and continued to affect him personally."[32] In *Toonen*, the HRCttee also emphasised the fact that the inclusion of the terminology "such as" in Article 26 indicates a non-exhaustive list of grounds of non-discrimination: reference to sex in the article also includes sexual orientation.[33] These principles were expanded in application of the law (Article 2(1)) in the context of partnership rights. The HRCttee found violations of Article 26 in a case where (without justifications) Australia had denied partnership benefits to the same-sex partner of a deceased veteran.[34]

More significantly, *Toonen* established a precedent for HRCttee, not only to adopt a positive approach towards the subject of sexual orientation in the face of individual communications, but also to raise this issue during reviews of State practices. In 1996, the HRCttee highlighted in its concluding observations for Sudan that homosexual acts were not "serious crimes" for which the death penalty could be imposed.[35] In the period between 2000–2006, in its review of 84 reports, the HRCttee raised the subject of discrimination on the basis of

---

Health and Rights, edited by Richard Parker and Peter Aggleton (London: Routledge, 2010), 459.

31 *Toonen v. Australia*, Communication No. 488/1992 March 31, 1994. As a result of this case, Australia was forced to change its law criminalising homosexual acts in the State of Tasmania.

32 *Ibid.*, ¶ 5.1.

33 See Sarah Joesph, "Gay Rights under ICCPR–Commentary on Toonen v Australia," *University of Tasmania Law Review* 13 (1994): 392, 398.

34 *Young v. Australia*, communication No. 941/2000 (CCPR/C/78/D/941/2000).

35 In the concluding observations for Sudan, the HRCttee highlighted that "[t]he imposition in the State party of the death penalty for offences which cannot be characterised as the most serious, including apostasy, committing a third homosexual act, illicit sex, embezzlement by officials, and theft by force, is incompatible with article 6 of the Covenant. Moreover, some forms of execution fail to comply with the prohibition against cruel, inhuman or degrading treatment or punishment, especially for women, contained in

sexual orientation no less than 13 times. The Committee has been critical of, *inter alia,* failings in including the category of sexual orientation in employment,[36] failing to include sexual orientation in broad anti-discrimination provisions,[37] and the lack of educational programmes and inequality in ages of consent between homosexual and heterosexual activity.[38]

3 Adjudication of the Rights of Sexual Minorities in the Muslim World: The Case of Pakistan

Having regard to the aggression and negativity directed at rights based on sexual orientation and gender identity within the Muslim world, it is hardly surprising to note the absence of any such references in international and national human rights instruments initiated by Muslim majority States. The Universal Islamic Declaration of Human Rights (1981),[39] the League of Arab States, the Arab Charter of Human Rights (2004),[40] as well as the Organisation of Islamic Cooperation (OIC)'s Cairo Declaration on Human Rights in Islam (1990)[41]

article 7 of the Covenant." Concluding observations of the Human Rights Committee, Sudan. 19/11/1997. CCPR/C/79/Add.85. (Concluding Observations/Comments) CCPR/C/79/Add.85, at 8.

36 "The Committee notes with concern allegations of widespread incidence of violent crime perpetrated against persons of minority sexual orientation, including by law enforcement officials. It notes with concern the failure to address such crime in the legislation on hate crime adopted at the federal level and in many States. It notes with concern the failure to outlaw employment discrimination on the basis of sexual orientation in many States. (articles 2 and 26)." Concluding Observations of Human Rights Committee regarding United States of America (18 December 2006) CCPR/C/USA/CO/3/Rev.1, at 25.

37 Concluding Observations of Human Rights Committee regarding Philippines (1 December 2003) CCPR/CO/79/PHL at 18; Concluding Observations of Human Rights Committee regarding Namibia 30 July 2004 CCPR/CO/81/NAM, at 22.

38 "The Committee considers that existing legislation on the minimum age of consent for sexual relations in respect of male homosexuals is discriminatory on grounds of sex and sexual orientation. It requests that the law be revised to remove such discriminatory provisions," Concluding Observations of Human Rights Committee regarding Austria 19 November 1998, CCPR/C/79/Add.103 at 13.

39 Adopted by the Islamic Council in Paris on 19 September 1981. For the full text see: *The International Journal of Human Rights* 2 (1998): 102.

40 League of Arab States, Arab Charter on Human Rights, May 22, 2004, reprinted in *International Human Rights Reports* 12 (2005): 893 (entered into force 15 March 2008).

41 Cairo Declaration on Human Rights in Islam, 5 August 1990, U.N. GAOR World Conf. on Human Rights, 4th Sess., Agenda Item 5, U.N. DocA/CONF.157/PC/62/Add.18 (1993).

refuse to acknowledge the existence of rights based on sexual orientation and gender identity. The OIC in particular has failed to consider the rights of LGBT communities as valid human rights claims.[42]

Amidst the developing global jurisprudence on sexual orientation and gender identity, contributions from the Muslim world have been limited.[43] A growing body of Muslim majority States are now parties to the primary international human rights treaties, where the relevant adjudicating bodies have made significant pronouncements on this subject.[44] There is nevertheless a dearth of case-law engaging Muslim majority States towards positive recognition of sexual orientation and gender identity, and it may well be the case that international human rights bodies favour a "margin of appreciation" approach or a culturally relativist approach in such cases.

Pakistan is a party to a number of international treaties with provisions relating to equality and non-discrimination, which could be applied to protect the rights of sexual minorities and LGBT communities. As of 1 April 2014, Pakistan has ratified or acceded to the ICCPR,[45] the Convention against Torture (CAT),[46] the International Covenant on Economic, Social and Cultural Rights (ICESCR),[47] the International Convention on the Elimination of All forms of Racial Discrimination (CERD,[48] the Convention on Elimination of Discrimination Against Women (CEDAW),[49] the Convention on the Rights of the Children (CRC),[50] the Optional Protocol to the Convention on the Rights

42 The human rights issues of interest of the OIC include mainly discrimination against Muslims, totally ignoring the existence of gender and sexual minorities. See "Organisation of Islamic Cooperation," http://www.oic-oci.org/page_detail.asp?p_id=168. See also William Clowns, "Universal – The UN, IOC and LGTB Rights," INPEC, 20 March 2012, http://inpec.in/2012/03/20/essay-universal-the-un-oic-and-lgbt-rights.

43 For a useful overview of Muslim State practices, see Lucas P. Itaborahy and Jingshu Zhu, *State-Sponsored Homophobia: A World Survey of Laws: Criminalisation Protection and Recognition of Same-Sex Love* (8th ed., IGLA, May 2013), http://old.ilga.org/Statehomophobia/ILGA_State_Sponsored_Homophobia_2013.pdf.

44 Michael O'Flaherty and John Fisher, "Sexual Orientation, Gender Identity and International Human Rights Law: Contextualising the Yogyakarta Principles," *Human Rights Law Review* 8 (2008): 207, 214.

45 New York, 16 December 1966 United Nations, 999 U.N.T.S. 171, 6 I.L.M. (1967) 368.

46 Convention against Torture and Other Cruel, Inhuman or Degrading Treatment or Punishment, New York, 10 December 1984 United Nations, U.N.T.S. 1465, p. 85.

47 New York, 16 December 1966, 993 U.N.T.S. 3; 6 I.L.M. (1967) 360.

48 New York, 7 March 1966 U.N.T.S. 660, p. 195.

49 International Convention on the Elimination of All Forms of Discrimination against Women, New York, 18 December 1979 U.N.T.S. 1249, p. 13.

50 Convention on the Rights of the Child, New York, 20 November 1989 U.N.T.S. 1577, p. 3.

of the Child on the involvement of children in armed conflict,[51] the Optional Protocol to the Convention on the Rights of the Child on the sale of children, child prostitution and child pornography[52] and the Convention on the Rights of Persons with Disabilities.[53] On 23 June 2010 Pakistan ratified the ICCPR and CAT. The ratification of the ICCPR provided a significant moment in the recognition of fundamental human rights, including the rights to non-discrimination and equality before the law. At the point of ratification of the ICCPR, Pakistan entered a reservation, and thereby attempted to limit the scope of protection offered by the treaty:

> [The] Islamic Republic of Pakistan declares that the provisions of Articles 3, 6, 7, 18 and 19 shall be so applied to the extent that they are not repugnant to the Provisions of the Constitution of Pakistan and the *Sharia* laws.

Subjected to intense objections from the international community regarding reservations based upon the *Sharia* and constitutional provisions, and immediately risking the European Union's ineligibility criterion of Generalised System of Preferences (GPS Plus Status) the then Prime Minister of Pakistan, Syed Yousaf Raza Gilani, effected the withdrawal of the Pakistan's reservations to the ICCPR in September 2011. Although the withdrawal of reservations brings the incorporated international treaty in line with the fundamental rights provisions in the Constitution of Pakistan 1973, there are considerable impediments in the practical implementation of the fundamental right to equality and non-discrimination. Furthermore, Pakistan has failed to become a party to the first optional protocol to the ICCPR, which could authorise individuals from sexual minorities to submit communications to the HRCttee.

Similarly, Pakistan has thus far refused to accede to or ratify the Optional Protocol to CEDAW which could authorise the committee on CEDAW to consider communications from "individuals or groups of individuals" complaining about, among other things, the violations of the right to sexual orientation and gender identity.[54] The protocol also authorises this committee to conduct

51 Adopted by the General Assembly 25 May, 2000. GA. Res. 263, U.N. GAOR, 54 Sess., Supp. 49; U.N. Doc. A/Res/54/263.

52 Adopted by the General Assembly 25 May, 2000. GA. Res. 263, U.N. GAOR, 54 Sess., Supp. 49; U.N. Doc. A/Res/54/263.

53 Convention on the Rights of Persons with Disabilities, New York, 13 December 2006 U.N. Doc. A/61/611.

54 The full text of CEDAW is available at http://www.ohchr.org/EN/ProfessionalInterest/Pages/OPCEDAW.aspx.

enquiries into "grave or systematic" violations of CEDAW, which may also include violations of sexual orientation and sexual or gender identity.[55] Although having signed and ratified CAT, Pakistan has not accepted the enquiry procedure under Article 20 of the Convention, nor has the State become a party to the Optional Protocol to CAT.[56]

In its foreign policy, Pakistan is a fervent supporter and leading member of the Organisation of Islamic Cooperation (OIC) – the premier organisation representing Muslim majority States, with its headquarters in Jeddah, Saudi Arabia – and its subsidiary organs (including Islamic universities, in Bangladesh, Niger, Uganda, and Malaysia and the "Islamic Fiqh Academy," also based in Jeddah). Under the auspices of the OIC, Pakistan has regularly launched attacks not only against sexual rights, but, even more substantially, against gender equality and the universality of women's rights. An indication of the problem was the process and timing of Pakistan's ratification of the CEDAW.[57] Pakistan's positioning in relation to CEDAW and women's rights provided further significant evidence of the State's lack of interest in sexual rights. Pakistan only ratified CEDAW on 12 March 1996 and at the time of ratification entered a broad declaration, according to which its accession was "subject to the provisions of the constitution of the Islamic Republic of Pakistan." It has been suggested that by inserting an ambiguous declaratory clause, the Pakistani State intended to hinder the effective implementation of women's rights as provided in the Convention.[58] Pakistan was also active in blocking avenues that promoted sexual orientation and gender identity, including the discouragement of any related advocacy campaigns. A consultative status before ECOSOC had been granted to the International Lesbian and Gay Association (ILGA) in 1993, which was revoked in 2006 as a consequence of pressure exerted by Pakistan, United States, Iran and other like-minded States.[59]

The pressure exerted by Pakistan and other OIC members was also evident during the Fourth World Conference for Women from 4–15 September 1995 (CSW), which was the first time where sexual and reproductive rights were

55 *Ibid.*, art. 8.

56 New York, 18 December 2002 GA Resolution A/RES/57/199 of 9 January 2003.

57 See Anne E. Mayer, "Islamic Reservations to Human Rights Conventions: A Critical Assessment," *Recht von de Islam* 15 (1998): 25, 35.

58 *Ibid.*

59 Julie Mertus, "The Rejection of Human Rights Framing: The Case of LGBT Advocacy in the US," *Human Rights Quarterly* 29 (2007): 1036, 1041; and Douglas Sanders, "Getting Lesbian and Gay Issues on the International Human Rights Agenda," *Human Rights Quarterly* 18 (1996): 67.

discussed.[60] Indeed, Pakistan as well as other OIC member States opposed all comments on sexual orientation at Beijing, interpreting all references to reproductive rights as occurring "in marriage."[61] Most of the Muslim majority States placed reservations upon the outcome document of the Summit, the Beijing Declaration.[62] Some States, such as Iran, pointed out that the implementation plan should take account of the different cultural and religious differences that exist in these countries;[63] others, such as Pakistan and the Maldives, placed reservations upon the final text of the Declaration.[64] Pakistan objected to the lack of a clear definition of the term "sexuality" and entered a reservation on the term and on paragraphs 232(f) and 97.

4 Pakistan and Human Rights Council Resolution 17/19 (2011)

Pakistan's official practices indicate a particular distaste towards the issue of sexual orientation and gender identity, considering homosexuality an "abnormal sexual behaviour."[65] Using religion as a pretext, Pakistan has taken the position that any advocacy of rights for LGBT communities amounts to reliance upon "vague and controversial notions" without "legal foundations in international law."[66] The Pakistani representative (acting on behalf of the OIC), while denying the application of any existing rights for LGBT communities, made the following point: "[the] international community only recognises those rights that are enumerated in UDHR which were codified in the subsequent international human rights instruments."[67] Additional opposition from Pakistan is based upon the apparent licentious behaviour that the provision of these rights would encourage, legitimisation of paedophilia and incest, a negative health impact and a weakening of the institution of family and society.

60 Report on the Fourth World Conference on Women ("CSW"), Final session of the main Committee. The Report of the CSW has been published by the International Institute for Sustainable Development (IISD), http://www.iisd.ca/vol14/enb1421e.txt.

61 CSW Report, Chap. IV (Strategic Objectives and Actions) and Closing Plenary.

62 *Ibid.*

63 CSW Report, Chap. II (Global Framework).

64 *Ibid.*, Closing Plenary.

65 See Pakistan (on behalf of the OIC), Panel Discussion Sexual Orientation and Gender Identity 22 Meeting, 7 March 2012; and AFP, "UN Rights Council Passes 'Historic' Gay Rights Resolution," *The Express Tribune*, 17 June 2012, http://tribune.com.pk/story/190874/un-rights-council-passes-historic-gay-rights-resolution.

66 *Ibid.*

67 *Ibid.*

As can be surmised from the earlier analysis, Human Rights Council Resolution 17/19 (2011) on sexual orientation and gender identity was a consequence of decades of struggle within the political organs of the UN. Pakistan's positioning and role throughout the process of adoption of a resolution on sexual orientation and gender identity presents significant elements of the State's psychological and moral repugnance for this issue. The first State-representatives' initiatives for the adoption of a resolution on sexual orientation and gender identity had commenced as early as August 2003.[68] At the 59th Session of the United Nations Human Rights Commission, Brazil had introduced a Resolution entitled "Human Rights and Sexual Orientation"[69] with the conservative aim of expressing concern at violence on grounds of sexual orientation and calling upon States and relevant bodies to provide due attention to these instances of violence. The draft Resolution, while suggesting that the international community build upon the rights already conferred upon the Universal Declaration of Human Rights for members of the LGBT communities, did not propose the establishment of any new standards or mechanisms for preventing instance of violence based on sexual orientation and gender identity.[70] While affirming the universality of human rights, the Resolution asserted the principle that LGBT people are entitled to the same human rights and protections as other human beings.

However, there was considerable opposition to this Resolution.[71] Pakistan, acting on behalf of the OIC, condemned it. Ambassador Umer of Pakistan sent an *aide memoire* and letter to all the delegates calling for a vote against the Resolution, since, in Pakistan's view, it was politically incorrect. The Ambassador argued that this "issue was not a 'proper subject' for consideration, that it created rights which were in direct confrontation with Islam and their legislation and that the Brazilian resolution 'would turn a great many countries into direct human rights violators'."[72] Pakistan argued that the Resolution was flawed procedurally and was directly insulting for the 1.2 billion Muslims around the globe. According to the International Gay and Lesbian

68 United Nations Press Release No HR/CN/1086 (Apr 15, 2004).

69 U.N. ECOSOC, Draft Resolution "Human Rights and Sexual Orientation," E/CN.4/2003/L.92 (2003).

70 See Timothy M. Garvey, "God v Gays? The Rights of Sexual Minorities in International Law as seen through the Doomed Existence of the Brazilian Resolution," *Denver Journal International Law and Policy* 38 (2009–2010): 659.

71 See U.N. ECOSOC, Proposed Amendments by Saudi Arabia, Pakistan, Egypt, Libya and Malaysia E/CN.4/2003/L.106–110 (2003).

72 IGLHRC "Sexual Rights & Sexual Orientation at the United Nations Commission on Human Rights" (Revised 2005) at p. 14.

Human Rights Commission, the text of the *aide memoire* was quite hateful.[73] Pakistan called for a "no-action motion" with a view that the Human Rights Commission takes no action on the Resolution with no consequent votes on the Resolution. The "no-action motion" strategy was, however, voted down by a narrow margin of 24 votes against, 22 votes in favour and 6 abstentions. A second vote taken on the final day of the session, whilst authorising retention of the Resolution on the Commission's Agenda nevertheless allowed for the postponement of the discussion on sexual orientation until 2004.[74]

Brazil's attempt to introduce a new resolution for the protection of sexual minorities within international human rights law during 2004 faced considerable opposition from Pakistan and like-minded States.[75] Pakistan, leading the charge on behalf of the OIC, went further, threatening Brazil with economic pressure and cutting off trade relations if the Brazilian government continued with the resolution.[76] Betsy Pisik, a political commentator writing in the *Washington Times*, noted that according to Scott Long, the director of homosexual, bisexual and transgender issues for Human Rights Watch, Brazil was placed under "extreme pressure" from Muslim majority States (particularly Egypt and Pakistan) so as to force the withdrawal of the Resolution that had been introduced before the Human Rights Commission.[77] During this period, in a letter distributed to all State Missions in Geneva by Pakistan, its representative asserted that "sexual orientation is not a human rights issue."[78] During the session, a cross-regional consensus was established within the Commission and it was agreed, without a vote, to defer consideration of the Resolution to the following session. In the Commission's 61st session in 2005 the Resolution, however, died a slow death, without any resolution having been considered or adopted.

---

73 *Ibid.*, 8.

74 *Ibid.*, 8.

75 Narayan, *supra* note 2, 341.

76 Betsy Pisik, "Homosexual Rights Resolution Withdrawn at United Nations," *The Washington Times*, 30 March 2004, http://www.washingtontimes.com/news/2004/mar/30/20040330-120645-4241r/?page=all; and Marie Juul Petersen, "Islamic or Universal Human Rights? The OIC's Independent Permanent Human Rights Commission," (Copenhagen: Danish Institute for International Studies- DIIS, 2012).

77 Betsy Pisik, "Homosexual Rights Resolution Withdrawn at United Nations," *The Washington Times*, 30 March 2004, http://www.washingtontimes.com/news/2004/mar/30/20040330-120645-4241r/?page=all.

78 See Letter from the Representative of the Permanent Mission of Pakistan, on behalf of the OIC (Geneva, 26 February 2004).

The debate on sexual orientation and gender identity was given impetus by the launch of the Yogyakarta Principles on the Application of International Human Rights Law in relation to Sexual Orientation and Gender Identity (Yogyakarta Principles) on 26 March 2007.[79] The subject was raised once again in the UN through the initiation of Resolution 17/19 by South Africa in June 2011. At the time of the introduction of Resolution 17/19 (2011), Pakistan expressed full opposition to the provisions of this resolution.[80] This opposition was maintained through the various stages of the Resolution and was evidenced in Pakistan's vote against the Resolution. As a leading member of the OIC, Pakistan's opposition to the 17/19 Resolution is reminiscent in many respects of the OIC's campaigns for the adoption of the UN Resolutions on "defamation of religions" (i.e., blasphemy).[81] It was also a reminder of the OIC's pressuring calls for an "end to Islamophobia" and, subsequently, the increased protection of Muslim minorities in Europe and the United States.[82] It is in this

---

79 The *Yogyakarta Principles* is the fruit of a meeting (6–9 November 2006) at the University of Gadjah Mada (Yogyakarta, Indonesia), where a group of experts discussed the treatment of gender and sexuality met to set some principles to develop on the application of international law of human rights in relation to sexual orientation and gender identity. Each of the principles comprises an indication of a State's duty vis-à-vis implementation of LGBT rights and subsequent obligations. These principles were presented by the International Commission of Jurists, supported by Amnesty International, Centre for Women's Global Leadership, Global Rights, European Region of the International Lesbian and Gay Federation, Human Rights Watch, International Service for Human Rights, during the fourth session of the Council of Human Rights in Geneva, in March 2007. See Paula L. Ettelbrick, Esq. and Alia Trabucco Zerán, "The Impact of the Yogyakarta Principles on International Human rights law Development," A Study of November 2007–June 2010, www.ypinaction.org.

80 Human Rights Council Res.17/19 of the Human Rights Council, 17th Sess., May 31–June 17, 2011, U.N. Doc. A/HRC/17/L.9/Rev.1 (June 15, 2011).

81 From 1999 to 2010, the main battleground between the OIC and western States was not on rights based upon sexual orientation and gender identity, but the "defamation of religions" debate, with resolutions voted alternatively within the General Assembly and the Human Rights Commission/Human Rights Council, calling for an end to Islamophobia and pressing to include blasphemy laws in freedom of expression limitations. See Javaid Rehman and Stephanie Berry, "Is 'Defamation of Religions' Passé? The UN, OIC and Islamic State Practices: Lessons from Pakistan," *George Washington International Law Review* 44 (2012): 431.

82 Javaid Rehman, "Islamophobia after 9/11: International Terrorism, *Sharia* and Muslim Minorities in Europe – The Case of the United Kingdom," *European Yearbook of Minority Issues* 3 (2005): 217.

sense that one should understand the walk-out by the Pakistani representative of the OIC block of the UN panel on discriminatory laws and practices of violence against individuals based on their sexual orientation and gender identity in March 2012,[83] and the subsequent statement by Pakistan regarding the OIC's position on LGBT rights. In submitting this statement, Pakistan's diplomat and the OIC's coordinator on human rights issues to the Council, Mr Zamir Akram, condemned LGBT rights. In clarifying Pakistan's and OIC's position, he noted that the OIC was concerned about "the attempts to create controversial 'new notions' or 'new standards' by misinterpreting the Universal Declaration of Human Rights and international treaties to include such notions that were never articulated or agreed to by the UN membership."[84] Furthermore, he noted that "[the OIC was] even more disturbed at the attempt to focus on certain persons on the grounds of their *abnormal sexual behaviour*, while not focusing on the glaring instances of intolerance and discrimination in various parts of the world, be it on the basis of colour, race, gender or religion[...]."[85]

Having been largely supported by the United States, one may legitimately question the real impact of the Resolution, (passed only by 23 States voting in favour, 19 against and 3 abstentions)[86] other than to corroborate the domination of western States in the Council as well as a continuation of the old political contest over human rights issues between the western and the OIC block. Indeed, the very recent consecration of LGBT rights within international law discourse does not refute the fact that queerness and sexual orientation and gender identity rights are subject to political pressure from both western and non-western States.

---

83 See Stephen Gray, "'Milestone' LGBT Discussion at UN Human Rights Council Welcomed despite Walkout," *Pink News*, 8 March 2012, http://www.pinknews.co.uk/2012/03/08/milestone-lgbt-discussion-at-un-human-rights-council-welcomed-despite-walkout/. See also, Robert Evans, "Muslim and African Nations Walk Out of UN Panel on Gay Rights," *Guardian.co.uk*, 7 March 2012, http://in.reuters.com/article/2012/03/07/un-gays-idINDEE8260GT20120307.

84 See Zamir Akram, Ambassador and Permanent Representative Coordinator of the OIC Group on Human Rights and Humanitarian Issues, H.E. Ms. Laura Dupuy Lasserre, President of the Human Rights Council, Geneva No.Pol/S0/2012 (14 February 2012, ¶ 5, http://blog.unwatch.org/index.php/2012/02/17/letter-from-uns-islamic-group-to-unhrc-president-opposing-panel-on-violence-against-gays/.

85 *Ibid.*, ¶ 6.

86 See U.N. Doc. A/HRC/17/L.9/Rev.1. See also UN Watch, "56 Islamic States Reject UN Debate on Anti-Gay Violence," 17 February 2012, http://blog.unwatch.org/index.php/2012/02/17/outrage-at-un-as-56-islamic-states-slam-gays-for-abnormal-sexual-behaviour-urge-silence-on-anti-gay-violence/.

5 Constitutional and Legislative Provisions Related to Sexual Orientation and Gender Identity

The Constitution of the Islamic Republic of Pakistan 1973 (as amended) does not contain explicit provisions ensuring protection on the basis of sexual orientation and gender identity.[87] Similarly, there are no clauses protecting LGBT communities. The Constitution, however, contains a fairly detailed set of fundamental human rights, which ensure the rights of all citizens of Pakistan. These fundamental rights, contained in chapter 1 of the Constitution, closely model the provisions of the UDHR and protect such fundamental rights as the right to security of persons,[88] safeguards as to arrest and detention,[89] the prohibition of slavery and forced labour,[90] the inviolability of the dignity of man,[91] the freedom of assembly[92] and the freedom of association.[93] Additional relevant provisions of the Constitution include Article 22(4), which provides that "[n]othing in this Article shall prevent any public authority from making provision for the advancement of any socially or educationally backward class of citizens." Since sexual minorities have been kept at a significant educational and social disadvantage, members of these communities have put forward claims based in this provision. Furthermore, Article 25 provides *inter alia* that "all citizens are equal before law and are entitled to equal protection of law [and] that there shall be no discrimination on the basis of sex."[94]

Article 27(1) states that "[n]o citizen otherwise qualified for appointment in the service of Pakistan shall be discriminated against in respect of any such appointment on the ground only of race, religion, case, sex, residence or place of birth." Amongst the Principles of Policy enunciated in chapter 2 of the Constitution are commitments of social justice and eradication of social evils. Article 38 commits the State *inter alia* to provide all citizens with facilities for work and adequate livelihood, and basic necessities of life, "such as food

87 See The Constitution of the Islamic Republic of Pakistan (1973) as amended and updated, http://www.pakistani.org/pakistan/constitution/.

88 *Ibid.*, art. 9.

89 *Ibid.*, art. 10.

90 *Ibid.*, art. 11.

91 *Ibid.*, art. 14.

92 *Ibid.*, art. 16.

93 *Ibid.*, art. 17.

94 The term "alone" was deleted by section 8 of the Constitution (Eighteenth Amendment) Act 2010 with effect from 19 April 2010. The amended constitutional provision broadened the non-discriminatory clause to prohibit all forms of non-discrimination including inter alia discrimination based on race, religion, age, medical condition and disability, etc.

clothing, housing, education and medical relief."[95] While sexual minorities can take strength from the aforementioned provisions, a number of constitutional and legislative enactments have been deployed and subsequently interpreted in a manner that undermines their rights. The Constitution of Pakistan, 1973 (Article 227) proclaims Islam as the official State religion and affirms the commitment of the State that all laws must be formulated in accordance with the injunctions of *Sharia*.[96] A Council of Islamic ideology oversees that all laws and administrative practices are in consonance with the *Sharia*.[97] In Pakistan, the *Hudood* ordinances – despite amendments through the Protection of Women (Criminal Laws Amendment) Act 2006 – continue to punish any form of extramarital relations, including the offense of *zina*.[98] Homosexual or same-sex intercourse is criminalised under the *Hudood* ordinances and would carry the punishment in accordance with these ordinances. In a State, with claims to enforce the *Sharia*, the varying interpretations of the *Sharia* may extend the punishment to death by stoning for consensual, private homosexual activity. Homosexual activities in Pakistan, however, not only offend *Sharia* and Islamic law principles, but, more ominously, sodomy has remained a criminal offence under the Pakistan Penal Code (Act XLV of 1860) (PPC). A relic of the British colonialism, the PPC punishes sodomy with possible prison sentences under the pretext of protecting public morality. Section 377 of the PPC provides:

> Whoever voluntarily has carnal intercourse against the order of nature with any man, woman or animal, shall be punished with imprisonment for life, or with imprisonment of either description for a term which shall not be less than two years nor more than ten years, and shall also be liable

---

95 Art. 38(d).

96 *Ibid*, Part IX: art. 227.

97 *Ibid.*, art. 228.

98 Introduced in 1980 by the military dictator General Muhammad Zia-ul-Haq, the *Hudood* Ordinances consist of the Prohibition (Enforcement of *Hadd*) Ordinance 1979; the Offence of *Zina* (Enforcement of *Hadd*) Ordinance 1979; the Offences against Property (Enforcement of *Hadd*) Ordinance 1979; and the Offence of *Qazf* (Enforcement of *Hadd*) Ordinance 1979. The *Hudood* Ordinances reinforce criminal laws for offences in relation to having sex outside of marriage (*zina*), false imputation of rape and property related offences. The apparent rationale for the introduction of the *Hudood* Ordinances had been to bring Pakistan's penal law in conformity with the *Sharia*. Notwithstanding the State's commitment of non-imposition of an exclusively Islamic code on non-Muslims, these Ordinances for most part also control the activities of non-Muslims alongside the majority Muslims. See Javaid Rehman, "Minority Rights and the Constitutional Dilemmas of Pakistan," *Netherlands Quarterly of Human Rights* 19 (2001): 417, 432.

> to fine. Penetration is sufficient to constitute the carnal intercourse necessary to the offense described in this section.[99]

As a result of criminalisation, many gay men and women have been punished, incarcerated, and extra-judicially executed. LGBT individuals are condemned to hiding their sexualities or taking the risk of revealing their identities. At the same time, there is considerable hypocrisy within Pakistani society. While there are significant numbers of homosexuals or bisexuals, those with influence or power are either able to go abroad or manage a private and secluded life. Pederasty is widespread in rural areas and, in many cases, this occurs with the consent of the elders in the family who offer their younger children for the use of adults in the community. Furthermore, sexual abuse – including the rape of men and children – is an unfortunately reality. In the current hostile environment in Pakistan, it is inconceivable to bring about any legal challenges to section 377.

However, section 377 has been the object of public interest litigation in neighbouring India, which also inherited the legislative provisions and, like Pakistan, retained these provisions. In *Naz Foundation v. Government of NCT of Dehli*,[100] the Foundation, in challenging the constitutionality of section 377, submitted that the provisions contained therein violated fundamental rights to equality, freedom of speech, the right to life and liberty. It was also argued that that these provisions resulted in driving sexual minorities and LGBT communities underground, generating fear and compromising efforts to deal with sexually transmitted diseases (STDs), including HIV/AIDS. On 2 July 2009, the Dehli High Court rejected the argument that homosexuality was contrary to public policy and popular morality in India. In reaching this conclusion, the Court relied extensively on the Yogyakarta Principles, as well as the jurisprudence of the ECHRts and HRCttee. The sense of victory for those campaigning for equality and non-discrimination on the basis sexual orientation and gender identity was, however, short-lived; the judgment of the High Court was overturned by the Supreme Court in December 2013. In reinstating the provisions of section 377, the Indian Supreme Court took the position that it was not for the Court to change or repeal the provisions of the penal code, but rather was for the Parliament to bring relevant changes if deemed necessary.[101] This

99 PPC, S.377.

100 *Naz Foundation v. Government of nct of Dehli* WP (C) No. 7455/2001 (2 July 2009), http://lobis.nic.in/dhc/APS/judgement/02-07-2009/APS02072009CW74552001.pdf.

101 *Suresh Kumar Koushal and another v. Naz Foundation* (11 December 2013) http://www.scribd.com/doc/190889099/SC-verdict-on-Article-377.

Supreme Court judgment sent shock waves all across the world, impacting on human rights activists as well as the judiciary in all countries. It was probably to counter such negativity that the Indian Supreme Court bench (consisting of Radhakrishnan J and Skiri J) delivered a monumental judgment on 15 April 2014. In the landmark judgment of *NALSA v. Union of India*, the Court recognised transgendered individuals as belonging to a "third gender" and also upheld all fundamental rights within the Indian constitutions for transgendered people.[102] Furthermore, a curative petition filed by the petitioners in the *Naz Foundation* judgment has been agreed to be heard by the Supreme Court in April 2014. [103]

6 Constitutional Protection for the *Hijras* of Pakistan

Homosexual activity between consenting adults remains a criminal offence in Pakistan, with members of the LGBT community liable to be prosecuted either under the *Hudood* Ordinances or under the PPC. With the religiously indoctrinated as well as statutory enshrined criminalisation of homosexual conduct, it has not been possible for the judicial system to offer any protection on the explicit basis of sexual orientation and gender identity. That said, Pakistani Courts have focused on the rights of a specific community, commonly known as *Hijras* or *khusras*. Within the context of South Asia and Pakistan, *Hijras* have a specific historical background with recognised biological traits. *Hijras* claim to have cultural and religious connections to South Asia dating back to at least seventh century invasions of the territory by the Arabs. The references to sexual liberty and diversity in the *Quran*, as well as the *Ahadith* references of the Prophet Mohammad on effeminate men are narratives integral to contemporary *Hijra* identities.[104] *Hijras* retained a vibrant presence in courts and *darbars* of the Muslim rulers of the Indian Sub-Continent, and their role as servants of the Mughal rulers is widely acknowledged. In contemporary terms,

---

102 *National Legal Services Authority v. Union of India*, (Writ Petition) (Civil) No 604 of 2013 (15 April 2014). For text of the Judgment see http://supremecourtofindia.nic.in/outtoday/wc40012.pdf.

103 http://www.livelaw.in/transgender-community-formally-recognised-third-sex-also-avail-benefits-socially-economically-backward-communities-supreme-court-directs-centre-stat/.

104 See Javaid Rehman and Eleni Polymenopoulou, "Is Green a Part of the Rainbow? *Sharia*, Homosexuality and LGBT Rights in the Muslim World," *Fordham International Law Journal* 37 (2013): 1, 18.

Hijras are frequently abandoned as children, left to be supervised in a community of other *Hijras* under the command and instructions of a leader, known as the "guru." *Hijras* have a limited role to play in social affairs, mainly as dancers at wedding parties or as entertainers. They also have a frequent presence in other festivities and their blessing during marriages, child birth and circumcision of males is taken to keep away future misfortunes.

Hijras remain a community that is ridiculed and socially and morally subjugated. *Hijras* have long suffered various human rights abuses, including torture and killings. Section 377 remains a primary instrument of repression and abuse by the State operated machinery. Begging and dancing, as well as prostitution – all for petty money – constitute probable professions for this improvised community. PPC is a significant tool with which to repress and obstruct the sexual lifestyle of the *Hijra* community. Although prosecutions and convictions under section 377 are rare, *Hijras* are commonly intimated, harassed and threatened by the law enforcing agencies. In a social and legal system rife with corruption and procedural irregularities, the *Hijras* as a vulnerable community are a natural target of abuse both by the police and society as a whole.

The sexual and biological aspects of *Hijra* identity remain shrouded in controversy. There are claims of genital disorder with some *Hijras* at birth, while others are castrated men. It is also the case that the traditional western concept of male and female, sexuality and homosexuality does not fit easily into the sexual structures and understanding of *Hijra* identity.[105] The official position (also endorsed by the Pakistani Supreme Court) is that *Hijras* are "eunuchs" or "castrated" men or people with genetic gender disorders. On the other hand, a wider understanding is that *Hijras* are biological males but take on female identities, choosing to dress like women. *Hijras* are not homosexuals, but are categorised as transgender men or cross dressers.[106] *Hijras* also belong to an "intersex" gender, a gender between male and female. The term "transgender" has been defined in a variety of ways. Essentially, it is taken to apply to:

> [S]omeone who doesn't fit within society's standards of how a woman or a man is supposed to look or act; for example, 'transgender' may be used to describe someone who was assigned female at birth but later realizes that label doesn't accurately reflect who they feel they are inside. This person may now live life as a man, or may feel that their gender identity

105 Amisha R. Patel, "India's Hijras: The Case for Transgender Rights," *George Washington International Law Review* 42 (2010) 835.

106 *Ibid.*, 839.

> can't be truly summed up by either of the two options we're usually given (male or female). They might feel like they're in between those two options; both male and female; or outside the two-gender system, entirely, neither male nor female.[107]

Similarly, it is important to note that:

> A transgender identity is not dependent upon medical procedures. In other words, some transgender people have surgeries or take hormones to bring their body into alignment with their gender identity, but many do not medically alter their bodies, and that doesn't mean they're not transgender.[108]

The *Hijra* identity in this wider sense relates to transgenderism and invokes protection accorded to transgendered people. There has been limited jurisprudence from domestic courts of Pakistan on the subject of sexual orientation and gender identity, although to its credit, Pakistan's apex court, the Supreme Court of Pakistan, has passed a number of orders to protect the rights of the *Hijras*. The first, initial steps towards protection of the *Hijra* community were undertaken in response to a petition filed by an Islamabad based lawyer, Dr Mohammad Aslam Khaki. In the petition submitted to the Pakistan Supreme Court (PSC) on 6 February 2009, Dr Khaki identified *Hijras* as eunuchs. In rationalising his initiation of the petition to the Court, Dr Khaki noted that he had started this action after he was "approached by the members of civil society [who] have drawn the attention towards the case of molestation, humiliation and arresting [of] the most oppressed section the society i.e. the eunuchs or people of Middlesex (also called she males) by the [Rawalpindi] Police."[109] The petition asserted that the "community of the Shemales is the most oppressed section of life whose...fundamental rights are infringed by the parents [,], society [,] and also the government."[110]

107 The Lesbian, Gay, Bisexual and Transgender Community Centre, "What is 'Transgender?'," http://www.gaycenter.org/gip/transbasics/whatistrans.

108 *Ibid.*

109 Cited in Jeffrey A. Redding, "From 'She-Males' to 'Unix': Transgender Rights and the Productive Paradoxes of Pakistani Policing," SRRN paper http://papers.ssrn.com/sol3/papers.cfm?abstract_id=1905070, 7.

110 See *Mohammad Aslam Khaki and another v. Senior Superintendent of Police (Operations) Rawalpindi and others*, Human Rights Constitutional Petition No: 43/2009, at 5.

The petition also noted the exclusion of "she-males" from a desirable and lovable home environment, with parents disowning them and forcibly exiling them to the "gurus" for exploitation.[111] It also asserted that "[t]he members of society claiming themselves to be the members of civil or Islamic society" violate shemales' "right to dignity as enshrined by the *Quran* as well as by Article 14 of Constitution of Islamic Republic of Pakistan."[112] The petition submitted that "legal and Islamic right to property and inheritance is negated as they are not given such inheritance from their parents."[113] In his petition, Dr Khaki had prayed to the Supreme Court to "restore and protect the fundamental rights of Shemales" so that they are able to join "mainstream of life."[114]

The response of the PSC was swift and varied. Amongst the various orders issued on 16 June 2009, the PSC ordered provincial governments to conduct a census of "She-males" in every province along with details of names and domiciles of the "She-males."[115] In a subsequent order issued by PSC, the Court confirmed that "'She–males' are citizens of this country and entitled to protection particularly under Articles 4 and 9 of the Constitution."[116] The PSC went on to caution the police to refrain from any abuse and misuse of powers against shemales, and ordered provincial governments to send to the Court recommendation for the "social uplift" of shemales.[117] The Court was sympathetic towards *Hijras*. The tone was benevolent and appealed to human emotions and sentiments. In its hearing held in August 2009, the Court noted that "[t]hey are creatures of Allah Almighty, therefore, their social life is to be respected."[118] In this hearing, PSC ordered provincial and federal governments to ensure that eunuchs are enabled to seek appropriate education and employment. The PSC also ordered the police to provide all possible protection to the eunuchs and cautioned against abuse and victimisation.[119]

In its order of 4 November 2009, the Court's approach showed a significant shift. While in its previous orders the Court had relied upon both the constitutional provisions and principles of the inherent dignity of mankind, in its order

111 *Ibid.*

112 *Ibid.*

113 *Ibid.*

114 *Ibid.*, prayer.

115 See also Redding *supra* note 109, 8.

116 See *Mohammad Aslam Khaki and another v Senior Superintendant of Police (Operations) Rawalpindi and others*, Constitutional Petition No: 43/2009, Order (14.07.2009), 6.

117 *Ibid.* at 6.

118 See *Mohammad Aslam Khaki and another v. Senior Superintendant of Police (Operations) Rawalpindi and others*, Constitutional Petition No: 43/2009, Order (17.08.2009) at 5.

119 *Ibid.*

of 4 November 2009, it adopted a narrow approach towards the *Hijras*. In consistently suggesting disability and gender disorder as the defining criterion of eunuch identity, the Court order adopted a different nomenclature.[120] More troubling, however, is the Court's approach of relating disability and physical deformity with gender disorder. The Supreme Court order of 4 November requires the Attorney General to:

> [P]repare some proposals on the basis of which the Federal and the Provincial Governments can conveniently recognize the status of eunuchs to be the respectable citizens and to protect their right of inheritance in moveable and immovable properties left by their parents/elders and their legal obligations to provide maintenance to them *on account of disability* due to which they are not being treated at par with other citizens of the country.[121]

This element of "gender disorder" and disability is more visible in the subsequent order of the Supreme Court issued on 20 November 2009. The Court order states:

> It is to be noted that this class of the society has been neglected merely *on account of gender disorder in their bodies*, otherwise they are entitled to enjoy all the rights granted to them by the Constitution being its subject, including their rights in inherited property because normally to deprive them from their such legitimate rights, sometime their families disowned them. As far as existing laws are concerned, there are no provisions on the basis of which they can be deprived from their legitimate rights to inherit the properties. Similarly NADRA [the National Database and Registration Authority] is required to adopt a strategy with the assistance of the concerned department of the Govt. to record exact status in the column meant for male or female after undertaking some medical tests based on hormones etc. They are also entitled for entering their names in the electoral list. As far as the question of casting the vote is concerned, it could be decided separately, because they can if need be, exercise the right of franchise etc.[122]

120 See also Redding *supra* note 109, 10–11.

121 See *Mohammad Aslam Khaki and another v. Senior Superintendant of Police (Operations) Rawalpindi and others*, Constitutional Petition No: 43/2009, Order (04.11.2009), 2, emphasis added.

122 *Mohammad Aslam Khaki and another v. Senior Superintendant of Police (Operations) Rawalpindi and others*, Constitutional Petition No: 43/2009, Order (20.11.2009) at 2, emphasis added.

The Court also correlated the "gender disorder" with other forms of disability and, while dispensing orders for federal and provincial governments to ensure employment for eunuchs, noted that "[a]s the government has already ensured the jobs to the disable[d] persons…similar policy can also be adopted."[123] The Court order revealed that the essential nature of the concern was to isolate and target those "faking" the eunuch identity from those with genuine gender disorders. The PSC had obtained information:

> that in the name of the unix [eunuchs] some male and female who [are] otherwise have no gender disorder in their bodies have adopted this status and commit crimes on account of which a bad name is brought to unix [eunuchs]. This aspect is to be checked by the police of the area where such like people are operating.[124]

The Court's tone was stark but more disappointing and alarming was the change of nomenclature. As noted already, the Court had in its earlier order of June 2009 deployed the terminology of "she-males." The language and terminology shifted to "eunuchs" in its order of 4 November, with the order of 20 November describing *Hijras* as "Unix," to a mixed terminology of "unix/ eunuchs" in the order of 23 December 2009. The PSC reiterated its concern of fake eunuch identities in its order of 23 December 2009.[125] The Court expressed concern that the "[i]nterior Ministry has not consulted with the NADRA for the purpose of recording exact status of unix in the column, meant for male or female after undertaking some medical tests based on hormones, therefore, on the next date of hearing progress in this behalf shall also be made."[126]

This order also reiterated respecting rights of [unix] eunuchs including inheritance rights, right to education,[127] employment opportunities and voting

123 *Ibid.*, at 3.

124 *Ibid.*, at 5.

125 See *Mohammad Aslam Khaki and another v. Senior Superintendant of Police (Operations) Rawalpindi and others*, Constitutional Petition No: 43/2009, Order (23.12.2009) at 2.

126 *Ibid.*, at 2.

127 The Court noted that "[t]he Provincial and the Federal Governments have also not taken steps for ensuring the admission of the unix in the educational institutions. The Secretary, Social Welfare Department, Sindh, Mr Iqbal Ahmed stated that steps are being taken for their admission and accommodation in the educational institutions. The remaining Provincial Governments through Secretaries Social Welfare Department are also directed to follow the same practice and ensure their admission in the educations institutions, because it is their basic and fundamental right to get education in the institution in terms of Article 22 read with Article 25 of the Constitution." *Ibid.*, at 4.

rights for the eunuchs.[128] The PSC order required the government to make progress on the issue of providing eunuchs with national identity cards confirming their distinct identity and recording this exact status (in the column of identity card) after "some medical tests based on hormones."[129] In terms of employment, the Court applauded the initiative by the government of Sindh for engaging the *Hijras* during the Polio vaccination scheme.[130] The Court encouraged other provincial governments to follow suit in engaging *Hijras* in such security operations as Polio vaccination project. The Court also applauded the Indian state government of Bihar in employing *Hijras* as dependable tax collectors from habitual defaulters and noted further plans of the Bihar government to provide literacy and vocational training for *Hijras* and for preparing *Hijras* for regular, appropriate employment.[131]

On 11 November 2011, the PSC ordered the Election Commission of Pakistan to enlist eunuchs as part of the voters list by contacting them. The then Chief Justice, Iftikhar Muhammad Chaudhry, directed NADRA to expedite procedures for issuing computerised national identity cards. In January 2012, the issues of paternity and gender on the national identity cards were resolved. The cards now bear the name of the father, with the gender column mentioning the status of "Khawaja Sara."[132] In April 2013, Pakistan's election tribunal allowed Bindya Rana (a transgender individual) to contest elections for a provincial Assembly seat in Karachi. Already in 2012, the PSC ruled that members of the transgender community have the right to family inheritance and that there must not be any deprivation of that right. The PSC also ruled for equal

128 The Court noted that the "[l]earned Attorney General stated that so far no progress has been made regarding entering the names of the unix in the electoral list. However, Mr. Aslam Khaki, learned ASC stated that names of so many unix have already been registered and some have also contested elections. The Election Authorities of the Province are directed to have a contact with the Secretaries Social Welfare Department and after getting the copy of the registration of the unix in the Provinces, they should enter their names in the voter lists on the basis of the I.D. Cards whatsoever they possess and if any change is recorded on the basis of NADRA's entries, the same shall also be carried out in the electoral lists. Copy of this order be also sent to the Chief Election Commission for making directions to the concerned authorities." *Ibid.*, 3.

129 *Ibid.*, 2.

130 *Ibid.*, 6.

131 Extract cited by the Court at 9.

132 "Gender Column added to CNIC forms for Transvestites, SHC told," Dawn.com, 15 December 2010, http://www.dawn.com/news/591097/gender-column-added-to-cnic-forms-for-transvestites-shc-told.

rights in all fields, including employment and education. The Court directed authorities to send copies of its order to Federal and provincial governments and also directed the manner in which the order was to be implemented.

7 Conclusions

This chapter has confirmed that rights relating to sexual orientation and gender identity remain politically contested. After decades of resistance and neglect, the UN finally became engaged in efforts to recognise and acknowledge rights based on sexual orientation and gender identity. Such efforts have, however, been subjected to political jockeying and manipulation. The adoption of Human Rights Council Resolution 17/19 (2011) provided some sense of achievement. Similarly, subsequent initiatives, such as the Human Rights Council's sponsored panel discussion on sexual orientation and gender identity, represent positive advances.[133] That said, it may be observed that a full acknowledgment of rights based on sexual orientation and gender identity remain a battleground within the UN human rights system and particularly for the Muslim world. Within most Islamic societies, there is considerable opposition to the notion of sexual minorities and more controversially the recognition of varied sexual orientation and identities. There is large-scale pessimism prevalent amongst human rights activists and experts: amidst the deep human rights crises prevalent in Muslim societies, rights of sexual minorities are not a priority for the States, civil societies or the human rights sector.[134]

This research has also demonstrated that stereotypical western notions of demarcating gay, lesbian or transgender identities can be counter-productive for the advancement or resolution of issues within the Muslim World.[135] In the case of Pakistan, as the present chapter has examined, there has been limited

133 This was the first global panel discussion on sexual orientation and gender identity which was held in the UN Human Rights Council on 7 March 2012. The Panel Discussion is available at http://www.unmultimedia.org/tv/webcast/2012/03/panel-discussion-sexual-orientation-and-gender-identity.html, 7 March 2012.

134 Interview with I.A. Rehman, Human Rights Commission of Pakistan, Lahore Secretariat (5 March 2014), notes on file with the author.

135 See Sonia Kaytal "Exploring Identity," *Yale Journal of Law and Feminism* 14 (2002): 97; Oliver Phillips "Constituting the Global Gay," in *Sexuality in the Legal Arena*, edited by Carl Stychin and Didi Herman (London: Athlone, 2000), 17; and Jeffrey A. Redding, "Human Rights and Homo-Sectuals: The International Politics of Sexuality, Religion and Law," *Northwestern Journal of International Human Rights* 4 (2006): 436.

jurisprudence from domestic courts. There is very limited understanding of the definition or biological identification of *Hijras* and yet with the PSC adjudication focused on the specific community of *Hijras*. Furthermore, the entire safeguard programme is designed, at least ostensibly, for a specific community of *Hijras* and perceived by the Supreme Court as "eunuchs" or "castrated" men or people with gender disorder. While focusing on assisting a tiny community with biological, physical gender "disorders," the Supreme Court was never concerned about the international legal rights of the LGBT communities and its pronouncements do not add anything to the protection of transgender communities more generally.[136] Even in so far as *Hijras* of Pakistan are concerned, the jury is still out. Despite some positive developments, *Hijras* continue to suffer at the hands of police officers: rape, sexual abuse and violence by law enforcement agencies is not uncommon.

136 Redding, *supra* note 109, 6.

CHAPTER 7

A Feminist Human Rights Perspective on the Use of Internal Relocation by Asylum Adjudicators

Nora Honkala

My first encounter with Professor Sandy Ghandhi was as a master's student in his module on international human rights. Indeed, it was *his* module. This is not just a cliché but also one that is demonstrative of his relentless belief in human rights being the idea of our time. Sandy taught the module inspirationally, seamlessly pulling together the immensity of theory and practice concerning the field, making it not only educational but also thoroughly enjoyable. Sandy's exceptional experience, intellectual rigour and capacity for hard work are often modestly hidden behind his casual charm and wit. As my doctoral supervisor and mentor, Sandy never waned in his enthusiasm for engaging with justice, finding words of encouragement during my moments of despair; and, most of all, for giving me the space to make up my own mind. I am fortunate to have begun my academic career under Sandy's mentorship.

1 Introduction

Women's refugee claims often concern complex human rights violations that necessitate a nuanced interpretation and application of refugee law. The United Nations High Commission for Refugees (UNHCR) offers guidance to adjudicators to take a liberal and humanitarian spirit in light of the object and purpose of the 1951 Refugee Convention. In this chapter, I examine the jurisprudence from two appellate level decisions: *FB* (Lone Women-PSG-internal relocation-AA (Uganda) considered) Sierra Leone [2008] UKAIT 00090[1] and *HC & RC* (Trafficked Women) China CG [2009] UKAIT 00027.[2] In both cases the adjudicators found there to be 'persecution' within the meaning of the Refugee Convention, but dismissed the appeals based on the availability of an internal relocation option.

1 Hereinafter *FB* (*Sierra Leone*).

2 Hereinafter *HC & RC* (*China*).

 | DOI 10.1163/9789004261181_009

In this chapter I seek to critique the adjudicators' reasoning with regard to the internal relocation option and argue that this reasoning evidences a problematically restrictive application of refugee law and process. Evidence from the two cases reveals that the reasoning does not adequately take into account the socio-legal realities of the nature of the asylum seeker women's human rights violations. As such, the chapter concludes that the interpretation of the law evident in these decisions falls short of the standard of taking into account the overall object and purpose of the Convention, as well as the general human rights context. What is proposed is to engage with the feminist critiques in order to understand the discrimination that such an approach can cause.

2 International Refugee Law Framework

The 1951 U.N. Convention Relating to the Status of Refugees and its 1968 Protocol form the foundations of the international refugee protection regime. Today, the Convention has 145 State party signatories and remains the sole international legally binding instrument that gives protection to refugees. The definition of a refugee contained in the Convention is one of the most widely-accepted international norms, and one that has also made its way into public consciousness.[3] Even though the Refugee Convention and its Protocol do not require the definition to be adopted by States, many nonetheless employ it in their domestic asylum systems.[4] The Convention defines a refugee as a person who:

> [O]wing to well-founded fear of being persecuted for reasons of race, religion, nationality, membership of a particular social group or political opinion, is outside the country of his nationality and is unable, or owing to such fear, is unwilling to avail himself of the protection of that country; or who, not having a nationality and being outside the country of his former habitual residence as a result of such events, is unable or, owing to such fear, is unwilling to return to it.[5]

---

3 Daniel J. Steinbock, "The Refugee Definition as Law: Issues of Interpretation," in *Refugee Rights and Realities: Evolving International Concepts and Regimes*, edited by Frances Nicholson and Patrick Twomey (Cambridge: Cambridge University Press, 1999): 13–36, at 13.

4 James C. Hathaway, "A Reconsideration of the Underlying Premises of Refugee Law" *Harvard International Law Journal* 31 (1990): 129.

5 Convention Relating to the Status of Refugees 1951, art. 1 A (2).

When a State makes a refugee status determination, the asylum seeker must prove that she has a well-founded fear of being persecuted *for reasons of* one or more of the enumerated Convention Grounds: race, religion, nationality, membership of a particular social group or political opinion. Persecution must be shown. A commonly accepted method is to show this by finding both "serious harm" and the "failure of State protection."[6] It is important to remember that the object and purpose of the Refugee Convention are humanitarian. As stated in its preamble, the goal of the Convention is to "assure refugees the widest possible exercise of these fundamental rights and freedoms...without discrimination."

The particular ways in which international refugee law is applied can have significant gendered consequences for the claims of many women. Although women can of course suffer from the same kinds of persecution as men, there is evidence that women have been unable to benefit equally from the protection afforded by the Refugee Convention.[7] Women's claims thus necessitate an understanding of the particular implications of gender in relation to their claims. There can be said to be two main ways in which women may not be afforded equal treatment under the Refugee Convention: first, that the usual interpretation of the Convention marginalises women's experiences and, secondly, that procedural and evidential barriers can decrease the quality of the decision-making process.[8] This chapter is concerned with the first of these obstacles.[9]

3 Feminist Engagement with International Refugee Law

The problems with the interpretation of the Refugee Convention stem from the fact that the Convention remains deeply rooted in its history. At the time of the drafting of the Convention, the relevance of gender was only discussed once.[10] The Yugoslav delegate proposed that the category "sex" be included in Article 3, which states that the Convention shall be applied "without discrimination as to race, religion or country of origin."[11] However, this suggestion was

6 Hathaway, *supra* note 4, at 129.

7 Heaven Crawley, *Refugees and Gender: Law and Process* (Bristol: Jordans, 2011): 5.

8 *Ibid.*

9 For thorough investigation into quality of initial decision-making in the UK, including the procedural barriers, see Helene Muggeridge and Chen Maman, "Unsustainable: The Quality of Initial Decision-Making in Women's Asylum Claims," *Asylum Aid*, January 2011, http://www.asylumaid.org.uk/wp-content/uploads/2013/02/unsustainableweb.pdf.

10 Thomas Spijkerboer, *Gender and Refugee Status* (Aldershot: Ashgate, 2000): 1.

11 Spijkerboer, *supra* note 10, at 1.

rejected as the feeling at the time was that "the equality of the sexes was a matter for national legislation."[12] The Chairman of the drafting committee, the U.N. High Commissioner for Refugees Van Heuven Goedhart, strongly doubted whether there would ever be any cases on account of sex.[13] Refugee women thus remained mostly invisible until the 1980s.

It was largely due to NGOs, feminist activists and academics that this invisibility of women asylum seekers was exposed and brought onto the international agenda. Feminists have indeed been criticising the supposed gender neutrality of the refugee definition since the 1980s.[14] The ways in which the Refugee Convention has been interpreted, particularly in Western industrialised States, have been heavily influenced by the historical context of the Convention itself. The model of the Convention's refugee definition is a sole, male, political exile, who was considered to be the main casualty of the Cold War era.[15]

Many women's claims do not fit this model and the fact that gender is not included as a Convention ground has been controversial. Feminists like Jane Freedman have argued that the absence of gender as a sixth category has meant that gender-related persecution has been trivialised, and demonstrates that it has not been taken as seriously as other forms of persecution on the basis of race, religion, nationality or political opinion.[16] On the other hand, it has also been argued that a separate category might lead all persecution done to women being "pigeon-holed," leading to perceptions that women's persecution is always something fundamentally different from that of men, and – by inference – something less important.[17] It is generally accepted, however, that the international climate is not conducive to the expansion of the refugee definition by way of including gender as a sixth category.[18] It is therefore imperative that the refugee convention is interpreted in a manner that is inclusive and

---

12 *Ibid.*, quoting the British delegate.

13 *Ibid.*

14 See, for example, Doreen Indra, "Gender: A Key Dimension of the Refugee Experience," *Refuge* 6, 3 (1987); and Jacqueline Greatbatch, "The Gender Difference: Feminist Critiques of Refugee Discourse," *International Journal of Refugee Law* 1 (1989): 517.

15 Jacqueline Bhabha and Sue Shutter, *Women's Movement: Women under Immigration, Nationality and Refugee Law* (London: Trentham Books, 1994).

16 Jane Freedman, *Gendering the International Asylum and Refugee Debate* (London: Palgrave Macmillan, 2007): 75.

17 *Ibid.*

18 Emily Copeland, "A Rare Opening in the Wall: The Growing Recognition of Gender-Based Persecution," in *Problems of Protection: The unhcr, Refugees and Human Rights in the 21st Century*, edited by Niklaus Steiner *et al.* (London: Routledge, 2003): 101–116, 101.

gender sensitive. Bhabha, Crawley and Goldberg have all argued for a more inclusive approach to defining what constitutes persecution.[19] The problem then is not the Convention definition but the way in which women's experiences are actually "represented and analytically characterised."[20] The cases of *FB* (*Sierra Leone*) and *HC & RC* (*China*) both show how the adjudicators use restrictive interpretation of the internal relocation principle and ignore the socio-legal realities of the women's experiences.

4 Gender and Internal Relocation Option

> A loved child has many names.[21]

The terms *internal relocation, internal protection, internal flight alternative, internal flight option* and *internal relocation option* all refer to a State created legal concept that in the 1980s quickly rose to become a stable hurdle in the refugee determination process. Albeit through varied tests, States around the world have embraced the internal relocation option as a mechanism to deny and restrict international protection to asylum seekers. Given that women's asylum claims are more likely than men's to involve non-State agent persecution, women are disproportionally affected by the application of the internal relocation option.

While the origins of the internal relocation option are not clear, what is often referenced is the UNHCR Handbook. The UNHCR in 1979 provided the following instructions:

> The fear of being persecuted *need not* always extend to the *whole* territory of the refugee's country of nationality. Thus in ethnic clashes or in cases of grave disturbances involving civil war conditions, persecution of a specific ethnic or national group may occur in only one part of the country.

---

19 Jacqueline Bhabha, "Boundaries in the Field of Human Rights," *Harvard Human Rights Journal* 15 (2002): 155; Heaven Crawley, "Engendering the State in Refugee Women's Claims for Asylum," in *States of Conflict: Gender Violence and Resistance*, edited by Susie M. Jacobs *et al.* (New York: Zed Books, 2000); Crawley, *supra* note 5; and Pamela Goldberg, "Anyplace but Home: Asylum in the United States for Women Fleeing Intimate Violence," *Cornell International Law Journal* 26 (1993): 565.

20 Heaven Crawley, "Gender, Persecution and the Concept of Politics in the Asylum Determination Process," *Forced Migration Review* 9 (2000): 17, 19.

21 Scandinavian proverb.

> In such situations, a person *will not be excluded* from refugee status merely because he could not have sought refuge in another part of the same country, if under *all* the circumstances it *would not have been reasonable to expect him to do so.*[22]

It is evident from the instruction that it was meant to *deter* States from excluding persons from refugee status merely because they could have sought internal protection elsewhere within the country.[23] However, since the 1980s States have used this instruction very restrictively, if not in bad faith. States have interpreted the instruction to mean that exclusion from refugee status *may* be justified and that the inquiry could include a retrospective analysis (i.e., whether the asylum seeker could have sought refuge in another part of the same country).[24] The UNHCR has subsequently issued further instructions to States in the application of a two-stage test, first on the "relevance analysis" and then on the "reasonableness analysis."[25] But as much as the UNHCR has since wanted to clarify the appropriate application of the internal relocation option, the instruction has taken on a life of its own, its dire consequences proving too difficult to rein in.

While the internal relocation option was not envisioned at the time of the drafting of the Refugee Convention, or indeed until around the 1980s when State policies regarding asylum were significantly more open, authorities in the field argue that the internal relocation option is consistent with international refugee law.[26] This is because, as Hathaway explains, "international protection is designed to provide a back-up source of protection" or surrogate protection to persons seriously at risk.[27] A refugee claims this international surrogate protection because her own State cannot or will not

22 UNHCR, *Handbook on Procedures and Criteria for Determining Refugee Status under the 1951 Convention and the 1967 Protocol Relating to the Status of Refugees*, reedited January1992, UNHCR, 1979, U.N. Doc. HCR/IP/Eng/REV.1, ¶ 91, emphasis added.

23 James C. Hathaway and Michelle Foster, "Chapter 6.1: Internal Protection/Relocation/ Flight Alternative as an Aspect of Refugee Status Determination," in *Refugee Protection in International Law; unhcr's Global Consultations on International Protection*, edited by Erika Feller *et al.* (Cambridge: Cambridge University Press, 2003): 357–417, 361.

24 *Ibid.*, 362.

25 UNHCR, *Position Paper on Relocating Internally as a Reasonable Alternative to Seeking Asylum (The So-Called "Internal Flight Alternative" or "Relocation Principle")*, 9 February 1999, http://www.refworld.org/docid/3ae6b336c.html, ¶¶ 13–14 and 15–17 respectively.

26 James C. Hathaway, "International Refugee Law: The Michigan Guidelines on the Internal Protection Alternative," *Michigan Journal of International Law* 21 (1999): 131.

27 Hathaway and Foster, *supra* note 23, 358.

provide protection.[28] A refugee can rely on this surrogate protection when she has shown that there is a lack of State protection. With the task of harmonising European Union policy on asylum, internal relocation has now also become codified in EU law, in Article 8 of the Recast Qualification Directive.[29] However, the EU approach to what it terms the "internal protection alternative" has been criticised as not conforming to international law.[30]

The development of the doctrine in the UK has taken influences from both international jurisprudence and EU law. In the UK, internal relocation option developed through three main cases: *Karanakaran*,[31] *Robinson*[32] and *Januzi*.[33] In *Karanakaran*, Sedley LJ explained that:

> [...] in most cases, [...], it is in relation to the asylum seeker's ability or willingness to avail himself of his home State's protection that the question of internal relocation arises. Because, however, unwillingness is explicitly related to the driving fear, it predicates a different set of considerations from inability, which may be indicated or contraindicated by a much wider range of factors.[34]

In *Robinson*,[35] the Court of Appeal looked towards international jurisprudence in addressing the specific question of reasonableness of relocation. The Court was informed by the Canadian case of *Thirunavukkarasu*, where the question of whether it "would be unduly harsh to expect this person to move to another less hostile part of the country" was considered to be part of the test to measure the "reasonableness" of the internal relocation option.[36] Woolf LJ

28 Dallal Stevens, *UK Asylum Law and Policy: Historical and Contemporary Perspectives* (London: Sweet & Maxwell, 2004): 328.

29 Recast Qualification Directive 2011/95/EV, 13 December 2011, http://www.ilga-europe.org/home/issues/asylum_in_europe/monitoring_eu_asylum_law/the_recast_qualification_directive_2011_95_eu, 9.

30 Hathaway and Foster, *supra* note 23. For a comprehensive analysis of the Recast Qualification Directive and its critique, see John Eaton, "The Internal Protection Alternative under European Union Law: Examining the Recast Qualification Directive," *International Journal of Refugee Law* 24, 4 (2012): 765.

31 *Karanakaran v. Secretary of State for the Home Department* [2000] EWCA Civ 11.

32 *R v. Secretary of State for the Home Department & Immigration Appeal Tribunal, ex parte Robinson* [1997] EWCA Civ 3090.

33 *Januzi (FC) v. Secretary of State for the Home Department* [2006] UKHL 5.

34 *Ibid.*, LJ Stedley ¶ 4.

35 *Robinson, supra* note 32.

36 *Thirunavukkarasu v. Canada (Minister of Employment and Immigration)*, [1994] 1 FC 589 (CA). http://www.refworld.org/docid/3deb87324.html.

also enumerated various tests that had previously been applied within the UK context.[37] Of note for present purposes was the last of these: "if the quality of the internal protection fails to meet basic norms of civil, political and socio-economic human rights," relocation was considered to be unavailable.[38] This part of the test suits a position that Hathaway and Foster have argued for, that consideration should be firmly placed on international human rights law standards.

Hathaway and Foster argue for a shift towards an "internal protection alternative" and reject the current UNHCR recommendation to analyse whether it is "reasonable" to require the claimant to avail herself of the "safety" of the proposed internal destination in favour of a commitment to assess the sufficiency of protection that is accessible to the asylum seeker there.[39] Their analysis has been accepted by international refugee lawyers and has been coined the "Michigan approach" following an international round table organised there.[40]

The reasonableness test is notoriously difficult to apply, lending itself to highly subjective interpretations. Hathaway has criticised it as being "prone to arbitrariness...[and] involving an unfocused and open-ended inquiry which is not anchored in the language or object" of the Refugee Convention.[41] However, it is the Michigan approach, informed by international refugee law and international human rights law, which the House of Lords rejected outright in *Januzi*. The House of Lords explicitly held that reasonableness of internal relocation should *not* be evaluated on the basis of the place of relocation meeting civil, political and socioeconomic rights.[42] According to Lord Bingham, neither the Refugee Convention nor the Qualification Directive's Article 8 requires a human rights approach as advanced by the Michigan Guidelines.[43] However, Lord Bingham was of the opinion that decisions should be guided by the UNHCR Guidelines, which do address "respect for human rights" and

---

37 *Robinson*, *supra* note 32, ¶ 18: "For example, (a) if as a practical matter (whether for financial, logistical or other good reason) the 'safe' part of the country is not reasonably accessible; (b) if the claimant is required to encounter great physical danger in travelling there or staying there; (c) if he or she is required to undergo undue hardship in travelling there or staying there; (d) if the quality of the internal protection fails to meet basic norms of civil, political and socio-economic human rights.".

38 *Ibid.*

39 Hathaway and Foster, *supra* note 22, 381.

40 Hathaway, *supra* note 26.

41 Hathaway and Foster, *supra* note 22, 387.

42 Eaton, *supra* note 30, 778.

43 *Januzi*, *supra* note 33, ¶¶ 15–20.

"economic survival."[44] In essence, then, Lord Bingham advances a position that – instead of the Michigan approach's non-discrimination principle – adjudicators should ask the question: can the claimant live a "relatively normal life"?[45]

Lord Bingham's analysis illustrates some of the difficulties in advancing a human rights approach in the UK context. Reasonableness analysis, of course, forms one of the foundational principles within common law traditions. However, it is arguable that grounding the application of the internal relocation test to international human rights standards is more desirable, particularly in the case of women asylum seekers where gender-based persecution is part of their claim. This is because human rights, if appropriately used, could provide a useful standard of measurement that is internationally recognised. In particular, advances made in the area of women's rights could better inform decisions made on asylum-seeker women's claims. Arguably, it provides a less subjective test than the manner in which the reasonableness test has so far been applied, which has discriminated against women.

Undoubtedly, however, a human rights approach does not offer a panacea in refugee determination processes. There is always the additional problem of trying to make individual caseworkers in the first instance, and later adjudicators and appellate tribunal members, actually apply a certain approach. Even when higher courts have created additional criteria for the application of the internal relocation option, they have not been able to control how the criteria are ultimately applied by the decision-maker.[46] Indeed, the Upper Tribunal has, as evidenced from the following cases, been extremely restrictive in its application of the internal relocation option.

What is argued here is that an alternative reading is not only possible, but also *needed* when considering the specific cases where the internal relocation option has been used to deny refugee status for women fleeing gender-based persecution. The Tribunal has used its internal relocation option tests so restrictively that it places an unnecessarily high standard for the asylum-seeker women to pass. The reasonableness analysis has been particularly susceptible to the Tribunal's problematic views on the dichotomy of victimhood and agency that stem from their Eurocentric and male-centred perspective. It is finally suggested that an assessment of the relocation option, if impossible to

---

44 UNHCR, *Guidelines on Internal Protection: "Internal Flight or Relocation Alternative" within the Context of Article 1 A (2) of the 1951 Convention and/or 1967 Protocol Relating to the Status of Refugees*, 23 July 2003, U.N. Doc. HRC/GIP/03/04, ¶¶ 28–30.

45 Eaton, *supra* note 30, 778.

46 Stevens, *supra* note 28, 329.

challenge *per se*, should be grounded in international human rights standards. If applied with gender sensitivity, it could improve the current state of the internal relocation option test.

5 *HC & RC (China)* and Internal Relocation

HC & RC (China) is a case involving a trafficked woman and her child from a rape. HC was born in the village of Nan Shan in Henei City in Anhui province in China, where she was looked after by her grandmother between the ages of 6, when she was orphaned, and 10, when her grandmother died. After her grandmother's death, HC left her home village and ended up in Sezhuan where she lived on the streets, scavenging for food and sometimes finding work. After moving to and working in a rural area as a domestic worker, she moved back to the city. For a few years, she moved around like this in search of work.

It was in 2005, at the age of 14 or 15, that she became involved in prostitution. She was employed washing dishes when she met a middle-aged woman who promised her well-paid work. She did not know what the work involved. She went on a journey by minibus with this woman and two other young girls and arrived at a house. After a few days she was told she had to take clients, she was being forced into prostitution. She saved money to facilitate an escape. She used this money to pay an agent believing that he would help her escape. However, this agent took her to Russia and forced her into prostitution. After getting pregnant, she was told to leave and she fled to the UK.

The case of *HC & RC (China)* evidences some of the problematic reasoning found in women's cases when adjudicators judge the "reasonableness" of the internal relocation option from a particular individualistic, Western male perspective. The adjudicators are able to come to the conclusion that the internal relocation option is possible for HC & RC by a limited engagement with the risk of re-trafficking and lack of State protection and by viewing the "reasonableness" of the internal relocation option from a narrow perspective that fails to engage meaningfully with the realities of the violations of the applicant's socio-economic rights.

In *HC & RC (China)*, the adjudicators narrate HC's experiences through a simplistic vision of agency, or lack thereof, and evidence a failure to understand the nature of trafficking. This narrative has little to do with the economic realities, global inequalities, disfranchisement and the ever increasing strictness with which State borders are policed, that make up the major forces behind global trafficking of women. The portrayal of the traditional trafficking victim is echoed in the current international approaches to trafficking. The larger story of the evolving legal framework on trafficking has been problematic. As argued elsewhere, the official presentation follows the cinematic representation of trafficking as highly gendered and reproduces stereotypical narratives of femininity and masculinity.[47] It is these larger narratives of victimisation and criminalisation that mask the very real global structural inequalities that produce the conditions for trafficking.

Notably, it is this stereotypical ideal of the "proper" victim that elicits the protection approach of the Western legal machinery. It is also the way in which HC's story is told, through the simplistic binary of victimhood and agency. She is represented as young and "naïve" as she recounts her lack of awareness that she would be forced into prostitution. The Home Office Presenting Officer (HOPO) argued that "when she [HC] was younger and more vulnerable she had not been abducted. She had ended up as a prostitute through naivety."[48] The implication seems to be that if she had been abducted, she would conform to the stereotypical image of trafficking victim, completely void of agency. HC, on the other hand, was "just" young and naïve. Although she might elicit some sympathy as an innocent victim at that stage, after coming to the UK and "growing up" HC, according to the HOPO, does not fit this mould anymore. Now, "she is aware of the position, if it were to arise again."[49] According to the HOPO narrative, she now has agency, she now *knows*, and she would not *consent* to being trafficked again. Eventually, it is the adoption of this reductive narrative based on the binary dichotomy of victimhood and agency that allows the Tribunal to reach the conclusion that she is not at risk of re-trafficking and that internal relocation option is available to her. The representation of HC's experiences is thoroughly divorced from the economic, political and social realities that are central to her claim.

It is this kind of reasoning that shows that the adjudicators are assessing the viability of internal relocation from a particularised individualistic and economically privileged Western position. It is as if the issue is as simple as, for example, moving house from Belfast to London might be for them as privileged, white males. This reasoning ignores the multitude of factors that affect practical access to protection elsewhere in the country of origin. In reality, women face multiple issues including financial, social, linguistic, familial and logistical that affect their ability/inability to relocate to another part of the

47 Rutvica Andrijasevic, "Chapter 11: The Difference Borders Make: (Il)legality, Migration and Trafficking in Italy among Eastern European Women in Prostitution," in *Uprootings/Regroundings: Questions of Home and Migration*, Sara Ahmed *et al.* (Oxford: Berg, 2003): 251–271, at 265.

48 *HC & RC (China)*, ¶ 36.

49 *Ibid.*, ¶ 36.

country of their origin.[50] It is not sufficient for the adjudicators to think that the persecution can be localised; the question needs to be a holistic assessment of whether there is any realistic likelihood of access to protection of their rights.

Equally, in finding that HC & RC would not become destitute on return to China, the adjudicators use very problematic reasoning. They seem to either not want or be capable of estimating the realities of a single mother in China. They mention that "Beijing is a city where single mothers clubs have been established."[51] Yet they did not reflect on whether HC could actually *access* these clubs. There is no consideration on who has access to these clubs or what their costs are. The existence of support to some people is not enough if it is not meaningfully accessible to the person in question. The adjudicators think that she can get domestic or agricultural work, but again do not consider how she will be able to get work and take care of her child at the same time as a single mother with no relatives in the country nor any economic resources of her own.

The adjudicators also brush aside the expert evidence that provides that she and her child are at a high risk of re-trafficking. The evidence from human rights NGOs is also ignored, even when they specifically addressed the lack of substantive protection from trafficking and exploitation of women "due to limited legislative definitions, administrative detention of prostitutes and policy execution."[52] They even ignored a United States State Department Report, used to provide evidence for the lack of State protection, which stated that, despite the general anti-corruption measures, the PRC government "did not demonstrate concerted efforts to investigate and punish government officials specifically for complicity in trafficking."[53] Key deficiencies that the Report noted were in the area of victim care and protection and tackling trafficking for involuntary servitude or forced labour which, as the expert Dr Sheehan explained, were the precise areas upon which HC and RC would rely for protection against re-trafficking.[54] The State Department Report further stated that protection and rehabilitation for trafficking victims was modest and that protection services remained "temporarily inadequate to address victim's needs."[55]

The adjudicators are able to side-line the evidence of a lack of protection of the rights of victims of trafficking by coming to the conclusion that HC would

50 See, for example, Gina Clayton, "Even If – The Use of the Internal Protection Alternative in Asylum Decisions in the UK," *Asylum Aid*, August 2014, http://www.asylumaid.org.uk/wp-content/uploads/2014/07/Even-If...Asylum-Aid-2014.pdf.

51 *Ibid.*, ¶ 91.

52 *Ibid.*, ¶ 11.

53 *Ibid.*, ¶ 15.

54 *Ibid.*

55 *Ibid.*, ¶ 16.

just not consent to being re-trafficked. The economic disadvantage and the possibilities of destitution are not addressed adequately as the adjudicators reason that she is in fact a "mere economic migrant." The adjudicators take the view that since she is an orphan and has lived on the streets, she "had accumulated considerable experience of fending for herself."[56] This leads them to decide that she will be able to relocate and that, even if she might "encounter economic difficulties," she will not "be permitted to sink into destitution," as they claim that she will be able to get some assistance from the All-China Women's Federation.[57] After all, the Tribunal reasons:

> the humanitarian object of the Refugee Convention was to secure a reasonable measure of protection for those with a well-founded fear of persecution in their home country or some part of it; it was not to produce a general levelling-up of living standards around the world; desirable though of course that was.[58]

The expert evidence on the "severe discrimination and considerable long-term social and economic disadvantages" is overridden in a particularly noteworthy manner. The Tribunal considers a newspaper article consisting of an interview of six single mothers in China. It states that "[i]t may very well be that she would encounter a degree of prejudice but, nonetheless, it is clear from the articles referring to the six single mothers mentioned above that, despite whatever prejudice they encountered, they were still pleased to have had their children, which demonstrates in our view that they had not encountered overwhelming prejudice."[59] It is not clear how the degree of a mother being pleased to have had her child demonstrates a correlation to the degree of societal prejudice. It is probably the case that many parents would be pleased to have had their children, no matter what society might say of them. Basing decisions on such a newspaper article trivialises the actual societal prejudice and discrimination that women face. This is doubly problematic as the adjudicators in this case also disregard the evidence from reputable human rights organisations as well as the country expert evidence.

This is despite the concerns of the expert evidence that HC's lack of family or social network and her poverty would make her a likely target for traffickers if returned to China. Dr Sheehan considered both "work and accommodation

56 *HC & RC (China)* ¶ 84.

57 *Ibid.*, ¶ 88.

58 *Ibid.*, ¶ 89.

59 *Ibid.*, ¶ 88.

to be activities fraught with risk for a young woman alone."[60] Some people-traffickers would typically disguise their actions with offers of legitimate work and/or accommodation. However cautious she might be, she would remain "extremely vulnerable to the many fake employment agencies and training providers in China, which were actually fronts for people-trafficking."[61] This is because the only relatively safe way to find work in China is to follow the recommendation of a family member or someone from the same home village or small town, an option which the appellant did not have: she would have no choice but to go to exactly the kind of agencies that traffickers exploited.[62]

The UNHCR Guidelines on Relocation note that internal relocation consideration should be a holistic exercise where the decision-maker looks at the individual personal circumstances, including past persecution or the fear of it, psychological and health condition, family and social situation and survival capacities.[63] In *HC & RC (China)*, the adjudicators, while not referring to the Guidelines, discuss each point and arrive at a restrictive view that invites criticism of selective use of evidence and purposeful exclusion. For instance, when considering her lack of family at place of relocation, it is not considered in the meaningful way in which the expert evidence for instance provides, i.e., the discrimination and real difficulties faced by lone women without family networks. Instead, the adjudicators use her lack of family to argue that – since in their view the principal reason for discrimination against trafficked women is that their families had lost face – as the appellant has no family, "this principal cause of discrimination would not arise."[64] This finding completely ignores the realities of structural discrimination, and specifically discrimination that is based on gender.

The adjudicators fail to recognise the real risk of violations of HC's socio-economic rights upon her return. The problem of not recognising systemic violations of economic and social rights, particularly in relation to women, is a reflection of a larger problem of international refugee law still seeming to consider civil and political rights violations as being of more importance. It reflects

60 *Ibid.*, ¶ 18.

61 *Ibid.*, ¶ 18.

62 *Ibid.*, ¶ 19.

63 UNHCR, *Guidelines on International Protection: Gender-Related Persecution within the Context of Article 1 A (2) of the 1951 Convention and/or its 1967 Protocol relating to the Status of Refugees* (May 2002), U.N. Doc. HCR/GIP/02/01. Baroness Hale drew upon on these Guidelines in *Secretary of State for the Home Department v K (FC) Fornah v. Secretary of State for the Home Department* [2006] UKHL 45.

64 *Ibid.*, ¶ 85.

the pervasiveness of the "traditional, single, male" refugee model. By privileging violations of civil and political rights, decision-makers are at risk of discriminating against women asylum seekers, especially those persecuted by non-State actors. Recognition of social and economic rights necessitates an understanding of the context, which arguably in the case of *HC & RC* (*China*) was repeatedly and decisively ignored. Such restrictive reasoning goes against the object and purpose of the Refugee Convention, to apply the Convention expansively so as to afford people the widest possible exercise of their rights without discrimination.

6 *FB* (*Sierra Leone*) and Internal Relocation Option

There is an underlying reason why the internal relocation option assessment disproportionally affects women's asylum cases. The reason is because women are more likely to have been persecuted by non-State actors. There is a presumption that if the persecution is by State actors, an assessment of internal relocation is not applicable. This is the preferable presumption. In cases where non-State actors are the persecutors, the presumption that the internal relocation option is automatically applicable is problematic. Much of the persecution of women is, indeed, by non-State actors due to the unequal social, economic and political situation of women in societies. In such cases, the adjudicators need to make a decision on whether there is effective, accessible and practicable State protection or whether the State of origin is unable or unwilling to offer protection to the asylum seeker. Too often, in women's cases, the adjudicators are fixated with localising the asylum seeker women's harm. In these cases, the persecution by non-State actors is constructed as something solely private and therefore localised.

FB was 16 years old from Sierra Leone when she arrived in the UK and claimed asylum. She lived in Bankala village with her parents and brothers. Her father had been killed in 1999 during the civil war. The appellant's mother was a sowei[65] and one of the women who carried out the ritual circumcision of young girls. When FB was about 16, she underwent female genital mutilation (FGM). She spent about five days recovering in a nearby village during which time she was told that her mother had died and she was to replace her mother as a sowei. On her return to her village she told of her reluctance to the local chief but he insisted that she go through the rituals to become a sowei, and

65 The leader of a female 'initiation society' of Sande/Bondo women.

that she would subsequently become one of his wives. She refused this and fled.

Initially, the Secretary of State refused her claim, as he did not accept that her contention that she would be forced into becoming a sowei and would be forced to marry the local chief engaged the Refugee Convention. The adjudicator rejected a risk of further FGM and thought it would not be unduly harsh for her to relocate. She applied to the Immigration and Asylum Tribunal on the basis that the adjudicator had made a series of legal errors. The application was dismissed on the basis that she was not a member of a particular social group, but on renewal, a reconsideration was ordered. Subsequently, her case turned on the finding of the availability of the internal relocation option.

In *FB* (*Sierra Leone*), situating the harm the claimant suffered in the private sphere is essential to the finding of the availability of the internal relocation option. Amnesty reports cited as evidence showed how women's civil, political, social and economic rights were being "violated on a daily basis" and that there was a "lack of formal protection" from the Sierra Leonean government.[66] Indeed, the Tribunal accepted that she fell within one of the five enumerated Convention grounds of membership of a particular social group.[67]

The problem for FB was that the adjudicators considered it "reasonable" for her to 'relocate'. *FB* (*Sierra Leone*) is symptomatic of cases in which the UK approach to reasonableness of internal relocation has resulted in a consideration that is centred on the applicant rather than State actions (or omissions). This means that the availability of the internal relocation option tends to be assessed based on the resources and opportunities available for the asylum seeker, rather than an examination of the actions of the State or its obligations.[68] This has led to Tribunals finding that the internal relocation option is available even when there is no indication that such protection will come from the State. For instance, in *JM* (*Kenya*) the adjudicators decided that the applicant could get protection from her "faith."[69] Even though the adjudicators undoubtedly meant the church community, this mention of the metaphysical shows the absurdity with which the adjudicators decide cases when using the reasonableness test. International refugee law, however, focuses on the State and its lack of protection. There is nothing that justifies this reliance on other

66 *Ibid.*, ¶ 47.

67 *Ibid.*, ¶¶ 69–71.

68 Siobhan Mullally, "Domestic Violence Asylum Claims and Recent Developments in International Human Rights Law: A Progress Narrative?," *International and Comparative Law Quarterly* 60, 2 (2011): 459, at 481.

69 *JM* (Sufficiency of protection- IFA- FGM) Kenya [2005] UKIAT 00050.

actors when the State is unwilling or unable to provide protection. It is the State that has the primary obligation to provide protection and the claimant should not be expected to seek protection from an entity that is not a legitimate or nominal government.[70] There is a need to concentrate on State responsibility in order to avoid the restrictive and inappropriate use of the reasonableness test.

Centring on the applicant, rather than the lack of State protection, coupled with simplistic binary framing of agency versus victimhood, makes it very difficult for asylum seeker women's complex experiences to be intelligible to the Tribunal. In *FB* (*Sierra Leone*), just as in *HC & RC* (*China*), the applicant's display of her agency, and the Tribunal's recognition of it, allowed the Tribunal arrive at the decision that she was thus able to relocate. The Tribunal in *FB* (*Sierra Leone*) stated: "whilst we would never wish to underestimate the vulnerability of young women in the position of the appellant, the appellant herself has shown both courage and resilience in facing her difficulties."[71] Furthermore, the adjudicators noted that they took "into account the particular skills that she had developed in the UK and the courage and resourcefulness she has displayed in coming here."[72] The adjudicators appear to insinuate that since FB has managed to come to the UK, she is equally as able to relocate to another part of her country of origin. With respect to the binary notions of victimhood and agency, there seems to be no successful position to take here. Between these binary notions, the asylum seeker cannot be at the same time vulnerable and have agency. This complexity is not acknowledged by the decision-making process.

The Tribunal considered that it would not be unduly harsh for FB to relocate to Freetown "partly because it is a cosmopolitan urban environment where the rural chiefs do not have so great an influence and where State authority is more evident."[73] Again, the Tribunal did not take seriously the extensive evidence from Human Rights Watch and other country reports in the case, which demonstrated the lack of State protection for gender-based violence throughout Sierra Leone. FB had two children in the UK and is being sent back as a single mother with two children with neither family connections nor prospects of employment. This is something which was considered in her evidence, but did not appear to make a difference to the final decision.

---

70 Ninette Kelley, "Internal Flight/Relocation/Protection Alternative: Is it Reasonable?," *International Journal of Refugee Law* 14, 1 (2002): 4, at 24.

71 *FB* (Sierra Leone) ¶ 83.

72 *Ibid.*, ¶ 87.

73 *Ibid.*, ¶ 76.

As in *HC & RC* (*China*), the adjudicators are able to arrive at this decision by looking at the persecution narrowly. By containing the non-State persecution within the private sphere, the adjudicators were able to *speculate* that FB could relocate to another part of Sierra Leone because the man she was being forced to marry was over 70 at the time and "might" be dead already.[74] In these situations the complicity of the State is not analysed in any meaningful way. The women in question are conceived as private subjects, constituted only through their relationship with these old men that "might" be dead already or, in the case of *HC & RC* (*China*), through HC's relationship with the trafficker who would not find her anymore. Conversely, these women are not subjects as themselves and in relation to their State, which is unable or unwilling to offer their rights protection. This portrayal ultimately has the consequence of delegitimising these asylum seeker women's cases. While it fits government policy, it produces discriminatory outcomes.

7 Conclusion

In 2011, on the anniversary of the Refugee Convention, the Committee of the Convention to Eliminate All Forms of Discrimination Against Women (CEDAW) adopted a statement that called for gender equality for refugees. The CEDAW Committee:

> [C]all[ed] on States to recognize gender related forms of persecution and to interpret the 'membership of a particular social group'[75] ground of the 1951 Convention to apply to women. Gender sensitive registration, reception, interview and adjudication processes also need to be in place to ensure women's equal access to asylum.[76]

The CEDAW Committee thus recognised that it is not only the interpretation of the Refugee Convention, but *gender-sensitive adjudication processes*, that are necessary for the protection of the rights of asylum seeker women.

74 *Ibid.*, ¶ 62. Similar reasoning was used by adjudicators in *MD* (Women) Ivory Coast CG [2010] UKUT 215 (IAC).

75 UNHCR Executive Committee recommended this already in 1985, see Executive Committee Conclusion No. 39 (XXXXVI)-1985 on Refugee Women and International Protection, 18 October 1985, ¶ K.

76 U.N. Committee on the Elimination of Discrimination Against Women (CEDAW), *CEDAW Statement on the Anniversaries of the 1951 Convention Relating to the Status of Refugees and the 1961 Convention on the Reduction of Statelessness*, 19 October 2011, http://www.refworld.org/docid/4ea13f012.html.

A human rights approach, in and of itself, is undoubtedly not free from difficulties of application, as can be seen in the case of the "reasonableness test" in internal relocation assessments. However, when it comes to women's rights, a human rights approach that takes into account the feminist critiques is preferable. The discriminatory effects of the current assessment of the internal relocation option in women's refugee status determination process must be challenged. The concerns of the disproportionate effect on women of the hierarchisation of human rights and the public/private divide that enables greater impunity of women's harm needs to be taken seriously. By doing this we can expose the ways in which the application of the internal relocation option has ultimately provided another means by which to restrict the movement of people.

CHAPTER 8

Persistent Objector Teflon?

Customary International Human Rights Law and the United States in International Adjudicative Proceedings

James A. Green

1 Introduction

The persistent objector rule provides that "[i]f whilst a practice is developing into a rule of general law [that is, customary international law], a State persistently and openly dissents from the rule, it will not be bound by it."[1] However, a number of writers have argued that persistent objection does not (or should not) allow a State to exempt itself from certain "fundamental" norms of international law.[2] Given the moral nature and asserted universality underpinning human rights norms, they – more than any other breed of international legal rule – have been said to fall into this category.[3]

1 "Statement of Principles Applicable to the Formation of General Customary International Law," Final Report of the Committee on Formation of Customary (General) International Law, International Law Association, London Conference, 2000, http://www.ila-hq.org/en/committees/index.cfm/cid/30, section 15.

2 See, for example, Patrick Dumberry, "The Last Citadel! Can a State Claim the Status of Persistent Objector to Prevent the Application of a Rule of Customary International Law in Investor-State Arbitration?," *Leiden Journal of International Law* 23, 2 (2010): 379, 379 and 397–98; Brian D. Lepard, *Customary International Law: A New Theory with Practical Applications* (Cambridge: Cambridge University Press, 2010), 230–237; and Oscar Schachter, "International Law in Theory and Practice," in 178 *Collected Courses of The Hague Academy of International Law* (Leiden: Martinus Nijhoff Publishers, 1982), 9, 37–38. See also *Fisheries Case* (United Kingdom v. Norway), reply submitted by the Government of the United Kingdom of Great Britain and Northern Ireland, 1950 I.C.J. Plead. II, 428–429 (28 Nov.).

3 See Louis Henkin, "Human Rights and State 'Sovereignty'," *Georgia Journal of International Law* 25, 2 (1996): 31, 38; Holning Lau, "Rethinking the Persistent Objector Doctrine in International Human Rights Law," *Chicago Journal of International Law* 6, 1 (2005): 496; Lepard, *supra* note 2, at 333–336; Lynn Loschin, "The Persistent Objector Rule and Customary Human Rights Law: A Proposed Analytical Framework," *University of California Davis Journal of International Law and Policy* 2, 2 (1996): 147; Jordan J. Paust, "The Complex Nature, Sources and Evidences of Customary Human Rights," *Georgia Journal of International and Comparative Law* 25, 1 (1995): 147, 152; Niels Petersen, "The Role of Consent and Uncertainty in the

 | DOI 10.1163/9789004261181_010

Can States exempt themselves from customary international law human rights standards through persistent objection? Certainly, a significant majority of scholars agree that the "escape hatch"[4] provided by the persistent objector rule cannot be opened in relation to *jus cogens* norms, and a good proportion of the widely recognised peremptory norms of the system have their basis in the field of international human rights law. However, not all human rights norms are peremptory: indeed, ultimately, very few of them are. The insulation from exemption that the *jus cogens* project provides only gets us so far.

Those looking to ensure the application of customary human rights standards even to dissenting States have thus faced a dilemma: whether to (1) make a dubious case for the peremptory nature of the human rights norm in question, so as to try to imbue it with the resultant protection from persistent objection that *jus cogens* status provides; or (2) accept that most human rights norms are *not* rules of *jus cogens*, but then assert that even non-peremptory human rights norms are immune from persistent objection. Either approach is highly problematic, and the third option – to allow for persistent objection to all but the handful of human rights norms that have indeed reached the level of *jus cogens* – runs counter to intuitive notions of justice, universality and morality at the very heart of the human rights concept.

This dilemma is herein considered with a particular focus on the practice of the United States in the context of international adjudication. The United States is the only State to have explicitly claimed to be a persistent objector with regard to human rights norms in international adjudicative proceedings. It did so twice before the Inter-American Commission on Human Rights (IACHR), in *Roach and Pinkerton v. United States* (1987)[5] and *Domingues v. United States* (2002).[6] In both of these proceedings before the IACHR, the United States asserted that it was exempt from any possible customary international law prohibition of the juvenile death penalty. More recently, the United States claimed persistent objector status before a North American Free Trade Agreement (NAFTA) arbitration tribunal, in *Grand River Enterprises v.*

Formation of Customary International Law," *Reprints of the Max Planck Institute for Research on Collective Goods*, 2010, http://www.coll.mpg.de/pdf_dat/2011_04online.pdf: 13–14; and Charles Quince, *The Persistent Objector and Customary International Law* (Denver: Outskirts Press, 2010), 62–63 and 76.

4 Ted L. Stein, "The Approach of the Different Drummer: The Principle of the Persistent Objector in International Law," *Harvard International Law Journal* 26, 2 (1985): 457, 472.

5 *Roach and Pinkerton v. United States of America*, 1987 Inter-Am. CHR, Resolution No. 3/87, Case 9647 (22 Sept.).

6 *Domingues v. United States of America*, 2002 Inter-Am. CHR, Report No. 62/02, Case 12.285 (22 Oct.).

United States (2011).[7] The United States' submission in *Grand River* was that it was exempt from a number of customary indigenous human rights – and particularly the right of "indigenous consultation" – by virtue of its repeated expressions of dissent. The claims made by the United States in these three adjudicative proceedings, and the respective responses of the IACHR and the NAFTA Tribunal, will be used to highlight the interplay between customary international human rights law and the persistent objector rule.

First, this chapter briefly sets out, in section II, the common understanding of the persistent objector rule. Section III then – also briefly – considers the notion of State exemption from international human rights law in general terms. The oft-made assertion that persistent objection is unavailing against *jus cogens* norms is considered in section IV. Analysis then turns, in section V, to the problem of non-peremptory human rights norms and, in particular, to dubious claims that have been made with regard to the *jus cogens* status of human rights provisions that are almost certainly not of that hallowed ilk. Section VI considers an alternative approach, being the argument that *all* human rights norms bind even persistent objectors, irrespective of peremptory status. Against this background of preceding analysis, section VI concludes by noting that perhaps the problem of persistent objection to human rights norms is not as pervasive as one might think.

Ultimately, this chapter seeks to shed some light on the relationship between international human rights law and the persistent objector rule. It aims to do so, one hopes fittingly, by adopting the approach so often taken by Professor Sandy Ghandhi in his analysis of the mechanics of international human rights law: at once both inherently humanist and with an eye on the maximisation of protection, while at the same time practical, pragmatic and – where necessary – sceptical.

2 The Basics of the Persistent Objector Rule

In predominant positivist understandings of the "horizontal" international legal system, States are not bound by law to which they have not consented to be bound.[8] Consent in the context of the formation of custom is usually

7 *Grand River Enterprises Six Nations Ltd* et al. *v. Government of the United States of America*, final award, 2011, UNCITL/NAFTA, http://www.naftalaw.org/Disputes/USA/GrandRiver/GRE-USA-Award-Merits.pdf (12 Jan.).

8 See Antonio Cassese, *International Law in a Divided World* (Oxford: Clarendon Press, 1986), 169; and James A. Green, "India's Status as a Nuclear Weapons Power under Customary International Law," *National Law School of India Review* (2012) 24, 1 (2012): 125, 139.

premised on silence as constituting tacit consent,[9] and it is here that the persistent objector rule is commonly seen as fulfilling a crucial role. At least theoretically, the rule preserves State autonomy – not to mention the positivist notion of a consent-based legal system – by providing States with a means of *withholding* consent.[10]

Perhaps because of its importance to the voluntarist conception of the international legal system, the persistent objector rule is ubiquitous within mainstream international law scholarship. It makes at least a cameo appearance in virtually every modern textbook on international law,[11] and has been famously endorsed, albeit briefly and as *obiter dicta*, in two merits decisions of the International Court of Justice (ICJ).[12] The rule is usually viewed as having two elements, both of which need to be satisfied for it to operate: (1) somewhat obviously, given the rule's name, objection must be *persistent*;[13] and (2) objection must occur *during the formation* of the norm.[14]

It is worth noting that, despite its ubiquity in the literature, the persistent objector rule certainly has its critics. Some point to the relatively low amount of State usage of the rule,[15] or the fact that objectors commonly find it politically difficult to maintain objection even when the technical legal elements for

9 See Olufemi Elias, "Persistent Objector," in *Max Planck Encyclopaedia of Public International Law*, VIII, edited by Rüdiger Wolfrum (Oxford: Oxford University Press, 2012), 280, 285, ¶ 3.

10 See Adam Steinfeld, "Nuclear Objections: The Persistent Objector and the Legality of the Use of Nuclear Weapons," *Brooklyn Law Review* 62, 4 (1996): 1635, 1655.

11 There are far too many such works to be cited here, but examples of key textbooks referencing the rule include James Crawford, *Brownlie's Principles of Public International Law* (8th ed., Oxford: Oxford University Press, 2012), 28; Martin Dixon, *Textbook on International Law* (7th ed., Oxford: Oxford University Press, 2013), 34–35; Robert Jennings and Arthur Watts, *Oppenheim's International Law, Volume I (Peace)* (9th ed., New York: Longman, 1996), 29; and Malcom N. Shaw, *International Law* (6th ed., Cambridge: Cambridge University Press, 2008), 89–91.

12 See *Asylum Case (Columbia/Peru)*, 1950 I.C.J. 266, 277–278 (20 Nov.); and *Fisheries Case (United Kingdom v. Norway)*, 1951 I.C.J. 116, 131 (18 Dec.).

13 Dino Kritsiotis, "On the Possibilities of and For Persistent Objection," *Duke Journal of Comparative and International Law* 21, 1 (2010): 121, 130.

14 Olufemi Elias, "Some Remarks on the Persistent Objector Rule in Customary International Law," *Denning Law Journal* 6 (1991): 37, 38.

15 See, for example, Jonathan I. Charney, "The Persistent Objector Rule and the Development of Customary International Law," *British Yearbook of International Law* 56 (1985): 1, particularly 11–16; Jeffrey L. Dunoff *et al.*, *International Law: Norms, Actors, Process: A Problem-Orientated Approach* (2nd ed., New York: Aspen, 2006), 78; and Stein, *supra* note 4, in general, but particularly at 459–463.

the rule's operation are met.[16] Others argue that because, for example, new States are not given the opportunity to object prior to the formation of customary law already in existence at their inception, the role that the majority ascribe for the rule (as the champion of State consent) is theoretically unsound.[17]

However, while these minority critiques must be acknowledged, they go beyond the scope of this chapter. The present author takes the view that the persistent objector rule does exist and is used by States, albeit perhaps not as regularly as one might expect. Irrespective of the rule's conceptual problems, States can exempt themselves from emerging norms of customary international law by way of a process of persistent objection.

3 State Exemption from Provisions of International Human Rights Law

As Ghandhi has highlighted, a significant amount of controversy has been generated in the literature (and amongst States) regarding reservations to human rights treaties.[18] Of course, treaty reservations – as inherent acts of exceptionalism – always have the potential to be controversial *per se*. Tensions over reservations are likely to be particularly acute in the context of human rights treaties, however, because their inherent aim is not just to

16 See, for example, Jonathan I. Charney, "Universal International Law," *American Journal of International Law* 87, 4 (1993): 529, 539; and Anthony D'Amato, "International Soft Law, Hard Law, and Coherence," *Northwestern University School of Law Public Law and Legal Theory Series*, No. 08–01 (2008): 17–19.

17 See, for example, and Patrick Dumberry, "Incoherent and Ineffective: The Concept of Persistent Objector Revisited," *International and Comparative Law Quarterly* 59, 3 (2010): 779, 797–798; and J. Patrick Kelly, "The Twilight of Customary International Law," *Virginia Journal of International Law* 40, 2 (2000): 449, 513 and 523–526.

18 See Sandy Ghandhi, "The Human Rights Committee and Interim Measures of Relief," *Canterbury Law Review* 13 (2007): 203, 233; and P.R. Ghandhi, "The Human Rights Committee and Reservations to the Optional Protocol," *Canterbury Law Review* 8 (2001): 13. Ghandhi specifically makes this point in relation to the controversy surrounding the Human Rights Committee's famous "General Comment on Issues Relating to Reservations made upon Ratification or Accession to the Covenant or the Optional Protocols thereto, or in Relation to Declarations under Article 41 of the Covenant," U.N. Doc. CCPR/C/21/Rev.1/Add.6 (2 Nov. 1994). See, more generally, Ryan Goodman, "Human Rights Treaties, Invalid Reservations, and State Consent," *American Journal of International Law* 96, 3 (2002): 531; and Catherine J. Redgwell, "Reservations to Treaties and Human Rights Committee General Comment No 24 (52)," *International and Comparative Law Quarterly* 46, 2 (1997): 390.

reconcile different national polices, but also different social, religious and moral systems.[19] Furthermore, it goes without saying that international human rights law aims to speak directly to a shared (or, at least, avowedly shared) morality: and questions of morality always raise the collective blood pressure of any society.

Human rights are "part of the concept of the international public order,"[20] and the moral and societal "weight" of such norms means that, for many, any kind of deviation by an individual State should be precluded.[21] Indeed, it is commonly argued (if far from entirely agreed) that human rights are *intrinsically universal* in nature.[22] Given their subject matter, many claim that they must, or at least should, apply to all States – and thus, of course, to all *people* – without exception.

In contrast to the voluminous literature on reservations to human rights treaties, there has been relatively little written on the possibility of persistent objection to customary international human rights law. Yet the irresistible force of moral universalism and immovable object of consent-based sovereignty collide just as obviously in this context too.[23] Persistent objection is, in many respects, the customary international law equivalent of reservations to treaties.[24] The mechanism of persistent objection allows a State to gain exemption from the otherwise universal binding force of the customary legal norm in question. Therefore, as with reservations and human rights in treaty law, the relationship between the persistent objector rule and human rights standards under customary international law is an inherently uneasy one.

The first port of call in trying to navigate this uneasy relationship is to consider the regularly repeated assertion that persistent objection cannot exempt a State from a peremptory norm of international law.

---

19 Anthony Aust, *Modern Treaty Law and Practice* (3rd ed., Cambridge: Cambridge University Press, 2013): 134.

20 Ian Brownlie, "The Decisions of Political Organs of the United Nations and the Rule of Law," in *Essays in Honour of Wang Tieya*, edited by Ronald St. John MacDonald (Dordrecht: Martinus Nijhoff Publishers, 1994), 91, 102.

21 Stephen Hall, "The Persistent Spectre: Natural Law, International Order and the Limits of Legal Positivism," *European Journal of International Law* 12, 2 (2001): 269, 301–305.

22 Jack Donnelly, "Human Rights as Natural Rights," *Human Rights Quarterly* 4, 3 (1982): 391, particularly 397–398.

23 Loschin, *supra* note 3, 161.

24 Bing Bing Jia, "The Relations between Treaties and Custom," *Chinese Journal of International Law* 9, 1 (2010): 81, 101–102.

4 Persistent Objection and Peremptory Human Rights Norms

Jus cogens norms are "fundamental legal norms from which no derogation is permitted."[25] It is therefore of no surprise that a significant proportion of the norms that are (or are at least claimed to be) of this "super-norm" character come from the field of international human rights law. The International Law Commission (ILC) stated in the context of its work on the law of State responsibility in 2001, that "[t]hose peremptory norms that are *clearly accepted and recognized* include the prohibitions of aggression, genocide, slavery, racial discrimination, crimes against humanity and torture, and the right to self-determination."[26] While this is almost certainly a non-exhaustive list, it provides us with a general picture of those norms for which the designation "*jus cogens*" is relatively uncontroversial. Notably, six of the seven norms listed by the ILC stem from international human rights law. It has already been mentioned that human rights have a community-centric, imperative and value-based nature, and the same can obviously also be said of peremptory norms: the two thus have an inherent interrelationship.[27]

This chapter is not the place to consider in detail the way in which peremptory norms of international law come into being,[28] but it is worth recalling the most widely quoted definition of *jus cogens* from Article 53 of the 1969 Vienna

25 Hilary Charlesworth and Christine Chinkin, "The Gender of *Jus Cogens*," *Human Rights Quarterly* 15, 1 (1993): 15, 15. Although there is significant support for the concept of *jus cogens* in doctrine, it is worth noting that there remains a good deal of general academic debate as to the scope, nature and, indeed, the very existence of *jus cogens* norms. See, for example, Robert P. Barnidge, Jr., "Questioning the Legitimacy of *Jus Cogens* in the Global Legal Order," *Israel Yearbook of Human Rights* 38, (2008): 199, 203–210; Gordon A. Christenson, "*Jus Cogens*: Guarding Interests Fundamental to International Society," *Virginia Journal of International Law* 28, 3 (1988): 585; Michael J. Glennon, "Peremptory Nonsense," in *Human Rights, Democracy and the Rule of Law: Liber Amicorum Luzius Wildhaber*, edited by in Stephan Breitenmoser *et al.* (Zürich: Nomos, 2007), 1265; and Prosper Weil, "Towards Relative Normativity in International Law?," *American Journal of International Law* 77, 3 (1983): 413. Suffice it to say here that the present author accepts the existence of *jus cogens* norms.

26 Report of the International Law Commission, 53rd Sess., 23 April-1 June and 2 July-10 August 2001, U.N. Doc. A/56/10 (2001): 85, emphasis added.

27 Antonio Cassese, *Five Masters of International Law* (Hart: Oxford, 2011), 25 (interview with René-Jean Dupuy: "human rights [can be seen as] *the basis for jus cogens*: if all men are equal, then by extension all peoples are equal"), emphasis added.

28 For a more detailed analysis of the manner in which *jus cogens* norms are created, see Alexander Orakhelashvili, *Peremptory Norms in International Law* (Oxford: Oxford University Press, 2006), 36–130.

Convention on the Law of Treaties (VCLT). Article 53 states that peremptory norms must be "accepted and recognized by the international community of States as a whole as a norm from which no derogation is permitted and which can be modified only by a subsequent norm of general international law having the same character."[29]

It is fairly clear that such acceptance and recognition on the part of the "international community of States as a whole" does not necessitate *universal* acceptance by States as to the peremptory character of any given norm. As the chairman of the Drafting Committee of the VCLT made clear in 1968, it is enough for "a large majority" of States to take such a position.[30] This notion of a "large majority" bestowing *jus cogens* status is, of course, rather at odds with a positivist conception of international law as being built on State consent.[31] Nonetheless, it is, for most, justified by the need to avoid a single State vetoing a peremptory norm accepted as such by all others.[32]

Acquisition of *jus cogens* status is the Holy Grail for any provision of human rights law: derogation becomes untenable, as does – aside from where a contrary norm of the same character later emerges – *change*. The particular consequence of peremptory status that is of relevance here, however, is that a significant majority of scholars argue that a State cannot exempt itself from a peremptory norm by way of persistent objection, even when the usual criteria

29 Vienna Convention on the Law of Treaties, Vienna, 23 May 1969, art. 53. Complementing art. 53 is art. 64 of the VCLT, which states: "[i]f a new peremptory norm of general international law emerges, any existing treaty which is in conflict with that norm becomes void and terminates." Admittedly, using Article 53 as the definition of *jus cogens* is not entirely satisfactory, see Erika de Wet, "The Prohibition of Torture as an International Norm of *Jus Cogens* and Its Implications for National and Customary Law," *European Journal of International Law* 15, 1 (2004): 97, 98–99.

30 Official Records of the United Nations Conference on the Law of Treaties, 1st Sess., 26 March-24 May 1968 (Summary Records of the Plenary Meetings and of the Meetings of the Committee of the Whole), A/CONF.39/C.1/SR.34 (1968): 472.

31 See Gennady M. Danilenko, "International *Jus Cogens*: Issues of Law-Making," *European Journal of International Law* 2, 1 (1991): 42, in general, but particularly at 48–57; and Lauri Hannikainen, *Peremptory Norms* (Jus Cogens) *in International Law: Historical Development, Criteria, Present Status* (Helsinki: Lakimiesliiton Kusannus, 1988), 49.

32 Rafael Nieto-Navia, "International Peremptory Norms (*Jus Cogens*) and International Humanitarian Law," in *Man's Inhumanity to Man: Essays on International Law in Honour of Antonio Cassese*, edited by Lal Chand Vohrah *et al.* (The Hague: Kluwer Law International, 2003), 595, 612. Cf., J. Brock McClane, "How Late in the Emergence of a Norm of Customary International Law May a Persistent Objector Object?," *International Law Students Association Journal of International Law* 13 (1989): 1, 25 (arguing that universal acceptance *is* required for the emergence of a new *jus cogens* norm).

for the rule's operation – persistence and timeliness – are otherwise met.[33] The ILC has articulated this majority view with particularly vehement language: "it is *inconceivable* that a persistent objector could thwart such a norm."[34]

The "classic" example from State practice illustrating that objection is unavailing in relation to a peremptory human rights norm is the widespread view that repeated dissent by South Africa and Rhodesia to the emerging customary international law norm prohibiting the policy of apartheid did not allow for those States to later continue to practice racial discrimination.[35] *Jus cogens* simply overrode the persistent objections of these States. Yet while apartheid may be by far the most commonly cited example of this phenomenon, perhaps of more note is the fact that ultimately *no State* has been able to maintain persistent objection to a peremptory norm.

In terms of legal theory, the rationale underpinning this position is based on a conceptualisation of the purpose of peremptory norms, as being aimed at protecting the most crucial values of common interest and moral imperative.[36]

---

33 This claim is ubiquitous, but to give just a few examples of those taking this view: Michael Byers, "Conceptualising the Relationship Between *Jus Cogens* and *Erga Omnes* Rules," *Nordic Journal of International Law* 66, 2 (1997): 211, 217 and 223; Christopher A. Ford, "Adjudicating *Jus Cogens*," *Wisconsin International Law Journal* 13, 1 (1994–1995): 145, 146–147; Peter Hulsroj, "*Jus Cogens* and Disarmament," *Indian Journal of International Law* 46, 1 (2006): 1, 8; Karen Parker and Lyn Beth Neylon, "*Jus Cogens*: Compelling the Law of Human Rights," *Hastings Journal of International and Comparative Law* 12, 2 (1989): 411, 418; and Christian Tomuschat, "Obligations Arising for States Without or Against Their Will," in 241 *Collected Courses of The Hague Academy of International Law* (Leiden: Martinus Nijhoff Publishers, 1993), 195, 307. See also *North Sea Continental Shelf* (Federal Republic of Germany/Denmark) (Federal Republic of Germany/the Netherlands), 1969 I.C.J. 3, 229 (20 Feb.) (Lachs, J., dissenting).

34 Report of the International Law Commission, 59th Sess., 7 May-5 June and 9 July-10 August 2007, U.N. Doc. A/62/10 (2007): 101, emphasis added.

35 See, for example, Omar Abasheikh, "The Validity of the Persistent Offender Rule in International Law," *Coventry Law Journal* 9 (2004): 40, 44; Luigi Condorelli, "Custom," in *International Law: Achievements and Prospects*, edited by Mohammed Bedjaoui (Dordrecht: Martinus Nijhoff, 1991), 179, 205; John Dugard, *International Law: A South African Perspective* (3rd ed., Cape Town: Juta & Co., 2008), 32; Maurice H. Mendelson, "The Formation of Customary International Law," in 272 *Collected Courses of The Hague Academy of International Law* (Leiden: Martinus Nijhoff Publishers, 1998), 155, 235–236; and Stein, *supra* note 4, 463 and 473–474.

36 See, for example, Quince, *supra* note 3, 39; Steinfeld, *supra* note 10, 1678; and John Tasioulas, "Customary International Law and the Quest for Global Justice," in *The Nature of Customary Law*, edited by Amanda Perreau-Saussine and James Bernard Murphy (Cambridge: Cambridge University Press, 2007), 307, 313.

It is understandably seen as undesirable, once "the international community as a whole" (meaning, as we have noted, *virtually* all States) has "accepted and recognised" any given international law norm as being of such importance that it cannot be derogated from, to allow a single State to gain exemption from that norm. Indeed, the very concept of a norm that cannot be derogated from is intuitively at odds with the persistent objector rule, the *raison d'etre* of which is derogation.[37]

Overall, then, it is relatively uncontroversial[38] to state that human rights norms that have been accepted and recognised as being peremptory – the prohibitions on torture, apartheid, genocide, slavery, *et al.* – are legally immunised from the possibility of State exemption through persistent objection.

5 Lengthen the List of Peremptory Human Rights Norms?

The problem is that this list of peremptory human rights norms – or at least the list of relatively uncontentious peremptory human rights norms – is rather short. The legal criteria for establishing any given norm as being peremptory are onerous: while universal acceptance is unnecessary, the test is nonetheless whether the *vast majority* of States of the world have accepted and recognised the norm as being peremptory.[39] Peremptory status for any given norm is difficult to be sure of.[40] As such, what we can be fairly sure of is that, as Lau concludes, "only a handful of human rights norms qualify as *jus cogens*, leaving the large majority of human rights laws susceptible to the persistent objector doctrine."[41]

---

37 See Ford, *supra* note 33, 146; and Kritsiotis, *supra* note 13, 133–134.

38 A small number of writers have criticised the majority view on the basis that denying exemption from *jus cogens* norms would amount to an erosion of the sovereign right of States to consent (or not) to rules of international law. See, for example, Cassese, *supra* note 8, 178; and Nieto-Navia, *supra* note 32, 612.

39 Christos L. Rozakis, *The Concept of* Jus Cogens *in the Law of Treaties* (Amsterdam: North Holland Publishing Company, 1976), 15.

40 James A. Green, "Questioning the Peremptory Status of the Prohibition of the Use of Force," *Michigan Journal of International Law* 32, 2 (2011): 215; and Christiana Ochoa, "Disintegrating Customary International Law: Reactions to *Withdrawing from International Custom*," *Duke Journal of Comparative and International Law* 21, 1 (2010): 157, 166 n.40.

41 Lau, *supra* note 3, 495, and at 498. See also Susan C. Breau, "The Constitutionalization of the International Legal Order," *Leiden Journal of International Law* 21, 2 (2008): 545, 547–548; Camilla G. Guldahl, "The Role of Persistent Objection in International Humanitarian Law," *Nordic Journal of International Law* 77, 1 (2008): 51, 62; Loschin, *supra* note 3,

One approach taken by those looking to ensure that human rights standards apply universally, even to persistent objectors, has therefore been to unilaterally lengthen the list of peremptory human rights norms. Rules that are almost certainly non-peremptory (based on any reasonable application of the VCLT Article 53 criteria) are thus at times argued to have acquired a peremptory character, specifically so that State persistent objection to them can be considered to be validly overridden. It is entirely understandable that writers "have strained to conclude that that a norm is *jus cogens*"[42] in instances where the norm in question is of particular moral importance – a designation that self-evidently includes provisions of international human rights law – without the rigorous application of the positivist criteria for the creation of peremptory rules.[43]

However, whatever the merit or moral "value" of any given legal rule, this does not in itself turn it into a peremptory norm; nor do pronouncements to this effect made by scholars, however numerous.[44] To allow for the uncritical and subjective selection of peremptory norms does more harm than good to the commendable goals of the *jus cogens* project. Without genuine acceptance and recognition by States, any avowed peremptory norm will not be treated as

---

163–164; and Bruno Simma and Philip Alston, "The Sources of Human Rights Law: Custom, *Jus Cogens*, and General Principles," *Australian Yearbook of International Law* 12 (1988–1989): 82, 103. Cf., *South West Africa Cases* (Ethiopia v. South Africa) (Liberia v. South Africa), Second Phase, 1966 I.C.J. 6, 298 (18 Jul.) (Tanaka, J., dissenting).

42 Lepard, *supra* note 2, 241.

43 For example, Steinfeld seemingly determines, with relatively little evidence, that the entire corpus of International Humanitarian Law and – even less convincingly – international environmental law, are peremptory in nature, so as to protect these rules against possible persistent objection by nuclear weapon States. Steinfeld, *supra* note 10, at 1640 and 1680–1685. See Guldahl, *supra* note 41, at 84 (rightly pointing out that Steinfeld's arguments in this regard are simply "untenable"). Another example is Tabassi's argument that the alleged customary comprehensive nuclear test-ban is a *jus cogens* norm, on which basis she then claims that possible persistent objector States (specifically India, Pakistan and the Democratic People's Republic of Korea) would nonetheless be required to refrain from nuclear testing, see Lisa Tabassi, "The Nuclear Test Ban: *Lex Lata* or *de Lege Ferenda*?," *Journal of Conflict and Security Law* 14, 2 (2009): 309, 347–350. However, this claim is obviously incorrect: see James A. Green, "India and a Customary Comprehensive Nuclear Test-Ban: Persistent Objection, Peremptory Norms and the 123 Agreement," *Indian Journal of International Law* 51, 2 (2011): 3, 29 (the "equivocal State practice and *opinio juris* in relation to customary status *simpliciter* [of the test ban] is impossible to equate to the near-universal acceptance and recognition of 'supernorm' status required for elevation to the hallowed group of peremptory international legal rules").

44 Barnidge, *supra* note 25, 205.

one by States, leaving a gap between what is peremptory on the page and what is peremptory in practice. We need to keep that gap a narrow one to avoid damaging the entire credibility of *jus cogens*.

This problematic "kitchen sink" approach to the identification of peremptory norms is highlighted by the practice of the United States in the context of international adjudication. As has already been noted, the United States is the only State to formally argue that it is an exempt persistent objector to human rights norms in adjudicative proceedings. The United States first made this claim in 1987 before the IACHR, in *Roach and Pinkerton*.[45] Here, the Commission was examining whether the imposition of the death penalty on the petitioners by United States' courts for crimes committed before their eighteenth birthdays (the petitioners indeed having been executed before the end of the proceedings), violated various provisions of the American Declaration of the Rights and Duties of Man 1948[46] "as informed by customary international law which prohibits the imposition of the death penalty for crimes committed by juveniles under eighteen."[47] The United States argued that, if a customary prohibition on the execution of persons who were less than eighteen years old at the time of the commission of the offense existed, it was nonetheless exempt from it as a persistent objector.[48]

First, the IACHR determined that if there was a customary international law prohibition on the juvenile death penalty, the United States would indeed not be bound by any such norm on the basis of its persistent objection.[49] Secondly, however, the Commission held that there was not only an established customary norm prohibiting the execution of juvenile offenders, but that this norm was peremptory in nature.[50] One would assume that this then meant that the Commission saw American objections as being unavailing (given that, as is the common consensus, the IACHR viewed the persistent objector rule as being inapplicable in relation to of *jus cogens*). Yet, in something of a *volte-face*, the IACHR went on to determine that – while a peremptory prohibition on

45 *Roach and Pinkerton*, *supra* note 5.

46 Specifically, the petitioners alleged violations of Article I (right to life), Article VII (special protection of children) and Article XXVI (cruel, infamous or unusual punishment), *ibid.*, ¶ 34.

47 *Ibid.*

48 *Roach and Pinkerton*, Memorandum of the United States to the Inter-American Commission on Human Rights in Case 9647, Inter-Am. CHR 147, OEA/ser.L/V./II.71, doc. 9 rev. 1, 15 (17 July 1981).

49 *Roach and Pinkerton*, *supra* note 5, ¶ 54.

50 *Ibid.*, ¶ 56.

juvenile executions existed – it was not clear that the age limit for identifying a "juvenile" for this purpose was necessarily set at *eighteen*.[51] The Commission felt that a new norm specifically prohibiting the executions of individuals aged *less than eighteen years* when their offense was committed was "emerging" at the time, but that this had not yet emerged.[52] This meant that the policy of the United States in executing sixteen year old offenders did not violate the (peremptory) customary legal prohibition after all.[53] The IACHR's report in *Roach and Pinkerton* therefore acts as authority for the view that persistent objection is unavailing in relation to human rights norms that have acquired peremptory status, but only, ultimately, in the abstract.[54]

This view was, however, further reinforced in the IACHR's 2002 decision in *Domingues*.[55] Following the Commission's report in *Roach and Pinkerton*, the claim was increasingly made that – from the early 1990s onwards – a norm prohibiting the execution of persons under the age of eighteen had crystallised into customary international law,[56] and there exists a good deal of evidence indicating that this was the case.[57] The increased general acceptance of the customary prohibition meant that the IACHR felt that it was on firmer ground in 2002, when next it was faced with the juvenile death penalty issue.

Domingues concerned a death sentence imposed by the state of Nevada on an individual who was sixteen at the time that he committed two homicides.[58] The United States once more argued that it was exempt from the prohibition on juvenile executions in relation to Mr Domingues – or, at least, was exempt

---

51 *Ibid.*, ¶ 60.

52 *Ibid.*

53 *Ibid.* Although the Commission nonetheless saw the United States as being in violation of Articles I and II of the American Declaration of the Rights and Duties of Man, at ¶¶ 61–65.

54 Dumberry, *supra* note 17, 788.

55 *Domingues, supra* note 6.

56 See, for example, Amnesty International, "United States of America: Open Letter to the President on the Death Penalty," 1994, http://www.amnesty.org/en/library/asset/AMR51/001/1994/en/dc29ca38-0b55-4014-8302-dfc1146a5ffb/amr510011994en.pdf, particularly the State practice referenced at 8.

57 The State practice supporting the establishment, in the early 1990s, of a customary norm prohibiting juvenile executions is set out in detail in Edward F. Sherman, Jr., "The U.S. Death Penalty Reservation to the International Covenant on Civil and Political Rights: Exposing the Limitations of the Flexible System Governing Treaty Formation," *Texas International Law Journal* 29, 1 (1994): 69, 88–90.

58 *Domingues, supra* note 6, ¶¶ 1–2.

from a rule that took eighteen rather than sixteen as the threshold for minority executions – on the basis that it was a persistent objector.[59]

Unlike in *Roach and Pinkerton*, by 2002 the IACHR felt comfortable in asserting that there was indeed a customary prohibition on the execution of juveniles (with the threshold for this specifically being eighteen years).[60] It then rejected the United States' claim of exemption from that customary norm on the basis, *inter alia*, that the prohibition on the execution of juveniles had the status of a norm of *jus cogens*:

> [T]he Commission considers that the United States is bound by a norm of *jus cogens* not to impose capital punishment on individuals who committed their crimes when they had not yet reached 18 years of age. As a *jus cogens* norm, this proscription binds the community of States, including the United States. The norm cannot be validly derogated from, whether by treaty or by the objection of a State, persistent or otherwise.[61]

In other words, in 2002, the IACHR was notably less equivocal than it had been in 1987: juvenile executions were prohibited by a *jus cogens* norm, and the United States was therefore in violation of that prohibition irrespective of its persistent objection. The United States Supreme Court subsequently ruled, in *Roper v. Simmons*[62] in 2005, that the juvenile death penalty was cruel and unusual punishment and was therefore unlawful under the American Constitution. This decision has been seen by some as likely being a direct result of the Commission's findings in its *Domingues* report,[63] and thus as conclusive evidence that persistent objection does not pay in relation to *jus cogens* rules.

The approach of the IACHR in both *Roach and Pinkerton* and *Domingues* certainly conforms to the general view of the immunisation from persistent objection provided to human rights norms by the acquisition of *jus cogens* status. More generally, the Commission can be applauded for its stance of direct opposition to the world's most powerful State on a crucial issue of human

59 See *Domingues v. United States*, Response of the Government of the United States to May 1, 2000 Petition, Case No. 12.185 (Michael Domingues), http://www.state.gov/documents/organization/16525.pdf, at 10–11; and *Domingues, supra* note 6, at ¶ 14.

60 *Domingues, supra* note 6, ¶ 83.

61 *Ibid.*, ¶ 85.

62 *Roper v. Simmons*, 2005, 543 U.S. 551.

63 See, for example, Sandra L. Babcock, "Human Rights Advocacy in United States Capital Cases," in *Bringing Human Rights Home, Volume 3*, edited by Cynthia Soohoo *et al.* (Westport: Praeger, 2008), 91, 105.

rights exceptionalism. Venturing momentarily into the light of biased moral certainty, before quickly retreating back into his hole of (admittedly fictional) legal impartiality, the present author would suggest that the execution of juvenile offenders is fundamentally and inexcusably *wrong*. On a human, instinctive level it is hard to criticise the Commission for flatly rejecting the assertion of an institutional right to kill children (or, slightly less repugnantly, adults who were children at the time when they committed the crime for which they are executed). Nonetheless, the decisions of the IACHR on the United States' claim of persistent objector status in relation to the juvenile death penalty must be assessed rather more critically than such a gut response allows.

It is worth noting, first, that the United States maintained its policy of juvenile executions for a full *three years* after the unequivocal *Domingues* decision. Perhaps this can be contextualised by the fact that this was generally viewed as a breach of international law, rather than being accepted as an example of an exempt persistent objector legitimately ploughing its own furrow.[64] Nonetheless, to the extent that *Domingues* and *Roach and Pinkerton* act as authority for the assertion that States cannot remain exempt from peremptory norms through persistent objection as a matter of law, the actual practice of the United States shows that it is possible to maintain such a position as a matter of *fact*, even if not indefinitely.

Perhaps more importantly, there has been significant debate as to the veracity of the IACHR's conclusion that the prohibition of juvenile execution is – or was at the relevant time – a super-norm.[65] It is almost impossible to dispute that the prohibition is now, and indeed has for some time been, a rule of customary international law. Whether it is a *jus cogens* rule is far less clear: "[w]hile most scholars would tend to agree that the juvenile death penalty is... established [in custom], few would agree that it is peremptory."[66] The test is whether the international community of States as a whole has "accepted and recognised" not merely that there is a customary prohibition on the juvenile death penalty, but that this prohibition is peremptory. It seems highly unlikely that this degree of consensus has occurred in practice.

---

64 See, for example, the United Nations Sub-Commission on the Promotion and Protection of Human Rights resolution 2000/17, 26th mtg., 17 August 2000.

65 See, for example, Curtis A. Bradley, "The Juvenile Death Penalty," *Duke Law Journal* 52, 3 (2002): 485, 537–539; Ochoa, *supra* note 40, 166 n.40; Quince, *supra* note 3, 75; and David Weissbrodt, "Execution of Juvenile Offenders by the United States Violates International Human Rights Law," *American University Journal of International Law and Policy* 3, 2 (1988): 339, 369–371.

66 Loschin, *supra* note 3, 169.

It was laudable of the IACHR to seek to block the United States' attempt to avoid compliance with a crucial norm of international human rights law through its persistent objection. In so doing, however, the Commission chose to elevate an almost certainly *non*-peremptory human rights norm to avowed peremptory status. This had the immediate legal effect of scuppering the United States' use of the persistent objector rule ("immediate" in the sense that this took a further three years), but it also has the disturbing secondary effect of undermining the very notion of *jus cogens*, by moving it into the realm of pure subjective naturalism.

The IACHR's approach is particularly unfortunate because a simpler, albeit rather more prosaic, solution was available. While there was certainly a pattern of objection on the part of the United States that would *prima facie* support its persistent objector claim,[67] in fact the United States' objections to the customary prohibition of the juvenile death penalty were insufficiently *consistent* for it to be considered an exempt persistent objector in the first place.[68] This was noted by the IACHR itself in *Domingues*:

> [T]he United States...rather than persistently objecting to the standard, has in several significant respects recognized the propriety of this norm by, for example, prescribing the age of 18 as the federal standard for the application of capital punishment and by ratifying the Fourth Geneva Convention without reservation to this standard.[69]

Ultimately, though, the IACHR saw this as something of an aside, given that its finding of *jus cogens* had already, for the Commission at least, "washed away" the American exemption.

---

67 Bradley provides *prima facie* evidence of the United States' persistent objection to an emerging customary international law norm on juvenile executions, with its objections starting well before any possible norm could have crystallised. See Bradley, *supra* note 65, particularly at 492–500.

68 The inconsistent practice of the United States in this regard was set out in significant detail in *Commonwealth of Pennsylvania v. Hector Huertas*, Motion to Preclude the Commonwealth from Seeking the Death Penalty Against a Juvenile and Consolidated Memorandum of Law, 2002 CP 0009–0941, CTD, 25–26. See also Dinah Shelton, "Application of Death Penalty on Juveniles in the US," *Human Rights Law Journal* 8 (1987): 355, 359; and Weissbrodt, *supra* note 65, 368, particularly n.158. Indeed, even some who have advocated the view that the United States should be exempt from the customary international law prohibition on juvenile executions have accepted that its practice was not always entirely consistent in this regard, see Bradley, *supra* note 65, 493.

69 *Domingues*, *supra* note 6, ¶ 85.

The credibility of the *Domingues* decision would have been significantly increased had the IACHR simply based its ultimate finding on the fact that United States had not been a sufficiently consistent objector. The bright lights of *jus cogens* were too big a draw, however. The finding of peremptory status on the part of the IACHR may actually have done more harm than good to the ability of human rights law to defend itself against persistent objection, playing into the hands of those who attack *jus cogens* as an "eye of the beholder" norm popularity contest.

6 A Teflon Coating for All Human Rights?

An alternative approach to dubious unilateral findings of peremptory status, similarly premised upon a moral absolutist and universalist view of human rights, is the claim that *all* human rights norms – be they peremptory or non-peremptory – are inherently immune from persistent objection.[70] Those taking this view accept that not all human rights provisions are peremptory, but argue that it is (or in some, rather more *lex ferenda* versions of this approach, should be) impossible to persistently object to them, nonetheless. The most notable exponent of this position is Holning Lau, who argued in 2005 that:

> The human rights regime's universality assumption is at odds with the effects of the persistent objector doctrine. By allowing individual States to exempt themselves from international human rights law, the human rights regime's universalist nature is necessarily compromised.[71]

A decade earlier, that famous champion of universal human rights, Louis Henkin, took the same view – albeit rather more bluntly: "the 'persistent objector' principle does not apply."[72]

The main challenge that has been raised to this idea of human rights being intrinsically exempt from persistent objection is the notion of State *consent* to international law-making. The persistent objector rule is supposed to preserve the voluntarist underpinnings of international law, and "[t]o abandon customary international law's strong positivist intellectual roots in favour of a new

70 See scholars listed in *supra* note 3.

71 Lau, *supra* note 3, generally, but quoted at 501.

72 Henkin, *supra* note 3, 38.

naturalism (whether expressed in the idiom of the 'rationality' or 'humanity' of favoured norms), would...be folly."[73]

Lau and Quince defend the theory that human rights are immune from persistent objection against this "negation of consent" argument by asserting that there is an element of "original consent" underpinning the international human rights law regime. In other words, they argue that by participating in the regime (for example, by signing and voting to adopt the Universal Declaration of Human Rights, or by ratifying the International Covenant on Civil and Political Rights), a State consents to the universal and intransgressible nature of *all* human rights law: thus meaning that consent in relation to any particular human rights norm has already been established.[74]

Customary international law theory is plagued with fictitious or overstated notions of consent,[75] but – even in that milieu – the idea of ultimate original consent to all human rights now and forever (including consent to human rights not yet formed or even *conceived of*) seems really rather a stretch. If this had any basis in truth, not only would reservations to human rights treaties be entirely and uncontroversially impermissible in all circumstances, but States would be formally required to become party to any new human rights convention as soon as it became open for signature: they would already have given their consent to be bound by the treaty. Quite simply, the original consent theory is nonsense.

Having said this, we know that universal consent is not required for the formation of *jus cogens* norms, but that they nonetheless cannot be persistently objected to. The commonly advanced rationale for prohibiting persistent objection to *jus cogens* is based on the moral universalism of peremptory norms and, given that the same trait is – many argue – inherent in all international human rights too, "ordinary" human rights should also be exempt from exemption. In other words, if the "consent issue" can be overcome regarding *jus cogens* norms because of the power of moral imperative, why cannot the same be true for human rights *in toto*? The fiction of the original consent theory is actually unnecessary, because true consent is itself a fiction in the context of customary international law. Why should there be a distinction here between *jus cogens* and other "moral" norms: why would we, it might be asked,

73 David Bederman, "Acquiescence, Objection and the Death of Customary International Law," *Duke Journal of Comparative and International Law* 21, 1 (2010): 31, 44.

74 Lau, *supra* note 3, 503–505; and Quince, *supra* note 3, 74 and 76.

75 See Jörg Kammerhofer, "Uncertainty in the Formal Sources of International Law: Customary International Law and Some of its Problems," *European Journal of International Law* 15, 3 (2004): 523, 533.

"limit unilateral exit for matters of slavery and piracy (which are generally agreed to be *jus cogens* norms) but not for child labor…?"[76]

Normatively, a difference may perhaps be found in the onerous positivist test for *jus cogens* norms to form. Such rules may not require universal acceptance, but they do require *near*-universal acceptance. That is why there are so few of them. Adhering to the positivist requirements of VCLT Article 53 helps keep the concept of *jus cogens* in touch with reality, and thus actually *protects* and *validates* its value-based agenda. *Jus cogens* norms are, or at least should be, natural law rules under careful positivist guard. Customary international human rights standards, in contrast, do not require the same high level of State acceptance and recognition, but just the usual basic preponderance of practice and *opinio juris* as for any custom. *Jus cogens* and other human rights norms can be distinguished precisely because peremptory norms are inherently different: they are, after all, peremptory.

Ultimately, though, the answer to the distinction between peremptory norms (which cannot be persistently objected to) and other human rights norms (which can) lies not in legal theory but in legal practice. No State has successfully maintained persistent objection in relation to a peremptory norm, whereas many *have* – and continue to – in relation to non-peremptory human rights norms.[77]

This is perhaps best illustrated by another claim of exempt persistent objector status made by the United States in the context of international adjudicative

---

76 Ochoa, *supra* note 40, 166 (a point made specifically in the context of discussing the proposal for allowing "subsequent objection" in Curtis A. Bradley and Mitu Gulati, "Withdrawing from International Custom," (2010) 120 *Yale Law Journal* 120, 2 (2010): 202). See also Henkin, *supra* note 3, at 38.

77 There are a number of successful persistent objector States to human rights norms. See, for example, the position of the United States in relation to the customary international law 'right to food'. The Special Rapporteur of the Commission on Human Rights on the Right to Food, in 2005, identified the United States as an exempt persistent objector state (*The Right to Food,* note by the Secretary-General, transmitting the interim report of the Special Rapporteur of the Commission on Human Rights on the right to food in accordance with General Assembly resolution 59/202, U.N. Doc. A/60/350, 23 footnote 44). This assertion by the Special Rapporteur then went unremarked upon by other UN member states, suggesting a general acceptance of the United States' exempt status, irrespective of the norm in question being one of international human rights law. Another example is China's reservation to Article 22(1) the Convention on the Rights of the Child (which has allowed Hong Kong scope to derogate from the rights of asylum seekers or refugee minors contained therein), as part of a pattern of persistent objection to the customary international law norm of *non-refoulement* (*C* et al. *v. Director of Immigration and Secretary for Security*, 2008, Hong Kong Special Administrative Region, CoA, CACV 132-137/2008: 187 and 197–198).

proceedings, specifically in the *Grand River* arbitration, considered by a tribunal under NAFTA Chapter 11.[78] The relevant claim was first put forward by the United States in 2008, but was maintained throughout proceedings until the Tribunal's final award in 2011 and, indeed, *beyond*.

The *Grand River* dispute related to the attempt by various federal states within the United States to reach a settlement with tobacco manufacturers for health-care costs stemming from smoking. The arbitration was instigated by a Canadian-registered tobacco company, Grand River (and some of its shareholders), which claimed that, for various reasons, this constituted discriminatory practice that breached a number of NAFTA provisions.[79] The salient aspect of the dispute for our purposes related to the claimants' contention that the practice of the United States was in breach of certain customary rights of indigenous investors, given the fact that many of the shareholders and employees of the Grand River company were Native American. This contention included what the claimants saw as an "obligation to pro-actively consult with [indigenous persons] prior to taking legislative action that will have a substantial impact upon them."[80] It was argued that that this customary human rights law obligation – which has its roots in Articles 19 and 38 of the United Nations Declaration on the Rights of Indigenous Peoples 2007[81] – had thus been breached by the United States.[82] It is worth noting that this obligation is indisputably a *non*-peremptory human rights norm of customary international law.

The United States provided a dual response: its primary argument was that there was insufficient State practice and *opinio juris* to find that there was a customary international law obligation to consult indigenous peoples in relation to investment.[83] As a secondary argument, however, the United States invoked the persistent objector exception:

---

78 *Grand River*, final award, *supra* note 7.

79 See *Grand River Enterprises Six Nations Ltd* et al. *v. Government of the United States of America*, notice of arbitration, 2004, UNCITL/NAFTA, http://naftaclaims.com/Disputes/USA/GrandRiver/GrandRiverNoticeOfArbitration.pdf, in particular, ¶¶ 61–80.

80 *Grand River*, claimants' memorial, merits phase, 2008, UNCITL/NAFTA, http://www.naftalaw.org/Disputes/USA/GrandRiver/GRE-USA-Merits-Memorial-R.pdf, particularly ¶¶ 184–192 and 213–217, quoted at ¶ 192.

81 United Nations Declaration on the Rights of Indigenous Peoples, U.N. Doc. A/RES/61/295 (13 Sept. 2007).

82 *Grand River*, claimants' memorial, *supra* note 80, ¶¶ 213–217. The claimants were admittedly not entirely unequivocal in regards to this claim, see *ibid.*, ¶¶ 180 and 188.

83 *Grand River*, counter memorial of the respondent, merits phase, 2008, UNCITL/NAFTA, http://www.naftalaw.org/Disputes/USA/GrandRiver/GRE-USA-Merits-Counter-Memorial-R.pdf: 127–129.

> [T]he United States clearly and consistently has articulated its view that...[the requirement of] consultation prior to the adoption of legislation does not reflect customary international law...[therefore] the United States cannot be bound by any consultation requirements.[84]

Certainly, the United States had maintained – and continues to maintain – a notable degree of dissent with regard to a number of "indigenous rights" that may be seen as binding under customary international law, of which the obligation in question here regarding indigenous consultation is just one.[85] Under the usual criteria for persistent objection – persistence and timeliness – it would seem that the United States can be correctly identified as an exempt "persistent objector."

The 2011 final award in the *Grand River* arbitration thus amounted to the first opportunity, in an adjudicative context, to test the assertion that human rights norms are inherently insulated from persistent objection, even when they are non-peremptory. The Tribunal first strongly implied that there was indeed a human right to indigenous consultation under customary international law.[86] However, the Tribunal then failed to pronounce on the claim of the United States that it was a persistent objector. Indeed, it did not even *take note* of this claim.

To an extent, "blame" for this should not be directed at the *Grand River* NAFTA Tribunal because it concluded that, to the extent that there was a customary rule of indigenous consultation, this did not to apply to individual investors and so its scope did not extend to the claimants.[87] In other words, the United States' possible persistent objection was not material to the Tribunal's decision, meaning that any finding on this issue would have been pure *dictum*. However, if human rights are as intrinsically and fundamentally immune from persistent objection as some would have us believe, one might expect that the Tribunal would have at least *acknowledged* this claim by the United States,

---

84 *Ibid.*, 128–129, references omitted.

85 See generally, Report of the Special Rapporteur on the Rights of Indigenous Peoples: The Situation of Indigenous Peoples in the United States of America, U.N. Doc. A/HRC/21/47/Add.1 (30 Aug. 2012). The United States is not a Party to the International Labour Organisation Convention concerning Indigenous and Tribal Peoples in Independent Countries (No. 169), Geneva, 27 Jun. 1969, and was one of only four States to vote against the General Assembly's adoption of the Declaration on the Rights of Indigenous Peoples, *supra* note 81 (143 States voting in favour).

86 See *Grand River*, final award, *supra* note 7, particularly at ¶ 213.

87 *Ibid.*

especially having seemingly indicated that the customary human right in question had indeed crystallised into law.

It is telling that the Tribunal stayed silent on this point, and is perhaps even more telling that the United States felt entirely comfortable asserting persistent objector status to a non-peremptory human rights norm throughout the proceedings. It is also of note there has been almost no academic commentary on the merits of the United States' persistent objector claim in the *Grand River* dispute,[88] and there has been no assertion made in the literature that the United States was (or even *should have been*) barred from maintaining its exempt status on the basis of a blanket immunity for all customary international human rights law.

The IACHR's dubious finding of peremptory status for the prohibition of the juvenile death penalty in both *Roach and Pinkerton* and *Domingues* also perhaps adds to the story here. That the Commission was willing to stretch credulity in this regard further indicates that that there is no additional exemption from the effects of the persistent objector rule for human rights norms *per se*. If, as some argue, all human rights norms possess some inherent form of persistent objector Teflon, then the IACHR would not have needed to concern itself with whether the prohibition of the juvenile death penalty was peremptory: the prohibition is indisputably a human rights norm, and so would have been universally binding even on dissenters. That the IACHR did not even consider this possibility is telling in itself.

Ultimately, there is no basis in practice for the claim that persistent objection is unavailing in relation to "ordinary" human rights law norms. Indeed, *Grand River* shows us that persistent objection to human rights norms is not only possible, but *unremarkable* in the cut and thrust reality of international legal interaction.

7 Conclusion

Where does this leave us? We know that persistent objection is unavailing in relation to *jus cogens* human rights norms, as the impossibility of exemption from the prohibition of apartheid demonstrates. However, the fact that the list of peremptory human rights is rather short means that this solution will rarely be available. This has led those looking to maximise the protections of human

88 Although see Luke Eric Peterson, "Persistent Objector Argument also at Issue in NAFTA Case," 14 July 2009, http://kluwerarbitrationblog.com/blog/2009/07/14/persistent-objector-argument-also-at-issue-in-nafta-case.

rights law and ensure its universal applicability down two different, but equally dangerous, paths: credibility-defying assertions of peremptory status for certain human rights norms, or unfounded claims as to the inapplicability of persistent objection to human rights law as a whole. Either approach involves an act of placing good intention-shaped paving stones on a road, and it is clear where that road leads. Our third option, of course, is to stoically accept that States can, and sometimes will, exempt themselves from customary international human rights norms.

This range of unpleasant choices mirrors the concern expressed by David Kennedy over what he has termed the "two related dangers of human rights work" – idolatry and pragmatism.[89] The idealism of idolatry manifests itself, for us, in difficult to maintain assertions of peremptory status or – worse still – insistence that any and all human rights are immune from persistent objection when this is clearly not the case in practice. Such blind faith damages rather than protects human rights law:

> [T]o hold the State to [a human rights] norm that is not peremptory, and to which the State has openly, consistently objected...could ultimately do more harm than good...[because] refusing to allow a State to opt out of a norm while the norm is still emerging could ultimately delay the implementation of certain human rights, rather than promote their cause.[90]

Conversely, pragmatism here inevitably leads to a general acceptance of the opposability of persistent objection to human rights, meaning possible undesirable gaps in the applicability of basic standards of protection.

In the interests of trying to avoid ending this chapter on too much of a low note, then, it is worth remembering that this issue – the conflict between human rights and the persistent objector rule – is easily overstated. *Jus cogens* human rights norms are protected, as we know, but so too are any treaty-based human rights to which the State has consented (including customary norms reflected in conventional instruments to which it is party). Rather obviously, "a State cannot claim persistent objector status to many basic or fundamental rights, as these are either peremptory or covered by treaty."[91]

---

89 David Kennedy, "The Human Rights Regime: Still Part of the Problem?," in *Examining Critical Perspectives on Human Rights*, edited by Rob Dickinson *et al.* (Cambridge: Cambridge University Press, 2012), 19, generally, but quoted at 22.

90 Loschin, *supra* note 3, 166–168.

91 *Ibid.*, 167.

It is also worth noting that the criteria for persistent objection are quite severe. Given that the rule necessarily represents an exception – and exceptions should be interpreted narrowly – this is no surprise.[92] A significant degree of persistence, unequivocalness and consistency of objection is required for a State to gain exemption by virtue of the rule. Plus, of course, objection must occur before the rule being objected to has crystallised as customary international law; meaning that unless objection has previously (persistently) occurred, all established human rights are already safe.

Moreover, while it is difficult to argue that there exists a *legal* rule that formally insulates human rights norms from persistent objection, the political pressure associated with human rights standards means that is practically untenable for most States to maintain exemption from them. There exists a special "rhetorical power" not just to the concept of *jus cogens*, but to human rights norms *per se*. The "influence of considerations of morality and desirability" makes persistent objection to human rights norms harder in fact, even if perhaps not in law.[93]

An excellent example of the difficulties for even developed States in maintaining objection to human rights norms is the position of Australia with regard to a number of customary international law rights of indigenous peoples.[94] Australia was, until 2009, undoubtedly a persistent objector to certain legal norms relating to indigenous rights,[95] which were almost certainly *not* norms of *jus cogens*. Nonetheless, given the fundamental nature of the human rights norms in question, increasing political pressure ultimately led to a reversal of the Australian position.[96] In other words, Australia found its persistent

92 Gideon Boas, *Public International Law: Contemporary Principles and Perspectives* (Cheltenham: Edward Elgar, 2012), 94–95.

93 Guldahl, *supra* note 41, 84.

94 There has been increasing agreement, particularly since the 1990s, that a number of "new" indigenous rights have attained the status of customary international law. See S. James Anaya, *Indigenous Peoples in International Law* (2nd ed., Oxford University Press: Oxford, 1996), 61–72.

95 See "Indigenous Rights Outlined by UN," BBC News, 13 Sept. 2007, http://news.bbc.co.uk/1/hi/in_depth/6993776.stm. Moreover, like the United States, Australia is not a Party to the ILO Convention No. 169, *supra* note 85, and was one of the four States to vote against the Declaration on the Rights of Indigenous Peoples, *supra* note 81.

96 In 2009, Australia explicitly endorsed the 2007 Declaration on the Rights of Indigenous Peoples, and apparently reversed its position on the customary status of a number of provisions contained within it. See "Experts Hail Australia's Backing of UN Declaration of Indigenous Peoples' Rights," United Nations News Centre, 3 Apr. 2009, http://www.un.org/apps/news/story.asp?NewsID=30382.

objector status overruled *de facto*, even though this was not the case *de jure* (because there was no conflict with a peremptory norm). Few States can sustain a game of tug-of-war against the pull of widely accepted human rights standards.

It is admittedly worth remembering – as is the case with so much in the international legal system – the important influence of power in this context. It is no coincidence that the only State to have asserted persistent objector status in international adjudicative proceedings is the world's sole superpower. Inevitably, powerful States will be able to maintain a stance of dissent more easily than others,[97] even in the face of human rights norms (and possibly, for a time at least, as shown by the juvenile death penalty example, in respect of *jus cogens* norms). This is a matter of fact, if not of law.[98] Yet the more positive side of this coin is that most States will *not* have the political clout to object to human rights norms. Even the United States will be unable to sustain objection against *jus cogens* norms (at least for long), and it is clear that "ordinary" human rights too have significant political pull (because of their significant *moral* pull), meaning that all States will struggle to stand apart indefinitely.

Therefore, Lau's conclusion, noted previously, that "the large majority of human rights laws [are] susceptible to the persistent objector doctrine"[99] is actually something of an overstatement. For those few States that are swimming against the current of human rights standards by way of persistent objection, there is nothing to stop political pressure from being applied on them (even after the norm in question has formed), to try to influence a renunciation of their isolationist position.[100] Indeed, political pressure *should* be placed on such States to conform, *especially* on powerful States. The law as it stands still currently allows for persistent objection to non-peremptory customary international human rights standards. But that doesn't mean that we have to like it.

97 Tasioulas, *supra* note 36, 313; and Guldahl, *supra* note 41, 84.

98 Bradley, *supra* note 65, 517.

99 Lau, *supra* note 3, at 495.

100 Loschin, *supra* note 3, 168.

CHAPTER 9

The Role of Truth Commissions in Adjudicating Human Rights Violations

Alison Bisset

1 Introduction

In 1998, Ghandhi remarked that the establishment of an international human rights court by the international community "would represent an enormous achievement."[1] Interestingly, that same year, a significant proportion of the international community finalised the Rome Statute of the International Criminal Court.[2] A permanent international criminal court was thereby created, which, while by no means concerned with all international human rights violations, has jurisdiction over the most serious international crimes of genocide, crimes against humanity and war crimes.[3] Although a different model to that of the court considered by Ghandhi,[4] the establishment of the International Criminal Court (ICC) undoubtedly represents a significant step forward in international efforts to provide accountability for the worst human rights violations. However, its creation appears to have had a stifling impact on the use of another adjudicatory mechanism: the truth commission.

Truth commissions have long been recognised as playing an important role in the adjudication of human rights violations in transitional States. Along with trials, reparations and justice reforms, they comprise the four principal

1 P.R. Ghandhi, *The Human Rights Committee and the Right of Individual Communication: Law and Practice* (Aldershot: Ashgate Publishing Co: 1998), 409.

2 Rome Statute of the International Criminal Court, A/Conf.183/9, 17 July 1998, (1998) 37 *International Legal Materials* 1002.

3 *Ibid.*, art. 5. Under Article 15(3) *ter* the ICC will exercise jurisdiction over the crime of aggression, subject to a decision by the States parties after 1 January 2017. ICC, Assembly of State Parties, Resolution RC/Res.6, The Crime of Aggression, adopted at the 13th plenary meeting on 11 June 2010.

4 The court considered by Ghandhi is concerned with adjudicating the compliance of States with their obligations under international human rights law. See Ghandhi, *supra* note 1, 408–409. The ICC, on the other hand, is concerned with assigning individual criminal responsibility for international human rights crimes.

 | DOI 10.1163/9789004261181_011

mechanisms of transitional justice and, in different ways, contribute to the transitional justice objectives of truth, justice, reparation and non-repetition.[5] Indeed, truth commissions are the most commonly used transitional justice mechanism, with over thirty having been established since the early 1970s.[6] Their worth lies not only in their clarification of the truth surrounding the commission of past violations, but in their focus on victims, contribution to the establishment of a rule of law culture and compilation of recommendations for reform.[7] They may have begun life as weak substitutes for criminal justice. However, more recent practice, in East Timor and Sierra Leone particularly, suggests that trials and truth commissions have different benefits to bring to transitional States and ought to be used together, rather than as alternatives.

Yet as transitional justice has entered into a new era under the ICC, the truth commission appears to be falling from favour. Of the eight situations currently being investigated or prosecuted by the Court, only a few have seen the establishment of truth commissions to adjudicate past violations.[8] The present chapter chapter examines this development and asks whether the current preoccupation with criminal justice for past human rights violations risks marginalising the valuable role that other transitional justice mechanisms can play. It will begin with an evaluation of the benefits delivered by trials and truth commissions in the adjudication of past violations, thereby demonstrating the desirability of their dual use. The chapter will then critically contrast pre and post ICC practice in order to demonstrate the decline in truth commission establishment following the creation of the ICC and consider the reasons for this decrease. It will be argued that the ICC era has, to date, been marked by a return to the belief that international criminal trials hold a position of unparalleled importance in the adjudication of human rights violations, with the

5 See Louis Joinet, *Set of Principles for the Protection and Promotion of Human Rights Through Action to Combat Impunity*, U.N. Doc. E/CN.4/Sub.2/1997/20/Rev.1 (1997) [Joinet Principles]; updated by Dianne Orentlicher, *Updated Set of Principles for the Protection and Promotion of Human Rights Through Action to Combat Impunity*, U.N. Doc. E/CN.4/2005/102.Add.1 (2005) [Updated Principles]; and *Basic Principles and Guidelines on the Right to a Remedy and Reparation for Victims of Violations of International Human Rights and Humanitarian Law* annexed to General Assembly Res. A/C.3/60/L.24 [Bassiouni Principles].

6 Generally, it is agreed that truth commissions have been established in the following States: Bolivia, Argentina, Uganda, Nepal, Chile, Chad, El Salvador, Germany, Sri Lanka, Haiti, South Africa, Ecuador, Guatemala, Nigeria, Uruguay, South Korea, Peru, Panama, Serbia and Montenegro, East Timor, Sierra Leone, Ghana, Democratic Republic of Congo, Paraguay, Morocco, Liberia, Kenya, Côte d'Ivoire, Togo and Mali.

7 See Section 2, *infra*.

8 See Section 3, *infra*.

result that transitional States may be denied the benefits brought by other adjudicatory mechanisms.

2 The Benefits of Trials and Truth Commissions

Trials and truth commissions fulfil different adjudicatory roles within transitional justice practice. The purpose of trials is, of course, to adjudicate particular crimes, making findings on the criminal culpability of individuals. They serve to deliver criminal justice for victims and enable States to fulfil their obligation to investigate and punish perpetrators.[9] Truth commissions, in contrast, investigate and clarify the nature and extent of past violations and are concerned with assigning institutional responsibility for their commission. Their establishment enables States to discharge their duty to investigate and provide victims, their families and the wider society with the right to know or the right to truth.[10] Yet in fulfilling their primary aims, it is believed that trials and truth commissions make distinct but complementary and overlapping contributions to the restoration of transitional States. Their impact is more complex and nuanced than simple delivery of truth and justice.

Transitional justice literature indicates that both trials and truth commissions play important roles in truth establishment. This is significant, as clarification of the truth about past events is considered essential in order for transitional societies to come to terms with their pasts, prevent recurrences of atrocities, and move forward to a reconciled future.[11] Trials deliver truth in specific cases, identifying the circumstances of particular crimes and those responsible for their commission. Thus, the contribution of trials lies in the establishment of micro truth, as they engage in close scrutiny of certain cases and focus on establishing individual culpability. In contrast, truth commissions work to provide an overarching view of past violations. They contribute

9 See the Joinet, Orentlicher and Bassiouni Principles, *supra* note 5.

10 UN Commission on Human Rights, *Study on the Right to Truth, Report of the Office of the United Nations High Commissioner for Human Rights*, 8 February 2006, U.N. Doc. E/CN.4/2006/91.

11 Mark Imbleau, "Initial Truth Establishment by Transitional Bodies and the Fight Against Denial," *Criminal Law Forum* 15 (2004): 159; Luc Huyse, "Dealing with the Past and Imagining the Future," in *Peacebuilding: A Field Guide*, edited by Luc Reychler and Thania Paffenholz (Boulder: Lynne Rienner Publishers, 2002), 327; and Tristan Anne Borer, "Truth Telling as a Peace Building Activity," in *Telling the Truths: Truth Telling and Peace Building in Post-Conflict Societies*, edited by Tristan Anne Borer (Notre Dame: University of Notre Dame Press, 2006), 1, 17–18.

to the establishment of macro truth, which encompasses the structural causes of past violations, the identification of broad patterns of violence and the intellectual authors of it.[12]

As indicated in the UN Study on the Right to Truth, there is an individual and societal dimension to the right to truth.[13] While individual victims and their relatives are likely to desire clarification of the details pertaining to particular cases, society as a whole is likely to focus upon the broader picture of the nature of the violations committed and the institutional responsibility for them. This is not to suggest that individuals have no interest in macro truths or society no interest in the micro truth of individual cases. There is a need for both micro and macro truth if the rights of victims and society are to be fulfilled and, consequently, there is a role for both truth commissions and trials. They have distinct but complementary contributions to make to truth establishment.

Likewise, both bodies are understood to contribute to the healing of victims through the provision of different forms of justice. Trials deliver the criminal justice that studies show the majority of victims desire.[14] As non-judicial bodies, truth commissions cannot meet the demands of victims for retributive, criminal justice. Yet because they do not operate under the procedural constraints of criminal trials, which require testimony from only a relatively small number of victims and exclude much of their account under exclusionary rules, truth commissions can offer victims a central role. Victim testimony is of primary importance for truth commissions as they build an overall picture of the abuses of the past.[15] Truth commissions can provide victims with a platform on which they can bring their experiences to the awareness of the public and, as formally established institutions, provide official acknowledgement of their suffering[16] Without overlooking the complexity and subjectivity of the

12 On micro and macro truth establishment, see Audrey R. Chapman "Truth Finding in the Transitional Justice Process," in *Assessing the Impact of Transitional Justice: Challenges for Empirical Research*, edited by Hugo Van der Merwe, Victoria Baxter and Audrey R. Chapman (Washington D.C.: United States Institute of Peace Press, 2009), 91.

13 UN Commission on Human Rights, *Study on the Right to Truth*, ¶ 58–60.

14 Ernesto Kiza *et al.*, *Victims of War: An Empirical Study on War-Victimization and Victims' Attitudes Towards Addressing Atrocities*, (Hamburg: Hamburger Edition Online, 2006), 97, http://www.his-online.de.

15 Priscilla B. Hayner, *Unspeakable Truths: Facing the Challenge of Truth Commissions*, (New York: Routledge, 2001), 28.

16 Martha Minow, *From Vengeance to Forgiveness: Facing History after Genocide and Mass Violence*, (Boston: Beacon Press, 1998), 58.

healing process,[17] it seems that together, truth commissions and trials can make a contribution in different ways to the overall process.

The work of both bodies can also be used to inform the content of reparations programmes and packages. Truth commissions have often used the recommendations element of their mandates to suggest the form that reparations should take and who should receive them, based upon their overview of past violations and those most affected.[18] Equally, the findings of trials can also be utilised to determine who should be eligible for reparations.

Finally, the work of trials and truth commissions can contribute to the longer-term objectives of reform and non-repetition. The very creation of both mechanisms is indicative of a break with the past, an acknowledgement that past abuses were wrong and an attempt to re-establish the orderly functioning of the State.[19] In addition, transitional States are believed to benefit from the assignation of responsibility that both produce. The individualisation of responsibility brought about through trials is believed to ease collective guilt and offer an avenue away from cycles of blame, revenge and recrimination. Trials are also said to deter violations, thereby maximising the possibilities for non-repetition of abuses.[20] While truth commissions are not concerned with individualising guilt, their focus on assigning institutional responsibility is considered equally important. Their assignation of institutional responsibility and consequent recommendations for reform of the institutions implicated is seen as a means of reducing the likelihood of violations being committed in the future.[21]

Trials and truth commissions therefore play complementary and mutually reinforcing roles within the transitional justice framework. Neither can deliver

17 Ruth Picker, *Victims Perspectives about the Human Rights Violations Hearings*, (Johannesburg: Centre for the Study of Violence and Reconciliation, 2005).

18 For an overview of the reparations recommendations made by truth commissions, see Priscilla B. Hayner, *Unspeakable Truths: Transitional Justice and the Challenge of Truth Commissions*, (2nd ed., New York and London: Routledge, 2011), Appendix 2, Chart 5. Some commissions, such as that in Morocco, have even been tasked with administering reparations programmes. See Mark Freeman, *Truth Commissions and Procedural Fairness* (Cambridge: Cambridge University Press, 2006), 35.

19 Ruti Teitel, *Transitional Justice* (Oxford: Oxford University Press, 2000), 28–30.

20 Minow, *supra* note 16, 40; Karl Jaspers, *The Question of German Guilt* (transl. E.B. Ashton), (New York: Dial Press, 1947), 39–41; and Dinka Corkalo *et al.*, "Neighbours Again? Intercommunity Relations after Ethnic Cleansing," in *My Neighbor, My Enemy: Justice and Community in the Aftermath of Mass Atrocity*, edited by Eric Stover and Harvey M. Weinstein (Cambridge: Cambridge University Press, 2004), 143–148.

21 Tricia D. Olsen *et al.*, "When Truth Commissions Improve Human Rights," *International Journal of Transitional Justice* 4 (2010): 457.

the benefits brought by the other and together they can make a significant contribution to the restoration of transitional States.

3 The Use of Trials and Truth Commissions

Although transitional justice discourse suggests important roles for both trials and truth commissions within transitional contexts, they have not always been used together, as complements. Truth commissions emerged as a means of adjudicating past violations in the early 1980s, as a number of States undertook the transition from authoritarian regime to democratic rule, often in the aftermath of violent internal conflicts. As these regimes fell, or voluntarily relinquished power, evidence of the systematic human rights violations committed under their rule came to light. Despite calls for criminal justice, fragile political settlements,[22] weak judicial systems[23] and the existence of national amnesty laws[24] precluded prosecutions in many States.

---

22 On the negotiated political settlement in South Africa, see Alex Boraine, "Truth and Reconciliation in South Africa: The Third Way," in *Truth v. Justice: The Morality of Truth Commissions*, edited by Robert I. Rotberg and Dennis Thompson (Princeton: Princeton University Press, 2000), 141–143; and Marianne Guela, "South Africa's Truth and Reconciliation Commission as an Alternate Means of Addressing Transitional Government Conflicts in a Divided Society," *Boston University International Law Journal* 18 (2000): 57. On the difficulties that faced the Chilean government following the overthrow of the Pinochet regime, see Jorge S. Correa, "Dealing with Past Human Rights Violations: The Chilean Case After Dictatorship," *Notre Dame Law Review* 67 (1992): 1455.

23 On the impediments to justice created by the judicial systems in El Salvador and Guatemala, see Mark Vasallo, "Truth and Reconciliation Commissions: General Considerations and a Critical Comparison of the Commissions of Chile and El Salvador," *University of Miami Inter-American Law Review* 33 (2002): 153, 159–160; Thomas Buergenthal, "The United Nations Truth Commission for El Salvador," *Vanderbilt Journal of Transnational Law* 27 (1994): 497, 534; Terry L. Karl, "El Salvador's Negotiated Revolution," *Foreign Affairs* 71 (1992): 147; and Andrew N. Keller, "To Name or Not to Name? The Commission for Historical Clarification in Guatemala, Its Mandate and the Decision not to Identify Individual Perpetrators," *Florida Journal of International Law* 13 (2001): 289, 294.

24 For discussion of the South American amnesty laws, see Jo Pasqualucci, "The Truth and Nothing But the Truth: Truth Commissions, Impunity and the Inter-American Human Rights System," *Boston University International Law Journal* 12 (1994): 321; and Naomi Roht-Arriaza, "Truth Commissions and Amnesties in Latin America: The Second Generation," *American Society of International Law and Proceedings* 92 (1998): 313.

As a concession that provided a means of investigating and acknowledging the past, while avoiding the controversy of pursuing individual criminal accountability, some States established truth commissions. Truth commissions were, therefore, created out of compromise, a conception that led critics to label them as weak, surrogates for justice and to accusations that they fostered a culture of impunity.[25] They have, however, garnered significant support since their beginnings as "flawed compromises," aided in no small part by South Africa's world-renowned Truth and Reconciliation Commission. A more sophisticated understanding of what they can contribute to transitional States has developed and, since the 1990s, their establishment has been considered in virtually every transitional context.[26] Post South Africa, truth commissions have been routinely equipped with broad mandates, large staffs and enhanced budgets. They have been bestowed with investigatory powers such as subpoena, search and seizure and witness protection, as well as the capabilities to conduct questioning under oath, to hold public hearings[27] and to grant confidentiality to those who offer testimony.[28] These attributes enable them to operate efficiently and to deliver the most meaningful results in terms of truth recovery, victim participation and recommendation formulation.[29]

Prosecution has undergone similar evolution. Particularly since the early 1990s, the commission of the most serious human rights violations has been accompanied by demands for their criminal prosecution. In situations where

---

25 Jonathan D. Tepperman, "Truth and Consequences," *Foreign Affairs* 81 (2002): 131.

26 Freeman, *supra* note 18, 11.

27 For example, the commissions of Nigeria (1999), Grenada (2001), East Timor (2001), Ghana (2002), Sierra Leone (2002), DRC (2004) and Liberia (2005) were all endowed with powers of subpoena. The commissions of Nigeria (1999), East Timor (2001), Ghana (2002) and the DRC (2005) were given powers of search and seizure and the commissions of Nigeria (1999), Grenada (2001), Peru (2001), East Timor (2001), Ghana (2002), Sierra Leone (2002), Morocco (2004), Paraguay (2004), the DRC (2004) and Liberia (2005) possessed the power to conduct public hearings. See Freeman, *supra* note 18, Appendix 1, Table A.1: Truth Commissions and their Key Powers.

28 In some cases the truth commission's mandate has stipulated that proceedings be conducted on a confidential basis. See Agreement on the establishment of the Commission to clarify past human rights violations and acts of violence that have caused the Guatemalan Population to Suffer, Oslo, 23 June 1994; Supreme Decree No. 065-2001-PCM, art. 7 on the establishment of the Peruvian TRC and Mexico Peace Agreements, Mexico City, 27 April 1991, art. 7 on the establishment of the Commission on the Truth for El Salvador. Other commissions have had discretion to grant confidentiality. See Sierra Leone, Truth and Reconciliation Commission Act 2000, s.7(3); East Timor, UNTAET Regulation No. 2001/10, s. 44.2.

29 See Hayner, *supra* note 18, Appendix 2.

trials were once deemed unfeasible and impracticable, more recent practice has seen the establishment of international criminal tribunals,[30] the creation of hybrid courts[31] and prosecutions in domestic courts.[32] In 1998, international consensus that it was essential for the most serious human rights crimes to be prosecuted resulted in the creation of the ICC, taking transitional justice into a new era of accountability.

The new millenium also brought developments in the way that trials and truth commissions were used in transitional States. As the ICC Statute came into force in July 2002, the transitional justice programmes implemented in East Timor and Sierra Leone saw truth commissions established alongside prosecutorial institutions as a complement to criminal justice. This dual model seemed to stem directly from the lessons of the past. There had been truth without criminal accountability in much of Latin America and States such as Argentina, Chile and Peru continued to see demands for justice in the courts.[33]

---

30 The Security Council created international tribunals for the former Yugoslavia and Rwanda. See Security Council Resolution 827 (1993), U.N. Doc S/RES/827 (1993), 25 May 1993; Security Council Resolution 955 (1994), U.N. Doc. S/RES/955 (1994), 8 November 1994.

31 United Nations Transitional Administration in East Timor (UNTAET) Regulation 2000/15, UNTAET/REG/2000/15, 6 June 2000, created the Special Panels for Serious Crimes; Special Court Agreement (Ratification) Act 2002 created the Special Court for Sierra Leone. General Assembly Resolution A/Res/57/228B on the creation of the Extraordinary Chambers for Cambodia, 13 May 2003. Hybrid institutions have also been created in Kosovo and Bosnia and Herzegovina. See United Nations Mission in Kosovo (UNMIK), Regulation 2000/64, U.N. Doc. UNMIK/REG/2000/64, 15 December 2000 on the creation of the 64 Panels and Security Council in Security Council Resolution 1503 (2003), S/RES/1503 (2003), 28 August 2003 on the creation of the War Crimes Chamber within the state court of BiH.

32 Amnesty International, *Universal Jurisdiction: The Duty to Enact and Enforce Legislation*, AI Index IOR 53/004/2001, 1 September 2001, Chapter 2 – The Evolution of the Practice of Universal Jurisdiction. On European attempts to prosecute, see Axel Marschik, "The Politics of Prosecution: European National Approaches to War Crimes," in *The Law of War Crimes – National and International Approaches*, edited by Timothy L.H. McCormack and Gerry J. Simpson (The Hague, London and Boston:, Kluwer Law International, 1997), 65–99.

33 See Ricardo Gil Lavedra, "The Possibility of Criminal Justice: The Argentinean Experience," in *The Role of the Courts in Transitional Justice: Voices from Latin America and Spain*, edited by Jessica Almqvist and Carlos Esposito (Abingdon and New York: Routledge, 2012), 56–81; and Yvan Montoya Vivanco, "Responding to Human Rights Violations Committed During the Internal Armed Conflict in Peru: The Limits and Advances of Peruvian Criminal Justice," in Almqvist and Esposito, *ibid.*, 159–184.

Similarly, criminal justice through the vehicle of the International Criminal Tribunal for the former Yugoslavia (ICTY), accompanied by trials at the domestic level, had been delivered for the former Yugoslavia, but efforts to establish truth commissions to accompany the pursuit of criminal accountability failed.[34] Deep divisions along ethnic lines remain within former Yugoslav States, with a number of "contested truths" prevailing among different groups.[35] Experiences at the international criminal tribunals had also shown that national level initiatives that engender a sense of local ownership and enable affected population engagement are to be preferred, where possible, over geographically distant and inaccessible international institutions.[36] The Sierra Leonean and Timorese models therefore seemed indicative of a more nunaced approach, which acknowledged that a number of different mechanisms, grounded at the national level, was likely to be needed to respond to the complex and varied needs of transitional States.

Instead of giving rise to a new practice of employing trials and truth commissions as part of a multi-faceted transitional package, the Sierra Leone and East Timor models seem to have marked both the beginning and end of coordinated, dual use. While the pursuit, if not the attainment, of criminal justice has gained some momentum under the ICC, the truth commission appears to be falling from favour. In contrast with the twelve year period 1990–2002, which saw the creation of nineteen truth comissions, the twelve years following the

---

34 Neil J. Kritz and Jakob Finci, "A Truth and Reconciliation Commission in Bosnia and Herzegovina: An Idea Whose Time Has Come," *International Law Forum* 3 (2001): 50; Jelena Pejic, "The Yugoslav Truth and Reconciliation Commission: A Shaky Start," *Fordham International Law Journal* 25 (2001–2002): 1; and Janine Natalya Clark, "Does Bosnia Need a TRC? Some Reflections on its Possible Design," *Ethnopolitics* 12 (2013): 225.

35 Janine Natalya Clark, "Reflections on Trust and Reconciliation: A Case-Study of a Central Bosnian Village" *International Journal of Human Rights* 16 (2012): 239; Janine Natalya Clark, "The ICTY and Reconciliation in Croatia: A Case Study of Vukovar, *Journal of International Criminal Justice* 10 (2012): 397; Janine Natalya Clark, "Collective Guilt, Collective Responsibility and the Serbs," *East European Politics and Societies* 22 (2008): 668; Janine Natalya Clark, "From Negative to Positive Peace: The Case of Bosnia and Hercegovina," *Journal of Human Rights* 8 (2009): 360; and Janine Natalya Clark, "The Limits of Retributive Justice: Findings of an Empirical Study in Bosnia and Hercegovina," *Journal of International Criminal Justice* 7 (2009): 463.

36 Matthew Saul, "Local Ownership of the International Criminal Tribunal for Rwanda: Restorative and Retributive Effects, *International Criminal Law Review* 12 (2012): 427; and Donna E. Arzt, "Views on the Ground: The Local Perception of International Criminal Tribunals in the former Yugoslavia and Sierra Leone," *The ANNALS of the American Academy of Political and Social Science* 603 (2006): 226.

operation of the ICC, 2002–2014, have seen the establishment of only nine new commissions.[37] Dual use is also in decline. Of the nine commissions established since those in Sierra Leone and East Timor and the creation of the ICC, only the Democratic Republic of Congo (DRC), Kenya and Côte d'Ivoire have seen any attempt at both prosecution and truth seeking, despite calls for prosecutions from the commissions of Paraguay,[38] Liberia[39] and Togo.[40] Even where there have been attempts at both truth seeking and prosecution in recent times, these stem from overlap between national truth commissions and ICC proceedings, rather than from a coordinated, national level, transitional response. Thus, it has tended to be haphazard and often unsuccessful. Consideration of the situations under investigation by the ICC clearly demonstrates this.

Due to its inability to investigate and prosecute past crimes, the DRC self-referred the commission of serious violations in parts of the country to the ICC while simultaneously operating a truth commission. Ultimately, that commission was unable to fulfil its mandate due to political interference and ongoing instability within the country.[41] Thus, while there have been some attempts at criminal justice under the mobile courts programme[42] and through the military justice system,[43] as well as to a lesser extent at the ICC,[44] the DRC has not benefitted from the operation of a truth seeking initiative.

Following the Kriegler and Waki Reports[45] into the 2007 post-election violence, it initially seemed that Kenya might emerge as the next State to establish

37 Paraguay (2004), Morocco (2004), Democratic Republic of Congo (2004), Liberia (2006), Kenya (2006), Togo (2009), Solomon Islands (2011), Côte d'Ivoire (2011) and Mali (2013).

38 *Informe Final, Comisión de la Verdad y la Justicia* (2008).

39 *Final Report of the TRC of Liberia* (Ghana: Twidan Graphics, 2009).

40 *La Commission Vérité, Justice et Réconciliation du Togo Rapport Final* (2012).

41 See International Center for Transitional Justice, Press Release, "The DRC Elections, Reconciliation and Justice," 27 July 2006.

42 Passy Mubalama and Simon Jennings, "Roving Courts in Eastern Congo," *Institute for War and Peace Reporting*, 13 February 2013.

43 Antonietta Trapani, "Complementarity in the Congo: The Direct Application of the Rome Statute in the Military Courts of the DRC," *DOMAC*, 12 November 2011.

44 Only Thomas Lubanga Dyilo and Germain Katanga have been convicted before the ICC for violations committed in the DRC. Lubanga's case is currently on appeal. In December 2011, Trial Chamber I declined to confirm charges against Callixte Mbarushimana and in December 2012, Mathieu Ngudjolo Chui was acquitted of the charges of war crimes and crimes against humanity. Bosco Ntaganda surrendered himself to the Court in March 2013 and charges against him were confirmed in June 2014.

45 Kriegler and Waki Reports on 2007 Elections, Summarised Version, Revised Edition (2009).

a truth commission and simultaneously pursue trials. However, it subsequently appeared that the Kenyan authorities were reluctant to prosecute the most serious violations and in 2010, the ICC opened investigations due to inactivity on the part of the Kenyan judicial system.[46] The Truth, Justice and Reconciliation Commission (TJRC) has now completed operations, while the slow pace of proceedings and failure to proceed in a number of cases means that those of the ICC are yet to properly get off the ground. Indeed, there is some doubt that the Kenyan cases will be completed before the ICC.[47] Even if there are eventually successful prosecutions for the violations committed in Kenya in 2007 to accompany the truth seeking undertaken by the TJRC, this will hardly constitute a model to be followed in the future. The Kenyan experience has been marked by domestic wrangling, accusations of corruption at the TJRC, outrage on the part of Kenya and the wider African Union at the ICC's intervention and a series of poor decisions by the ICC Office of the Prosecutor (OTP).[48]

Efforts to undertake truth seeking in the other situations being investigated by the ICC have been similiarly limited. Despite repeated calls for a truth commission in Uganda, and studies which demonstrate that victims seek clarification of the truth, no commission has been created.[49] No arrests have been made in connection with the ICC warrants issued for Lord's Resistance Army leaders in 2005 and although there have been efforts to strengthen the domestic judicial system, prosecutions have not yet been forthcoming.[50] In Sudan, a number of initiatives emerged from the Comprehensive Peace Agreement between the Government of Sudan and the Sudan People's Liberation Movement in 2005, but these were focussed on the achievement and

---

46 Decision Pursuant to Article 15 of the Rome Statute on the Authorization of an Investigation into the Situation in the Republic of Kenya, ICC-01/09, 31 March 2010.

47 Charges have already been droppped or have not been confirmed against three of the six indictees in the Kenyan situation and, as of January 2014, a Status Conference has been arranged to consider the issues raised by relevant parties and participants following the Prosecutor's request for a three month adjournment. T he 5 February 2014 trial date in the case against Uhuru Kenyatta has been vacated.

48 For discussion of the Kenyan situation, see Chandra Lekha Sriram and Stephen Brown, "Kenya in the Shadow of the ICC: Complementarity, Gravity, Impact," *International Criminal Law Review* 12 (2012)" 219–244.

49 International Center for Transitional Justice and the Human Rights Center, *Forgotten Voices: A Population Based Survey on Attitudes About Peace and Justice in Northern Uganda*, (Berkeley: International Center for Transitional Justice and the Human Rights Center, University of California, 2005), 35; OHCHR, *"The Dust Has Not Yet Settled": Victims' Views on the Right to Remedy and Reparation. A Report from the Greater North of Uganda*, 2011.

50 "Uganda: War Crimes Trials Face Challenges," *Human Rights Watch*, January 2012.

maintenance of peace, rather than investigations of the past.[51] The ICC issued warrants of arrest for four Sudanese officials, who remain at large, and three Darfuri rebels, who appeared voluntarily before the Court. Sudanese courts have not prosecuted past violations. Thus no one has been held accountable for the violations committed in Darfur.[52]

There was some attempt in the Central African Republic (CAR) at embarking upon a truth seeking process in 2003, under Bozize's National Transitional Council.[53] However, the commission's limited temporal mandate meant that it could not engage in the broad based truth seeking undertaken by the majority of modern commissions.[54] The commission itself called for the continuation and completion of its work under a different structure at the National Reconciliation Conference in October 2003.[55] The CAR self-referred to the ICC in 2004, resulting in the indictment of one individual for crimes against humanity and war crimes. Four others have been indicted for offences against the administration of justice.[56] At the national level, there have been no attempts at either truth seeking or criminal accountability since.

In Libya, referred to the ICC by the UN Security Council in February 2011, a Fact-Finding and Reconciliation Commission was established in 2012[57] with a mandate to investigate past crimes. Having made little progress, in December 2012, along with the national Human Rights Committee, the UN Development Programme and the UN Support Mission in Libya (UNSMIL), this body hosted a conference on Truth and Reconciliation in Libya: The Way Forward. The conference resulted in the adoption of recommendations, which called on the government to create conditions for truth seeking and to pass a new law on

51 The Comprehensive Peace Agreement between the Government of the Republic of the Sudan and the Sudan People's Liberation Movement/Sudan People's Liberation Army, 2005.

52 Sigall Horovitz, "Sudan: Interaction Between International and National Judicial Responses to the Mass Atrocities in Darfur," *DOMAC*, 19 April 2013.

53 "Central African Republic," Rule of Law in Armed Conflicts Project, Geneva Academy of International Humanitarian Law and Human Rights, April 2012.

54 It should be noted that the leading works on truth commissions do not recognise the CAR TRC as a truth commission. See Freeman, *supra* note 18; Eric Wiebelhaus Brahm, *Truth Commissions and Transitional Societies: The Impact on Human Rights and Democracy*, (Abingdon and New York: Routledge, 2010); and Hayner, *supra* note 18.

55 "Reconciliation Commission Recommends Government Shakeup," *IRIN*, 6 October 2003.

56 *The Prosecutor v. Jean-Pierre Bemba Gombo, Aime Kilolo Musamba, Jean-Jacques Mangenda Kabongo, Fidele Babala Wandu and Narcisse Arido*, Case No. ICC-01/05-01/13.

57 Libya, National Transitional Council, Law 17 (2012).

transitional justice making provision for criminal justice and reform.[58] There has, however, been little progress on these issues, with the majority of attention focussed on the jurisdictional struggles between Libya and the ICC over al-Senussi and Saif al-Islam.[59] Indeed, NTC Law 38 of May 2012 grants full amnesty for "military, security or civil actions dictated by the February 17 Revolution that were performed by revolutionaries with the goal of promoting or protecting the revolution."

Although not a State party to the ICC Statute, Côte d'Ivoire accepted the jurisdiction of the Court in 2010 in relation to the human rights violations committed between 2002 and 2010. In 2011, President Outtara established a Commission for Dialogue, Truth and Reconciliation (CDVR) to identify the root causes of the conflict, acts and patterns of violations, and ways for the country to overcome its legacy of violence through reconciliation.[60] The CDVR submitted its report in November 2013. However, its short, two-year mandate, insufficient financial resources, alleged political interference and perceived lack of neutrality on the part of the Chairperson meant that it concluded leaving much work still to be done.[61] It is claimed that it focussed unwisely on the structural causes of the crisis, most of which were already known, rather than on uncovering the truth surrounding the violations.[62] Moreover, the failure to hold public hearings means that victims feel excluded and the general populus disengaged. Reconciliation remains a long way off.[63] There have been three indictments at the ICC, all of which remain pre-trial and, at the national level, only Gbagbo loyalists have been charged by the Ivorian courts to date.[64]

In Mali, investigations by the ICC OTP were opened in July 2012 following referral of the situation by the Malian government. As yet, no indictments have been issued. In March 2013, the Council of Ministers announced the creation of a Dialogue and Reconciliation Commission, since replaced by the Dialogue, Truth and Reconciliation Commission. However, it lacks a clear mandate and adequate resourcing and is suspected to have been established predominently as a means of convincing the international community of Mali's commitment

58 Recommendations of the Conference on Truth and Reconciliation, held in Tripoli, 12–13 December 2012, ¶ 3 and 7(a).

59 *Libya: From Repression to Revolution*, edited by M. Cherif Bassiouni (Leiden: Martinus Nijhoff Publishers, 2013), 289–400.

60 Ordinance No. 2011-167, 13 July 2011.

61 "Côte d'Ivoire Truth Panel Seen Faltering," *IRIN*, January 13, 2014; "Côte d'Ivoire Reconciliation at 'Dead End'," *Mail and Guardian Africa*, 24 July 2013.

62 *Ibid.*

63 Côte d'Ivoire, July 2013 Monthly Forecast, Security Council Report, 28 June 2013.

64 "Côte d'Ivoire Truth Panel Seen Faltering," *IRIN*, 13 January 2014.

to address past violence in order to attain foreign aid.[65] Affected communities have not been consulted on the mechanisms or actors that should be involved in the reconciliation process.[66] Recent studies by Oxfam reveal that few are even aware of the commission and those who are express reservations about its composition, legitimacy and impact.[67] There are no national initiatives underway to ensure criminal accountability.

Finally, although not subject to ICC investigations, truth commissions are proposed for Tunisia, Sri Lanka and Nepal. These plans have similarly raised a host of concerns relating to the transparency of the selection processes, the independence of the commissioners and the scope of the truth commissions' mandates.[68] Prosecutions for serious violations do not look to be forthcoming in any of these States. These issues, which are similar to those encountered in Côte d'Ivoire and Mali, are of concern. Truth commissions created in the absence of victim consultation, with narrow mandates and without impartial and independent commissioners fall short of the standards internationally recognised as essential for them to serve as effective transitional justice mechanisms.[69]

Overall, the pursuit and standard of truth seeking seems to have become less of a priority in the ICC era. Even where there have been efforts to create truth commissions, the well-equipped, independent bodies of the late 1990s and early 2000s seem to be disappearing. They are being replaced by politically manipulated, under-resourced institutions, which have lost the important victim-centric focus that featured in previous transitions. This is a peculiar and concerning development in transitional justice practice. Studies show that truth commissions, when created in accordance with international standards, often make a real contribution to the establishment of a historical national record and to the fulfilment of the right to truth.[70] Moreover, the best

---

65 Mark Tran, "Mali's New President Faces Tough Test as He Strives for Reconciliation," *The Guardian*, 18 September 2013.

66 Ilaria Allegrozzi and Elise Ford, *Piecing Together the Jigsaw: Prospects for Improved Social Relations Following the Armed Conflict in Northern Mali*, Oxfam Research Reports, September 2013.

67 *Ibid.*

68 UN General Assembly, Written statement submitted by the International Commission of Jurists, a non-governmental organization in special consultative status, A/HRC/24/NGO/28, 22 August 2013; "In Tunisia, Appointing Strong Commissioners is the Next Step in Uncovering Truth," *International Center for Transitional Justice*, 4 February 2014.

69 Orentlicher Principles, *supra* note 5; and Eduardo Gonzalez and Howard Varney, *Truth Seeking: Elements of Creating an Effective Truth Commission*, International Center for Transitional Justice, 2013.

70 *UN Study on the Right to Truth*, U.N. Doc. E/CN.4/2006/91 (2006), ¶ 48–61.

prospects for long term respect for human rights and democracy come when truth commissions are utilised in conjunction with other transitional justice mechanisms.[71] The current decline in truth commission creation and quality is therefore surely a step backwards.

4 The Impact of the ICC?

Given the decline in truth seeking – and particularly the establishment of strong and well-resourced commissions – following the creation of the ICC, it seems logical to ask whether the retreat from truth seeking can be attributed to a renewed focus on prosecution. Undoubtedly, the establishment of the permanent International Criminal Court has brought universal attention to criminal trials as a means of responding to the most serious human rights crimes. However, the complex legal framework of the ICC Statute has done much more than simply create an international institution with power to prosecute genocide, crimes against humanity and war crimes[72] when committed on the territory or by nationals of States parties.[73] It has prioritised prosecution at national and international levels, with implications for States and non-States parties alike.

The complementarity principle, which underpins the prosecutorial regime envisaged by the ICC Statute, impacts on the ways in which States parties respond to ICC crimes. Complementarity works to ensure that primary responsibility for the prosecution of the crimes set out in the Statute remains with national courts.[74] Under the Statute, domestic courts are given presumptive jurisdiction.[75] The ICC is obliged to declare a case inadmissible where it is being or has been investigated or prosecuted by a State that has jurisdiction over it and a decision has been taken not to prosecute.[76] Only in circumstances where States are "unable or unwilling genuinely to carry out the investigation or prosecution"[77] does jurisdiction fall to the ICC. This respects the sovereign

71 Olsen *et al.*, *supra* note 21, 457.

72 Art. 5.

73 Art. 12(2).

74 Arts. 1 and 17.

75 See Gerry Simpson, "Politics, Sovereignty and Remembrance," in *The Permanent International Criminal Court – Legal and Policy Issues*, (Portland, Oregon: Hart Publishing, 2004), edited by Dominic McGoldrick *et al.*, 47–65, 55.

76 Arts. 17(1)(a) and (b).

77 Art. 17.

right of States to prosecute their own nationals and crimes that occur on their territory. While this may not, at first glance, appear revolutionary, complementarity does in fact alter and, to a large extent, *dictate* national priorities. If States parties wish to avoid intervention by the ICC then they have to ensure that, should the crimes within the Statute be committed, they undertake proceedings aimed at bringing those responsible to criminal justice. Already, this has prompted a wave of domestic legislative activity as States parties have sought to ensure that they at least have the legislation necessary to enable them to prosecute the crimes within the Statute.[78]

However, the ICC Statute impacts beyond normal treaty boundaries. The Statute makes provision for non-States parties to accept the jurisdiction of the Court with regard to specific situations.[79] Indeed, this is the case with Côte d'Ivoire, which although a non-State party has accepted the ICC's jurisdiction in relation to the violations committed since March 2004.[80] Perhaps most importantly, the UN Security Council has power under the Statute to refer situations to the ICC, when acting under Chapter 7 powers, even where this involves States that are not party to the treaty.[81] Thus, the Court's reach extends beyond its States parties and those which voluntarily accept its jurisdiction. This power, in particular, has the potential to put prosecution at the centre of collective international responses to the commission of international crimes and has already been used in the Security Council referrals of the situations in Darfur[82] and Libya[83] to the Court. Moreover, the power of referral may give rise to a greater focus on prosecutorial policies even in non-States parties, where they seek to avoid intervention by the ICC.

---

78 For discussion of some implementing legislation, see Goran Sluiter, "Implementation of the ICC Statute in the Dutch Legal Order," *Journal of International Criminal Justice* 2 (2004): 158; Juliet Hay, "Implementing the Rome Statute in New Zealand," *Journal of International Criminal Justice* 2 (2004): 533; Max du Plessis, "South Africa's Implementation of the ICC Statute: An African Example," *Journal of International Criminal Justice* 5 (2007): 460; and Fannie Lafontaine, "Canada's Crimes Against Humanity and War Crimes Act on Trial: An Analysis of the Munyareza Case," *Journal of International Criminal Justice* 8 (2010): 269. See also David Turns, "Aspects of National Implementation of the Rome Statute: The United Kingdom and Selected Other States," in McGoldrick *et al.*, *supra* note 75, 337–389.

79 Art. 12(3).

80 Letter reconfirming the acceptance of ICC jurisdcition, Abidjan, December 14, 2010, www.icc-cpi.int.

81 Art. 13(b).

82 UN Security Council Resolution 1593 (2005), 31 March 2005.

83 UN Security Council Resolution 1970 (2011), 26 February 2011.

Thus, at both ideological and practical levels, prosecution has taken on a position of unparalleled significance as a consequence of the complementarity regime and the wider ICC framework. For at least States parties, prosecution must be the primary objective in addressing past atrocities. Otherwise, as illustrated in the Kenyan situation, they risk the assumption of jurisdiction by the Court. The Security Council power of referral means that even States that do not subscribe to the ICC model risk prosecution before it. Truth commissions, and the creation of other transitional justice mechanisms, seem necessarily secondary considerations.

Yet, examination of recent transitional justice practice suggests a complicated picture. It is not simply that the focus on prosecution brought about by the ICC regime has resulted in an oversight of the benefits of truth seeking at national levels. Rather, it seems that since the creation of the ICC, there has been a general regression in national level transitional justice activity. Arguably, complementarity has not worked as envisaged.[84] States parties have not carried out domestic prosecutions, preferring instead to refer their own situations to the ICC.[85] Rather than enhancing domestic level accountability, the ICC has become a means for States to side step their responsibilities to prosecute. The decline in truth commission establishment and standards is symptomatic of this regression. As demonstrated in Section 3, in many of the States where ICC investigations and prosecutions are underway, and in some where they are not, there have been attempts to establish or operate truth commissions. However, many, if not all, of those attempts have been wanting in the political and financial commitments necessary to sustain robust truth seeking initiatives.

A similar malaise can be seen at the international level under the UN. The international determination to provide redress for the most serious human rights violations that led to the formation of the *ad hoc* tribunals, the establishment of truth commissions for El Salvador, Guatemala and Peru and the creation of multifaceted transitional programs for Sierra Leone and East Timor seems to have waned. Security Council attention is now focused on whether sufficient support can be found to refer a situation to the ICC. There too, the ICC model seems to offer an easy means of passing responsibility.

---

84 William A. Schabas, "Prosecutorial Discretion v. Judicial Activism at the International Criminal Court," *Journal of International Criminal Justice* 6 (2009): 731; William A. Schabas, "Complementarity in Practice: Some Uncomplementary Thoughts," *Criminal Law Forum* 19 (2008): 5. For critique of this position, see Darryl Robinson, "The Controversy over Territorial State Referrals and Reflections on ICL Discourse," *Journal of International Criminal Justice* 9 (2011): 355.

85 DRC, Uganda, CAR and Mali have all referred their own situations to the ICC.

Even where it has jurisdiction, the ICC can only achieve so much and progress to date can hardly be described as inspiring. Over almost 12 years, it has assumed jurisdiction in eight situations, commenced 21 cases and brought proceedings against 34 individuals.[86] However, only two cases have resulted in conviction.[87] Charges have been dropped against five individuals,[88] nine remain at large,[89] there has been one acquittal,[90] one ruling of inadmissibility,[91] one refusal to surrender to the Court[92] and one vacation of the trial date.[93] Moreover, international prosecutions, while symbolically significant and a means of contributing to the right to justice, cannot act as a substitute for meaningful national level redress. Nor can they alone discharge the obligations of States or fulfil the rights of victims in the aftermath of serious human rights violations.[94] The reality is that for many transitional States, there is currently very little effort to address past violations, either at national or international levels. This failure to deal with the past limits the prospects for long term healing and repair.

---

86 See www.icc-cpi.int.

87 *The Prosecutor v. Thomas Lubanga Dyilo*, Judgement Pursuant to Article 74 of the Statute, ICC-01/04-01/06-2842, 14 March 2012; and *The Prosecutor v. Germain Katanga*, Judgement Pursuant to Article 74 of the Statute, ICC-01/04-01/07-3436, 8 March 2014.

88 Charges have been dropped against Callixte Mbarushimana (DRC); Bahar Idriss Abu Garda (Sudan); Henry Kiprono Kosgey (Kenya); Mohammed Hussein Ali (Kenya); Francis Kirimi Muthaura.

89 The accused remain at large in the following cases, *The Prosecutor v. Joseph Kony, Vincent Otti, Okot Odhiambo and Dominic Ongwen*, ICC-02/04-01/05 (Uganda); *The Prosecutor v. Ahmad Muhammad Harun ("Ahmad Harun") and Ali Muhammad Ali Abd-Al-Rahman ("Ali Kushayb")*, ICC-02/05-01/07 (Sudan); *The Prosecutor v. Omar Al Bashir*, ICC-02/05-01/09 (Sudan); *The Prosecutor v. Abdel Raheem Muhammad Hussein*, ICC-02/05-01/12 (Sudan); *The Prosecutor v. Sylvestre Mudacumura*, ICC-01/04-01/12 (DRC).

90 *The Prosecutor v. Mathieu Ngudjolo Chui*, Judgement Pursuant to Article 74 of the Statute, ICC-01/04-02/12-3, 18 December 2012.

91 On 11 October 2013, Pre-Trial Chamber I decided that the case against Abdullah Al-Senussi is inadmissible before the ICC as it was currently subject to domestic proceedings conducted by the Libyan competent authorities and that Libya is willing and able genuinely to carry out such investigation.

92 On 31 May 2013, Pre-Trial Chamber I rejected Libya's challenge to the admissibility of the case against Saif Al Islam Gaddafi and stated that Libya is under an obligation to surrender to the Court. An appeal against that decision is pending.

93 See *supra* note 47.

94 UN Human Rights Council, *Right to Truth, Report of the Office of the High Commissioner for Human Rights*, A/HRC/5/7, 7 June 2007, 5–7.

5 Conclusion

The establishment of the ICC represents an enormous achievement. However, this achievement should not be allowed to overshadow the lessons learned from transitional justice practice. Those lessons show that the operation of a range of mechanisms will be required to bring about healing and repair in transitional States, and that domestic level initiatives that inspire local ownership are likely to have advantages over distant, international institutions. This chapter has shown that transitional justice practice following the creation of the ICC reflects something of a departure from these previously accepted principles.

Although significant in its creation, the progress of the Court itself has been disappointing, although this perhaps simply reflects the reality of the complexities and constraints of international criminal justice.[95] Despite significant disillusionment with it,[96] the ICC seems to have refocused attention at the international level, resulting, albeit unintentionally, in a lack of effective redress at national levels. Indeed, there is a distinct absence of effective transitional justice mechanisms in almost all of the States in which the ICC is involved. Instead of creating an enhanced system of accountability, the ICC regime seems to have given rise to one of transitional justice "offloading," where both States and the UN Security Council use the Court as a means of transferring responsibility for addressing past violations.

A trend of particular concern in this general national level regression is the decline in the establishment and quality of truth commissions and the consequent implications for the fulfilment of the right to truth in transitional States. Re-evaluation of transitional justice practice in light of the accountability deficit that has arisen at national levels following the creation of the ICC is required. Ghandhi's scholarship holds valuable lessons for this reassessment. While he was not averse to the creation of an international human rights court, Ghandhi's work teaches primarily of the necessity of providing effective redress for human rights violations through credible systems, which are accessible to victims.[97] Moreover, it demonstrates the valuable contribution that

95 Payam Akhavan, "The Rise and Fall and Rise of International Criminal Justice," *Journal of International Criminal Justice* 11 (2013): 527.

96 Mireille Delmas-Marty, "Ambiguities and Lacunae: The International Criminal Court Ten Years on," *Journal of International Criminal Justice*, 11 (2013): 553.

97 Ghandhi, *supra* note 1, 285–288.

quasi-judicial bodies, as opposed to courts, can make to the promotion and protection of human rights.[98]

In the field of transitional justice, it is time to refocus attention at the national level, reconsider the ways in which human rights violations are being responded to and the priority assigned to the various mechanisms designed to address them. Criminal trials, both national and international, must continue to play a part in transitional programmes and contribute to the delivery of justice. However, the significance of trials must be kept in context and multi-faceted programmes that aim to fulfil all four transitional objectives implemented. Truth commissions can, and should, be utilised within these. Their modes of operation make them visible, inclusive, victim oriented mechanisms. Their work in human rights adjudication not only assists truth recovery but acts as a springboard for the fulfilment of the rights to reparation and non-repetition. The benefits associated with their operation cannot be delivered by criminal trials and certainly not by a few international prosecutions at the ICC. Both will be required if the rights of victims are to be fulfilled and transitional States are to stand the best chance of long term peace and stability.

98 For example see Ghandhi, *ibid.*, 25 on the significance of the work of the Human Rights Committee in producing General Comments.

CHAPTER 10

Adjudicating Human Rights in the Preventive Sphere

Malcolm D. Evans

1 Adjudication and the "Pull" of the Judicial

The prevention of human rights abuses is what the "idea" of human rights is, ultimately, all about. Yet many of the tools that have been developed to address violations of international human rights obligations are increasingly "remedial" in nature, and there is an increasing tendency to highlight their "judicial" or "quasi-judicial" nature. There seems to be a widely held view that the international mechanisms for the promotion and protection of human rights remain in some ways incomplete – or at the very least, inadequate – if they have not been perfected through an apotheosis into the judicial sphere.[1] Indeed, the entire idea of "adjudicating human rights" may be a reflection of this impulse. It is undoubtedly the case that there has been a trend for the mechanisms which are attached to regional human rights instruments to progress in this direction: the European, Inter-American and African regional systems were all originally established without Courts of general jurisdiction but have moved in that direction over time. Yet it was nearly 50 years after it was first mooted that individual petition to the European Court of Human Rights was established as a matter of right within all contracting parties to the European Convention on Human Rights.[2] It still remains the case that the jurisdictional reach of the Inter-American Court is far from complete within

1 It is, however, notable, and somewhat ironic, that the merits of the European system having been re-invented as a largely judicial system (see *infra* note 4) is now being reappraised. See, for example, several of the contributions to *The European Court of Human Rights Between Law and Politics*, edited by Jonas Christoffersen and Mikael Rask Madsen (Oxford: Oxford University Press, 2013), including at 103 the observation by Sir Antony Lester that "with hindsight it was a mistake to abolish the Commission."

2 The idea had first been raised in 1948 during the initial discussions which led to the adoption of the ECHR. It finally came about with the entry into force of Protocol No 11 to the ECHR (ETS No 155) in November 1998. See generally Ed Bates, *The Evolution of the European Convention on Human Rights: From Its Inception to the Creation of a Permanent Court of Human Rights* (Oxford: Oxford University Press, 2010).

 | DOI 10.1163/9789004261181_012

the Inter-American system,[3] and whilst the African system currently boasts a plurality of Human Rights Courts, few African States are actually within their reach.[4] At the regional level, then, and despite the focus which it receives, the "judicialisation" of international human rights protection is far from being achieved.[5]

If this is so at the regional level, the process has not really begun at the international level, if that level is to be equated with the UN machinery for human rights protection. As is well known, there is no international court of human rights and, despite the occasional calls for the creation of such a body,[6] there appears to be no realistic possibility of this coming to pass within a meaningful time frame.[7] Nevertheless, and perhaps starting from a different base, there has been a similar sense of progression towards the judicial within the UN

3 Of the 35 member States of the Organisation of American States, currently only 23 are a party to the 1969 American Convention on Human Rights, which provides for the establishment of the Inter-American Court of Human Rights. Individuals do not have the right to refer cases to the Inter-American Court, this being reserved for the Inter-American Commission or States Parties by virtue of Article 61 of the Convention, and only in respect of those States which have accepted the jurisdiction of the Court to do so under Article 62.

4 The African Court of Human and People's Rights was established by the 1998 Protocol to the 1981 African Charter on Human and Peoples' Rights and became operational in 2006. In 2004 the African Union decided to merge this Court with the newly established African Court of Justice but, before this occurred, a further Protocol was adopted in 2008 on the establishment of a new African Court of Justice and Human Rights. The African Court is currently still operational, with 25 of the 53 member States of the African Union accepting its jurisdiction. The 2008 Protocol establishing the new Court of Justice and Human Rights is not yet in force.

5 For a more general comment on the role of regional courts see Malcolm Evans, "The Future(s) of Regional Court of Human Rights," in *Realizing Utopia*, edited by Antonio Cassese (Oxford: Oxford University Press, 2012).

6 For a recent initiative see Julia Kozma, Manfred Novak and Martin Scheinin, *A World Court of Human Rights – Consolidated Draft Statute and Commentary* (Vienna: Neuer Wissenschaftlicher, 2010). See also Manfred Novak, "The Need for a World Court of Human Rights," *Human Rights Law Review* 7, 1 (2007): 7; and Andrew Clapham, "Overseeing Human Right Compliance," in Cassese, *supra* note 5, 318, 323–324.

7 The far more modest proposal by the then UN High Commissioner for Human Rights to establish a single unified UN Treaty Body made in 2006 was swiftly abandoned and has not been returned to in the latest round of discussions within the UN concerning institutional development within the human rights system. For the proposal see the Concept Paper on the High Commissioner's Proposal for a Unified standing Treaty Body, U.N. Doc. HRI/MC/2006/CRP 1 (2006); and for comment see Michael O'Flaherty and Claire O'Brien, "Reform of the UN Human Rights Treaty Monitoring Bodies: A Critique of the Concept Paper of the High Commissioner's proposal for a Unified Standing Treaty Body," *Human Rights Law Review* 7, 1 (2007): 141.

treaty body system. The individual communication procedures which were originally found in some of the human rights treaties have now been extended to all[8] – with the exception of the Optional Protocol to the Convention against Torture, the aims of which are very different and which will be explored in detail below. Whilst participation within the individual communications procedures remains optional, and take-up varies considerably between the treaties, the general trend remains one of expansion.[9]

However, debate has long surrounded the nature of the outputs of that process[10]: although frequently described as "quasi-judicial,"[11] neither the primarily written process nor the "views" formulated at its conclusion are obviously judicial in nature. Whilst "views" reflect the factual findings of the Committee and allow it to expand on its understanding of the treaty obligations, they are not generally regarded as being judicial, nor are they considered to be so by the Human Rights Committee itself.[12] Whether they are or are not "judicial" is somewhat beside the point: the point is that it is often believed that the standing of the Committee's outputs would be enhanced if they were considered to be of a judicial nature.[13] Why? It certainly is true that compliance with the

---

8 See, for example, Geir Ulfstein, "Individual Complaints," in *UN Human Rights Treaty Bodies*, edited by Helen Keller and Geir Ulfstein (Cambridge: Cambridge University Press, 2012), 73. Of the nine relevant conventions, six provided for individual communications procedures from the outset. Individual Communications procedures were added to the Convention on the Elimination of Discrimination against Women by an Optional Protocol in 1999 (in force December 2000), the International Covenant on Economic, Social and Cultural Rights (CESCR) by an Optional Protocol in 2008 (in force from May 2013) and to the Convention on the Rights of the Child (CRC) by an Optional Protocol in 2011 (in force April 2014).

9 In 2000 there were only three such procedures whereas today there are nine, eight of which are operative. The number of States bound by these procedures are: CERD, 55; ICCPR, 115; CESCR, 15; CAT, 66; CEDAW, 105; CRC, 11; CRPD, 83; CED, 17.

10 Commenting on its early work, McGoldrick was able to pose as a question to be addressed: "Is it to fulfil the role of a judicial body…?" See Dominic McGoldrick, *The Human Rights Committee* (Oxford: Oxford University Press, 1990), 120.

11 Jane Connors and Markus Schmidt, "United Nations," in *International Human Rights Law*, edited by Daniel Moeckli, Sangeeta Shah, Sandesh Sivakumaran (2nd ed., Oxford: Oxford University Press, 2014), 381.

12 See UN Human Rights Committee, *General Comment No. 33: Obligations of States Parties under the Optional Protocol to the International Covenant on Civil and Political Rights*, 25 June 2009, U.N. Doc. CCPR/C/GC/33, ¶ 11, in which the Committee said that "[w]hile the function of the Human Rights Committee in considering individual communications is not, as such, that of a judicial body, the views issued by the Committee under the Optional Protocol exhibit some important characteristics of a judicial decision."

13 Rodley has observed that the procedures used when considering individual communications are modelled on judicial practice. with "both parties are given full opportunity to

views of the UN human rights treaty bodies is quite poor. But this is also true of some judicialised regional systems and there is no reason to believe that re-categorising outputs as judicial would necessary improve compliance.

More important, however, is the need to understand that being "quasi-judicial" – or "judicial in spirit" – does not mean that such mechanisms are to be seen as being "not quite, but almost there"; with "there" being recognition *as* judicial. It is not the role of the treaty bodies to be judicial – they are not – but it is their role to act within their own sphere of competence with the same degree of autonomy and authority as judicial bodies exercise within theirs. It is in this sense that they should be understood as acting "quasi-judicially," which is to say, acting "as if" they were judicial. As Ghandhi himself has put it, and as noted by Christopher Waters in the Introduction to this volume, "[the Human Rights Committee] must be seen to be acting in a manner which approximates, as nearly as possible to the way in which a court acts, when exercising its functions under the O.P. Accordingly, the Committee strives to make its decisions conform to a judicial pattern, to produce cogent *rationes decidendi* and develop a consistent jurisprudence."[14] Such an approach frees one from the pressure to continue down the path of seeking unnecessarily to "judicialise" these processes in the belief that this will enhance their utility in fulfilling their functions and in achieving the overarching goal of securing compliance with human rights commitments. They are perfectly capable of doing so as they are.

There is, however, a danger that the treaty bodies may themselves give the impression that their role is one of "adjudicating" human rights, in some judicial rather than "judicially inspired" sense. In the context of the individual communications processes this is understandable and possibly inevitable: being "quasi-judicial" in such a process does mean acting "as if" one were making a judicial finding on the basis of the evidence placed before the body in question. The reporting process is, however, very different and, as this is the

---

respond to each others' pleadings and the Committees' deliberations are indistinguishable from those of a court." He comments that the HRC adopts its views "in a judicial spirit." See Nigel Rodley, "International Human Rights Law," in *International Law*, edited by Malcolm Evans (4th ed., Oxford: Oxford University Press, 2014), 783, 811. This is drawn from *General Comment No. 33*, *supra* note 12, ¶ 11, which also says that "[t]hese [views] are arrived at in a judicial spirit, including the impartiality and independence of Committee members, the considered interpretation of the language of the Covenant, and the determinative character of the decisions."

14 P.R. Ghandhi, *The Human Rights Committee and the Right of Individual Communication: Law and Practice* (Aldershot: Ashgate Publishing Co, 1998), 395. See also Introduction to this volume, at note 9.

core obligatory process provided for within the treaties, any move towards judicialising that process is of particular significance.

Once again, taken over time, there has been considerable development in the operation of the reporting processes. In the early years of the system, the process involved a presentation of the State report to the relevant committee, followed by a question and answer session concerning the extent to which the report indicated that the State was in compliance with its substantive obligations under the treaty in question. That exchange *was* the outcome of the process. There was no other output save the record of the conversation. Whatever views might be held as to its effectiveness,[15] the nature of the process was clearly "conversational" (however stilted those conversations might have been). If judgments were made, they were largely made in the mind, and if they were articulated it was largely by implication.

This changed with the introduction of "concluding observations," first by the Human Rights Committee in 1992, and subsequently by all the treaty bodies engaged in reporting processes.[16] Concluding Observations themselves formally make a series of "recommendations" to the State party, but the very structure of the documents has an "adjudicatory" flavour: setting out factual and procedural issues, noting positive and negative factors, and culminating in a series of recommendations that are grounded in the treaty body's assessment of the country situation. This was mirrored by the process itself becoming categorised as an "examination" of State parties' reports. If this were a conversation concerning compliance, it was now different in kind from that which had previously occurred, and expectations surrounding the process have, in consequence, shifted.

A further shift is, perhaps, reflected in the emerging practice pioneered by the Committee against Torture in 2007 of adopting "Lists of Issues Prior to Reporting."[17] The essence of this optional procedure is that the treaty body

15 For an overview and evaluation of the process in its early years see McGoldrick, *supra* note 10, 62–119, who commented at 100 that "only time will reveal whether the HRC's failure to draw up specific reports on each State party and general comments addressed to particular State parties are fundamental defects in the reporting procedure." See also Nigel Rodley, "The Role and Impact of Treaty Bodies," in *Oxford Handbook of International Human Rights Law*, edited by Dinah Shelton (Oxford: Oxford University Press, 2013), 621, 628–629.

16 For an interesting account of the change, and the background to it, see Christian Tomuschat, *Human Rights: Between Idealism and Realism* (2nd ed., Oxford: Oxford University Press, 2008), 180–183.

17 For a summary of the background and an evaluation of the possible further development of this approach, see U.N. Doc. CAT/C/47/2 (27 September 2011).

determines the issues which it wishes to discuss with the State in question. The latter is then invited to respond only to those issues, rather than to the full range of Convention obligations. The logic is impeccable, in that it focuses the discussion on those issues which the treaty body considers to be most pressing. Nevertheless, it presupposes that the relevant committee has been able to identify those issues accurately and it has the inevitable consequence of heightening the adjudicatory feel to the process, in that the State is being, in effect, asked to justify its actions in the areas of concern, rather than report more generally on its fulfilment of its convention obligations. The most recent development in the UN human rights treaty system, General Assembly Resolution 68/268 (9 April 2014) (concerning the Strengthening of the Treaty Body System), both endorses and encourages this practice.[18]

None of this should be taken as being in any sense critical of these developments in the operational practice of the treaty bodies. On the contrary, they are to be applauded. It does, however, need to be recognised that these developments do point in the direction of a more adjudicative conception of their role and function, and so further contribute – albeit from a very different starting point – to the "juridification" of the mechanisms of compliance. Once again, there seems to be a latent "pull" in this direction. Among the many possible reasons for this, the interconnection of two powerful factors is to be highlighted. The first of these is the progression from adjudication to judgment: the second is the perceived force of legal determination in effecting change.[19] It becomes almost irresistible to conclude that the most effective response to non compliance is legally binding adjudication and that mechanisms need to be somewhere upon this pathway and assisted in their journey along it. And non-compliance with the existing findings of such bodies is seen as merely reinforcing the need for haste in doing so.

There are, however, a number of issues that need to be raised at this point. The first concerns the move from adjudication to legal judgment. There are other possible responses to determining that a human rights obligation is being breached than moving towards the issuance of a "finding" on the matter. Within the UN system, for example, the response often takes place within the political processes established by the Human Rights Council. Thus the

18 This approach is now increasingly being referred to as the "Simplified Reporting Process."

19 Many writers consider it a weakness that the outputs of the treaty bodies are not "legally binding" and contributes to their lack of impact. See, for example, Clapham, *supra* note 6, 321 (suggesting that the monitoring functions of the treaty bodies are inadequate to deliver "compliance").

Universal Periodic Review (UPR) process[20] increasingly draws on the work of the human rights treaty bodies, as does discussion concerning the establishment of Special Procedure mandates, both thematic and country specific.[21] These may be equally useful channels for responding to the "adjudication" of the situation made by the treaty bodies in their work. It is necessary to guard against the temptation to think that because a process is established by law and concerns compliance with legal obligations that the output of that process, to be effective, needs to be couched in legal forms.

A second issue flows out of this, and concerns the role of the treaty bodies in facilitating change through constructive dialogue. The reporting process is a form of exchange – albeit in fairly stylised form – which is intended to promote compliance through dialogue. Whilst it is certainly helpful for the treaty bodies to formalise particular recommendations which flow from this discussion, there are genuine questions to be asked about the manner in which those recommendations are couched. It is undeniable that the recommendations issued by treaty bodies have increased exponentially in length and detail over recent years.[22] Rather than offer an opportunity to assist States parties in improving their compliance by offering practical recommendations, there is a sense in which they have become more of a vehicle through which to articulate opinions concerning compliance, elaborating upon the nature of the obligations of States parties and the manner in which they might be being breached and remedied.[23] As a result, the way in which they function as a tool to assist in

---

20 For an insightful overview of the UPR process, and its points of differentiation from the Treaty processes (and from arguments for a Court of Human Rights), see Nadia Bernaz, "Reforming the UN Human Rights Protection Procedures: A Legal Perspective on the Establishment of the Universal Periodic Review Mechanism," *New Institutions for Human Rights Protection*, edited by Kevin Boyle (Oxford: Oxford University Press, 2009), 75.

21 It is, however, also true that in the first years following the establishment of the Human Rights Council there was a reluctance to establish new country-specific mandates, but that now seems to be in the past. See Ted Piccone, "The Future of the United Nations Special Procedures," in *Routledge Handbook of Human Rights Law*, edited by Scott Sheeran and Sir Nigel Rodley (London: Routledge, 2013), 725, 728–729; and Allehone M. Abebe, "The Role and Future of the Human Rights Council," in Sheeran and Rodley, *ibid.*, 743, 749–751.

22 This is demonstrated by the most cursory of comparisons between the first sets of concluding observations issued in the early 1990s, which averaged some 3 of 4 pages and contained 4 of 6 recommendations, with more recent concluding observations running into 15 or 20 pages containing dozens of detailed recommendations, and which are clearly as much the product of prior research as they are the outcome of the dialogue.

23 Cf. Walter Kälin and Jörg Künzli, *The Law of International Human Rights Protection* (Oxford: Oxford University Press, 2009), 211 ("[a]lthough the tone of these recommendations

compliance has changed somewhat. It may be that, as a result of the Treaty Strengthening Process, this may change yet again going forward, as there is increasing pressure to reduce both the length and number of recommendations made. If so, it will almost certainly result in a reorientation of their focus.

A related point which needs emphasising is that the dialogue between the State and the treaty body, and its outcome, is (or ought to be) merely the beginning of a process aimed at achieving improved compliance. The treaty bodies themselves recognise this, and it is reflected in the establishment of follow-up procedures by a number of treaty bodies which operate across the reporting cycle: the matter is not left fallow until the State in question appears once more before the Committee. At the same time, achieving compliance with the recommendations of the treaty bodies is not merely a task for the treaty bodies themselves. The role played by the Human Rights Council through UPR and the Special Procedures has already been mentioned, but the Office of the High Commissioner plays a vital role through the provision of technical advice and assistance, capacity building and, increasingly, through its field missions.[24] To this must be added the myriad activities by civil society organisations, and aid and assistance programmes which draw on the outputs of the treaty bodies in order to justify and drive change. In short, the impact of the work of the treaty bodies is magnified many times over by the work of others and there is a diffuse set of relationships, all of which contribute to compliance. The substantive point which needs to be taken from this is that if the nature of treaty body work becomes increasingly "judicialised," this changes fundamentally the manner in which others are able to integrate that work into their own, and to the extent that this may make it more difficult for them to do so it runs a risk of lessening the broader utility of those outputs.[25]

A final issue concerns the role of the international human rights bodies in preventing violations from occurring in the first place. Few of the bodies are actually designed to focus upon prevention, though all have preventive dimensions. In addition, the work of the UN thematic Special Rapporteurs has long been rooted in urgent action procedures, intended to allow them to intervene

---

is restrained, they often amount to clear directives to lawmakers and the executive branch").

24 For an overview see Michael O'Flaherty, *The Human Rights Field Operation: Law, theory and Practice* (Aldershot: Ashgate, 2007); and Michael O'Flaherty and Daria Davitti, "International Human Rights Field Operations: A Fast Developing Human Rights Tool," in Sheeran and Rodley, *supra* note 21, 169.

25 For a similar point in relation to the Inter-American system, see Clara Sandoval, "The Inter-American System of Human Rights and Approach," in Sheeran and Rodley, *supra* note 21, 427, 441–442.

in situations where persons within the scope of their mandates are at risk, as well as where there is evidence that the rights of persons are being, or have been, violated.[26] Similarly, under the individual communications procedures, treaty bodies have developed their practice of making awards of interim protection which are likewise intended to have a preventive effect.[27]

However, to return to the statement made at the commencement of this chapter, "[t]he prevention of human rights abuses is what the 'idea' of human rights is, ultimately, all about." The problem with "adjudication" as the vehicle through which to develop responses to non-compliance with human rights obligations is that it tends to pre-suppose that there has been, or may have been, a violation before the work of the human rights mechanisms commences. This approach certainly allows for the protection of human rights, in the sense that violations of or non compliance with human rights obligations are addressed and – let us say – the "human rights equilibrium" is restored. In this sense, "human rights" are protected. The reporting processes adopt a different approach, seeking to ensure compliance through co-operative dialogue but, as has been seen, the manner in which these processes have developed runs the risk of pulling them into an "adjudicative" frame of reference.

Yet there is a zone that lies before protection, and which involves prevention – not in the sense of remedial responses but in terms of seeking to forestall violation. It is remarkable how underdeveloped this strand of thinking remains, given that the term "prevention" is liberally applied in the human rights context, and as long ago as 1948 figured in the title of the *Convention on the Prevention and Punishment of the Crime of Genocide*. There is one area, however, in which the idea of prevention has firmly taken root. This concerns the prohibition on torture,[28] which will form the focus of the remainder of this

26 For a helpful and authoritative overview, see David Weissbrodt, "UN Charter-based Procedures for Addressing Human Rights Violations: Historical Practice, Reform and Future Implications," in *The Delivery of Human Rights: Essays in Honour of Professor Sir Nigel Rodley*, edited by Geoff Gilbert, Françoise Hampson and Clara Sandoval (London: Routlegde, 2011), 13.

27 Increasingly termed "provisional measures of protection," in the light of criticism that too many requests for interim measures were being made. See Connors and Schmidt, *supra* note 11, 359, 382.

28 Admittedly, this is not a universally held view. Somewhat unusually, Rodley has argued that "prevention is protection by another name." Indeed, he seems to dismiss the role of prevention as it is developed in this chapter as being little more than a device to save the errant State from exposure and, as such, amounts to a compact in which not holding the State to account is its reward for compliance. It is otherwise difficult to understand his comment that "in the case of torture, prevention is not better than cure." This rather misses the point that prevention is actually intended to prevent. See Nigel Rodley,

chapter. The following section will look at the "preventive approach" to the prohibition of torture, to be followed by a consideration of some of the challenges involved in generating "preventive recommendations" in order to shed light on how the idea of "adjudication" contributes towards the realisation of the human rights ideal in the preventive context.

2 The Preventive Approach to Torture

Prevention is a substantive obligation of States parties under Article 2(1) of the UN Convention against Torture (UNCAT), which provides that "[e]ach State Party shall take effective legislative, administrative, judicial or other measures to prevent acts of torture in any territory under its jurisdiction" and in 2008 the Committee against Torture (CAT) issued a General Comment on the "Implementation of Article 2 by States Parties."[29] In 2007, in the context of the *Bosnian Genocide* case,[30] the International Court of Justice (ICJ) commented on the scope of the preventive obligation found in Article I of the Genocide Convention,[31] and in doing so also referred to Article 2 of the UNCAT.

Prevention has also emerged as a discrete area of work in its own right, with its own mechanisms and methodologies as developed in the work of the European Committee for the Prevention of Torture (CPT) established under the European Convention for the Prevention of Torture and Inhuman or Degrading Treatment or Punishment (ECPT) and by the UN Subcommittee on Prevention of Torture (SPT) under the UN Optional Protocol to the Convention against Torture (OPCAT). The Optional Protocol entered into force in 2006 and the SPT met for the first time in 2007: so it is fair to say that, although there had been some 20 years experience of preventive work at the regional level, 2007–2008 marked a moment when the idea of torture prevention received a new prominence upon the broader international stage. But it did so in two very different ways and, whilst recognising that there is slight misuse of terminology in doing so (as both are grounded in legally binding treaty obligations), for the purposes of this chapter it is helpful to distinguish between the "legal"

"Reflections on Working for the Prevention of Torture," *Essex Human Rights Review* 6, 1 (2009): 21, 29.

29 See CAT/C/GC/2 (24th January 2008).

30 *Application of the Convention on the Prevention and Punishment of the Crime of Genocide* (Bosnia and Herzegovina v. Serbia and Montenegro), 2007 I.C.J. 43 (26 Feb.).

31 Art. I provides that "[t]he Contracting Parties confirm that genocide…is a crime under international law which they undertake to prevent and punish."

obligation to prevent and "preventive approaches" to the realisation of the prohibition of torture, since "adjudication" plays a very different role in relation to them.

2.1 *The Legal "Obligation"*

In 2007 the ICJ gave its judgment in the *Bosnia Genocide* case. The heart of the case concerned whether Serbia and Montenegro (at that time) were responsible for allegedly genocidal acts, including the massacre at Srebrenica. The Court ultimately decided that Serbia had not exercised a sufficient degree of control over the Bosnian Serb forces to be directly responsible for their activities.[32] However, it also decided that Serbia had not done all that was within its power to dissuade the Bosnian Serb forces from undertaking genocidal acts, and so concluded that Serbia was in breach of its obligation under the Genocide Convention to "prevent."[33] This indicates that a State can be internationally responsible for failing to do all that it might do dissuade others from engaging in genocidal acts. The reasoning used by the Court translates over fairly precisely into situations in which States fail to do all that they might to dissuade others from engaging in acts of torture.

The *Bosnian Genocide* case is of considerable significance as a possibly unique example of a State being found responsible for breach of a preventive obligation in inter-State litigation in a human rights context. It provides insight into the normative force of prevention and, even if international law is unlikely to prove a convenient procedural vehicle for holding States to account for their failures to prevent, it underlines the significance of ensuring that all States take their preventive responsibilities seriously. But what does it mean to take prevention seriously?

An important element of the *Bosnian Genocide* case is that it shows that the preventive obligation is not met merely by complying with other convention obligations concerning the criminalisation, prosecution and punishment of those responsible.[34] Although Article I of the Genocide Convention does refer

32 See *Bosnian Genocide* case, *supra* note 30, ¶ 415. This was based on its rejection of the "overall control" test in favour of the "effective control" test (¶¶ 200–406), an approach strongly criticised in Antonio Cassese, "The *Nicaragua* and *Tadić* Tests Revisited in the Light of the ICJ Judgment on Genocide in Bosnia," *European Journal of International Law* 18, 4 (2007): 649.

33 *Bosnian Genocide* case, *supra* note 30, ¶ 438.

34 In 2012 the ICJ found, for the first time, a State to have been in breach of these obligations under the UNCAT arts. 6(2) and 7(1) in *Questions Relating to the Obligation to Prosecute or Extradite* (Belgium v. Senegal), 2012 I.C.J. 422 (20 Jul.).

to States undertaking "to prevent and to punish," the ICJ was clear that these were separate concepts. The Court said that:

> [I]t is not the case that the obligation to prevent has no separate legal existence of its own; that it is, as it were, absorbed by the obligation to punish, which is therefore the only duty the performance of which may be subject to review by the Court. The obligation on each contracting State to prevent genocide is both normative and compelling. It is not merged in the duty to punish, nor can it be regarded as simply a component of that duty. It has its own scope...[35]

It is, then, necessary to do more than prosecute, since prevention is a broader concept: the question is, how broad? The Court expressly drew a parallel with, *inter alia*, Article 2 of the UNCAT, whilst noting that "[t]he content of the duty to prevent varies from one instrument to another, according to the wording of the relevant provisions, and depending on the nature of the acts to be prevented."[36] Nevertheless, the basic contours of content of the legal obligation to prevent as set out by the Court would seem to be easily transferable into the context of the prevention of torture. The question is whether this is appropriate.

The Court observed that "a violation of the obligation to prevent results from mere failure to adopt and implement suitable measures to prevent genocide from being committed. In other words...[a] violation of the obligation to prevent results from omission."[37] In so saying, the Court was intending to draw a distinction between prevention and complicity. It had already decided that Serbia was not itself responsible for complicity in genocide, which, for the Court, and like the ban on Genocide itself, was a negative obligation that required the State to refrain from undertaking the prohibited course of action. However, it took the view that "the duty to prevent places States under positive obligations, to do their best to ensure that such acts do not occur."[38]

Put in this way, there is no question of the preventive obligation being considered to be "absolute," in the sense that the prohibition on torture is an absolute. But when should States "do their best" to prevent? The Court thought that:

35 *Bosnian Genocide* case, *supra* note 30, ¶ 427. It is interesting to compare this with the approach of the CAT in its *General Comment No. 2*, which moves in the opposite direction, expressly linking prevention to punishment, as will be seen below.

36 *Ibid.*, ¶ 429.

37 *Ibid.*, ¶ 432.

38 *Ibid.*, ¶ 432.

> [A] State may be found to have violated its obligation to prevent even though it had no certainty, at the time when it should have acted, but failed to do so, that genocide was about to be committed or was under way; for it to incur responsibility on this basis it is enough that the State was aware, or should normally have been aware, of the serious danger that acts of genocide would be committed.[39]

In addition, the Court looked to the degree of influence that the Federal Republic of Yugoslavia (FRY) authorities (as they then were) exercised over the Bosnian Serbs, "owing to the strength of the political, military and financial links between the FRY on the one hand and the Republika Srpska and the VRS (the Bosnian Serb Army) on the other."[40] It also took the view that "they could hardly have been unaware of the serious risk of it once the VRS forces had decided to occupy the Srebrenica enclave."[41] As a result, the Court concluded that "[i]n view of their undeniable influence and of the information, voicing serious concern, in their possession, the Yugoslav federal authorities should, in the view of the Court, have made the best efforts within their power to try and prevent the tragic events then taking shape, whose scale, though it could not have been foreseen with certainty, might at least have been surmised."[42] However, it seemed to the Court that they had failed to do so,[43] noting that "for a State to be held responsible for breaching its obligation of prevention, it does not need to be proven that the State concerned definitely had the power to prevent the genocide; it is sufficient that it had the means to do so and that it manifestly refrained from using them."[44]

So drawn, the parameters of the preventive obligation are narrow. In order to be held internationally responsible for its failure to prevent, the State needs to have sufficient influence over those who are directly responsible and to be aware of a serious danger that such acts might be committed. In such cases, it becomes incumbent on the State to make "the best efforts within their power to try and prevent the tragic events then taking shape." Are these really the legal contours of the preventive obligation? And is this what prevention is about?

---

39 *Ibid.*, ¶ 432.

40 *Ibid.*, ¶ 434.

41 *Ibid.*, ¶ 436.

42 *Ibid.*, ¶ 438.

43 *Ibid.*, ¶ 438: "the Respondent has not shown that it took any initiative to prevent what happened, or any action on its part to avert the atrocities which were committed."

44 *Ibid.*

Of course, the *Bosnian Genocide* case was dealing with the potential responsibility of a State for failing to prevent a prohibited act from occurring within another. It was not addressing the content of the preventive obligation of a State with regard to acts of genocide occurring within its own jurisdiction. The Court fell back on the obligation to prevent precisely because, on the facts of the case, the acts in question could not be attributed to the FRY, according to its understanding of the principles of State responsibility.[45] It provided an alternative ground of responsibility under the Genocide convention in a situation in which the State could not be held responsible for the unlawful act *per se*. Had the acts in question been attributable to the FRY, it would appear to be otiose to consider the breach of the preventive obligation as a separate head of liability: if one is responsible for genocide – or torture – then one is also responsible for a failure to prevent it.

It would be entirely possible to reframe the discussion opened up by the Court in the *Bosnian Genocide* case in the context of the direct responsibility of the State for its own failure to take effective preventive measures, where issues such as influence and information ought not to be as relevant – if relevant at all. In a sense, however, such an approach to the emerging legal concept of prevention stands at a tangent to that dimension of "prevention" which is most uniquely "preventive." Naturally, rendering the prohibition of torture – and genocide – effective will involve challenging impunity and holding perpetrators to account.[46] But prevention ought also to involve interventions designed to ensure that the point at which the prohibition is breached is never reached. What is revealing about the approach taken by the Court in the *Bosnian Genocide* case is that its approach to the legal conceptualisation of prevention does not actually aim at prevention at all: it may offer a way of holding States to account for a failure to prevent, but it remains necessary for an act of genocide – or torture – to have occurred before the breach of the obligation to prevent becomes apparent. In short, it needs something on which "to bite."[47] And from a "preventive perspective," this amounts to a failure, since the essence of the preventive approach lies in the attempt to ensure that that "something" does not happen in the first place.

45 See *supra* note 32.

46 For recent works highlighting the on-going need to challenge impunity in the face of deep seated historical practices, see Ian Corbain, *Cruel Britannia: A Secret History of Torture* (London: Portobello Books, 2012); and Alfred W. McCoy, *Torture and Impunity* (Madison: University of Wisconsin Press, 2012).

47 To this extent, it is reminiscent of the view of prevention held by Rodley, and criticised above at *supra* note 28.

It is, then, interesting to turn to the General Comment issued around the same time by CAT in order to see if it takes a different path. As has been seen, Article 2(1) of the UNCAT provides that "[e]ach State Party shall take effective legislative, administrative, judicial or other measures to prevent acts of torture in any territory under its jurisdiction." Whereas in the *Bosnian Genocide* case the Court was keen to distance the preventive obligation from the obligation to punish with which it is connected in Article I of the Genocide Convention, the CAT appears to be keen to establish the interconnection of the preventive obligation with the other substantive provisions of the UNCAT. Thus it stresses that, in its view, Article 2(1) "obliges each State party to take actions that will reinforce the prohibition against torture through legislative, administrative, judicial, or other actions that must, in the end, be effective in preventing it."[48] Rather than being an end in itself, the General Comment immediately projects the preventive obligation as being a means of buttressing the prohibition. This in itself is hardly problematic: the entire point of the preventive obligation is to ensure that the prohibition is respected. The real question is how. Article 2(1) does no more than indicate an open-ended variety of forms that such preventive measures might take. It does not purport to set out what the substantive content of the preventive obligation is.

For some, this might be done by identifying what might be called "complementary obligations" which buttress the prohibition of torture, and which have legal standing in their own right. Obvious examples would include procedural rights for detainees, fair trial rights, minimum standards of treatment and so on, all of which are familiar from other instruments and all of which contribute towards prevention. But is anything added by elevating these buttressing protections into a legal framework of prevention? Does it assist? Or is it an unnecessary diversion from the primary thrust of preventive work?

The problem is nicely illustrated by returning to the CAT's General Comment on Article 2. It highlights the absolute nature of the prohibition, its extraterritorial effect, questions of attribution, superior orders, vulnerable groups and when, in Section III, it turns to the "[c]ontent of the legal obligation to take effective measures to prevent torture," its primary focus is on the importance of criminalising torture in accordance with the Convention's provisions.[49] Of course, these contribute to prevention, but it is striking that the General Comment has relatively little to say about prevention other than through a reiteration of the substantive provisions of the Convention itself.

48 *General Comment No. 2*, ¶ 2.

49 *Ibid.*, ¶¶ 8–12.

It does, however, acknowledge the importance of ensuring that detainees benefit from "certain basic guarantees," "some of which" are set out in the UNCAT[50] and it also recognises that "[e]xperience since the Convention came into force has enhanced the Committee's understanding of the scope and nature of the prohibition against torture, of the methodologies of torture, of the contexts and consequences in which it occurs, as well as of evolving effective measures to prevent it in different contexts."[51]

Nevertheless, the breach of the preventive obligation is still seen through the lens of the occurrence of an act of torture: "[i]f measures adopted by the State party fail to accomplish the purpose of eradicating acts of torture, the Convention requires that they be revised and/or that new, more effective measures be adopted."[52] In short, whilst acknowledging their evolving understanding of the preventive impact of other measures, the Committee has found it difficult to present the content of a legal obligation to prevent other than by elaborating existing legal obligations and highlighting their preventive potential against the background of violation.

2.2 *Preventive Approaches*

There is another way of addressing the issue of prevention that is not focussed upon ensuring that States fulfil their international commitments concerning the prohibition. Compliance with the prohibition is the result of torture prevention, but torture prevention – though a legal obligation in and of itself – does not need to focus upon compliance with legal obligations, nor indeed, if it is to be effective, should it. This is the insight which is to be drawn from the work of the European Committee for the Prevention of Torture and the UN Subcommittee for Prevention of Torture. The work of both these bodies centres on their conducting unannounced visits to places of detention and the production of confidential reports submitted to the State concerned setting out a series of recommendations.[53] It is beyond the scope of this chapter to

50 *Ibid.*, ¶ 13.

51 *Ibid.*, ¶ 14.

52 *Ibid.*, ¶ 4.

53 An equally important element of the OPCAT is that it requires States to establish independent "National Preventive Mechanisms" which are to undertake preventive visits at the national level. It is beyond the scope of this chapter to consider this aspect of the OPCAT. For a recent exploration of this aspect of the OPCAT see Elina Steinerte, "The Jewel in the Crown and Its Three Guardians: Independence of National Preventive Mechanisms Under the Optional Protocol to the UN Torture Convention," *Human Rights Law Review* 14, 1 (2014): 1.

explore the work of these bodies in detail,[54] but it is important to emphasise two critical elements of their work.

First, the work of both bodies is grounded in co-operation, both legally and practically. This is made explicit in the ECPT, Article 3 of which provides that: "[i]n the application of this Convention, the Committee and the competent national authorities of the Party concerned shall co-operate with each other."[55] It is also reflected in the ultimate "sanction" available to the CPT, which is to issue a "public statement," being conditional on the State party having failed to co-operate (which includes the refusal to improve the situation in the light of the CPT's recommendations).[56] Likewise, OPCAT Article 2(4) requires that "[t]he Subcommittee on Prevention and the States Parties shall cooperate in the implementation of the present Protocol" and the failure to co-operate or improve the situation can likewise result in the issuance of a public statement, or – and unlike the position under the ECPT – the publication of the visit report.[57] This focus on co-operation is not vacuous rhetoric. At a practical level, the operation of a system of preventive visits cannot really function effectively without the co-operation of the State party.[58] If a State wishes to

54 For detailed studies of the background to, and work of, these bodies, see Malcolm Evans and Rod Morgan, *Preventing Torture: A Study of the European Committee for the Prevention of Torture and Inhuman or Degrading Treatment or Punishment* (Oxford: Oxford University Press, 1998); and Rachel Murray et al., *The Optional Protocol to the UN Convention Against Torture* (Oxford: Oxford University Press, 2011).

55 See also the *Explanatory Report to the ECPT*, ¶ 20 ("[i]n the application of the Convention, the Committee and the State concerned are obliged to co-operate. The purpose of the Committee is not to condemn States, but, in a spirit of co-operation and through advice, to seek improvements, if necessary, in the protection of persons deprived of their liberty").

56 ECPT art. 10(1). The CPT has been parsimonious in the issuance of Public Statements, having done so only six times. The first was in 1992 in respect of Turkey (CPT/Inf (93) 1) and was followed by another in respect of Turkey in 1996 (CPT/Inf (96) 34). There then followed three public statements in respect of Russia as regards the Chechen Republic in 2001 (CPT/Inf (2001) 15); 2003 (CPT/Inf (2003) 33); and 2007 (CPT/Inf (2007) 17). The most recent was in respect of Greece in 2011 (CPT/Inf (2001) 10).

57 OPCAT, art. 16(4). To date, the SPT has neither sought to issue a public statement nor publish a report under such circumstances. One factor in this may be that the decision to do so is – oddly – to be taken by the UN Committee against Torture rather than by the SPT itself. This is a legacy of the idea that the SPT was to have been a "subcommittee" of the CAT, rather than a fully fledged independent treaty body. It is to be hoped that this does not prove an unnecessary fetter on the ability of the SPT to utilise this important procedure effectively.

58 At the most banal level, meetings with officials have to be arranged, visas waived (or acquired), credentials issued and information given in advance of any visit if it is to be

frustrate the work of either committee whilst undertaking a visit then it is easy enough for it to do so.[59] Moreover, the process arising out of a visit envisages an on-going exchange between the State and the Committee in question concerning the implementation of recommendations, most evidently in OPCAT Article 12(4) by virtue of which States parties undertake to "examine the recommendations of the Subcommittee on Prevention and enter into dialogue with it on possible implementation measures."[60]

Second, and as a reflection of this, the work of both bodies is not intended to be "adjudicative" in a judicial or quasi-judicial sense. This is a matter which will be returned to in the final section of this chapter, but for now it is important to note that this is expressly recognised in the Preambles to both instruments, which reflect the belief that "the protection of persons deprived of their liberty against torture and inhuman or degrading treatment or punishment could be strengthened by non-judicial means of a preventive character based on visits."[61] The borrowing between these texts is very clear at this point. There was great concern during the drafting of the ECPT – largely expressed by the European Court of Human Rights – that the CPT should not have any judicial or quasi-judicial function (the Court being concerned that the CPT might as a result usurp its own judicial function by determining whether States were or

---

productive. For the current practice see the *Guidelines of the Subcommittee on Prevention of Torture and Other Cruel, Inhuman or Degrading Treatment or Punishment in Relation to Visits to States Parties* (CAT/OP/12/4, adopted November 2010, and which are currently under revision), and in particular Guidelines 4, 6 and 7 and 10 which add detail to what is expected by way of co-operation.

59 Obvious examples would be officials turning up late for meetings; less obvious examples would include unnecessary bureaucratic delays in entry procedures to places of detention, "missing" files, keys, etc., subtle misinformation regarding key issues, etc., all of which speak to a reluctance to co-operate fully.

60 See also OPCAT art. 22, which similarly requires that there be a dialogue with the National Preventive Mechanism concerning possible implementation measures. As regards the SPT, this follow up combines written exchanges (typically a reply from the State and a response from the SPT) with, when possible, face to face discussion, often facilitated by other UN presences and bodies with an interest in supporting the work of the SPT. The SPT is also able to propose that a follow-up visit be undertaken, and has done so on two occasions, to Paraguay in 2010 and to Cambodia in 2013. It has announced that a further follow-up visit may take place in 2014. Each such visit generates its own written follow-up process. All written documentation can be made public with the consent of the State and full details are available at http://tbinternet.ohchr.org/_layouts/TreatyBodyExternal/CountryVisits.aspx.

61 ECPT, 4th Preamble. The 7th Preamble of OPCAT is virtually identical in substance.

were not in breach of the ECHR).[62] It was as a result of this pressure that the Preamble underlines the preventive role and distinguished this from the judicial functions of the Court.

In practice, and over the years, the Court has in fact come to draw heavily on the factual findings of the CPT, as well as drawing upon the CPT's evaluations in support of its own findings.[63] It is difficult to see why it was in fact necessary to underscore the non-judicial nature of the work of the SPT under the OPCAT, since as it had no such proximity to a judicial body within the UN system there was no real reason to seek to differentiate it in this fashion. Nevertheless, the reference is both useful and revealing, as it again underscores the extent to which the work of prevention is not to be equated with the more formalised processes focussed on assessment of compliance and determination of non-compliance.

There has, however, been an interesting difference in approach between the CPT and SPT in the manner in which they have developed their preventive work, (for which there are doubtless many reasons). In essence, the CPT has chosen to pursue the practice of developing statements of standards which guide it in its preventive work. These standards have been set out in its various "substantive sections" of the CPT's annually issued General Reports and have been released in a consolidated format as "The CPT Standards."[64] Though defying uniform description, many of these statements are dispositive in nature and set out a relatively clear template against which compliance can be assessed. This methodology has been consistently used by the European Committee, which in its Reports routinely draws upon these standards as reflecting "safeguards" against ill-treatment and considers the extent to which they are reflected in law as well as in practice. The SPT, on the other hand, has not gone down this route. Its published reports certainly call on States to

62 See Evans and Morgan, *supra* note 54, 118–122.

63 For an overview of early practice see Jim Murdoch, *The Treatment of Prisoners: European Standards* (Strasbourg: Council of Europe Press, 2005), ¶¶ 46–52. For a recent example see *Vinter v. UK* (9 June 2013), 63–64 and 116 where, when deciding that a whole life sentence without review amounted to a violation of art. 3 the Grand Chamber drew attention to this being also the opinion of the CPT, expressed in a report arising from a visit to Switzerland. See also *Tymoshenko v. Ukraine* (30 July 2013), ¶¶ 185–186 and 215, in which the Court quoted at length from the report arising out of its visit to the pre-trial detention unit where the applicant was being detained, and in which concerns were noted regarding the delay in access to external medical care, but not as to the quality of that care as such. The Court concluded that there had been no violation of ECHR art. 3 on the facts.

64 For the most recent version, see *The CPT Standards: "Substantive" Sections of the CPT's General Reports*, CPT/Inf/E (2002) 1 – rev 2013.

ensure that such safeguards are established as a matter of law, but it has not itself set out its vision of what preventive standards might be. Rather, it has adopted a completely different, contextual approach, reflected in 2012 paper on its "Approach to the Concept of Prevention."[65] The title of this paper is not accidental. Reflecting on the comments of the ICJ in the *Bosnian Genocide* case and of the CAT in its General Comment, the SPT observes that whilst "[i]t is of course both possible and important to determine the extent to which a State has complied with its formal legal commitments as set out in international instruments and which have a preventive impact...[this] will rarely be sufficient to fulfil the preventive obligation: it is as much the practice as it is the content of a State's legislative, administrative, judicial or other measures which lies at the heart of the preventive endeavour."[66]

In what is probably its single most significant comment on the subject of prevention, the SPT then says:

> ...there is more to the prevention of torture and ill-treatment than compliance with legal commitments. In this sense, the prevention of torture and ill-treatment embraces – or should embrace – as many as possible of those things which in a given situation can contribute towards the lessening of the likelihood or risk of torture or ill-treatment occurring.[67]

Such an approach is not really amenable to legal conceptualisation, and in consequence, the SPT concludes that:

> The purpose of such reports and recommendations is not only to bring about compliance with international obligations and standards but to offer practical advice and suggestions as to how to reduce the likelihood or risk of torture or ill-treatment occurring and will be firmly based on, and informed by, the facts found and circumstances encountered during the visits undertaken.[68]

---

65 CAT/OP/12/6 (30 December 2012), the full title of which is the rather unwieldy: "The Approach of the Subcommittee on Prevention of Torture to the Concept of Prevention of Torture and Other Cruel, Inhuman or Degrading Treatment or Punishment under the Optional Protocol to the Convention against Torture and Other Cruel, Inhuman or Degrading Treatment or Punishment."

66 *Ibid.*, ¶ 2.

67 *Ibid.*

68 *Ibid.*, ¶ 4. The remainder of the document then goes on to get out ten "Guiding Principles" that inform the practical application of its preventive mandate.

This represents a real innovation in the practice of international bodies involved in human rights protection. The SPT is seeking to tread a rather different path from that of the CPT, as well as that of other human rights bodies, by focussing on the preventive impact of the recommendations its chooses to make rather than upon the recommendation of compliance with applicable standards. Whilst an examination of SPT published reports shows that it does of course routinely recommend that States fulfil their international obligations, and in particular with their obligations under CAT, it also indicates that it is increasingly focussing on making recommendations which are "tailored to the situations which they address in order to offer the greatest practical guidance possible."[69] This is not to suggest that the CPT and other bodies do not do so – they do;[70] the point is that the SPT is making this its starting point, and in doing so currently eschews the approach of articulating standards *per se*.[71]

3 A New Approach to Adjudication in the Preventive Context?

The preventive approach adopted by the SPT differs, then, from the articulation and elaboration of preventive obligations. The preventive obligation, as found in Article 2 of CAT, provides a background to the work of the Committee but does no more than this. Like the ECPT, the OPCAT is essentially procedural

69 *Approach to the Concept of Prevention*, *supra* note 65, ¶ 5(f).

70 By way of a recent published example, see the Report of the CPT to Denmark arising out if its visit to Greenland in 2012 (CPT/Inf (2013) 3), ¶ 6: "The first request concerned the small, oppressive and nearly completely flooded yard, in which inmates from the remand and security sections of Nuuk Prison were expected to take their daily exercise. The delegation asked the Danish authorities to confirm, within one month, that the above-mentioned yard had been taken out of service and that all prisoners were offered the possibility of genuine physical exertion in adequate conditions (e.g. using the larger yard)."

71 Nor has the SPT followed the path of other UN human rights treaty bodies in issuing General Comments. Rather, it has used its Annual Reports to highlight "issues of note" arising from its work, and in a part of each Report devoted to "Substantive Sections" has set out its thinking on a range of issues which, it its view bear upon the execution of a preventive mandate. These have included the "Approach to the Concept of Prevention" (4th Annual Report (2011), CAT/C/46/2) and, more recently, reflections on "The importance of human rights education in the prevention of torture"; "The correlation between legal aid, a system of public defence and prevention of torture" (5th Annual Report (2012), CAT/C/48/3); "The role of judicial review and due process in the prevention of torture in prisons" and "Indigenous justice and the prevention of torture" (6th Annual Report (2013), CAT/C/50/2); and "Torture and Corruption" (7th Annual Report (2013), CAT/C/52/2).

in nature,[72] focussing on establishing mechanisms for preventive work. It is somewhat ironic that the CAT, which focuses on means and mechanisms to assist in the realisation of the prohibition of torture, contains no express prohibitive obligation, but does contain an obligation to take effective preventive measures, whereas the OPCAT, which focuses on means and mechanisms the prevention of torture, does not contain the preventive obligation.[73] Whilst this makes it easier for the SPT to focus on maximising the preventive impact of its work, it also presents dangers as well as opportunities. As the SPT has put it, "the Subcommittee is conscious that there is no logical limit to the range of issues that, if explored, might have a preventive impact."[74] But one cannot focus on everything, and so it goes on to say that "it believes that it is appropriate to focus on those issues which, in the light both of its visit to the State party in question and its more general experience, appear to it to be most pressing, relevant and realizable."[75] This approach has consequences for the place of "adjudication" in the work of the SPT and, through its experience, perhaps for others working within the framework of international human rights machinery.

The role of a visiting body is, ultimately, to observe and recommend. The question is what to recommend on the basis of the observations made. It does not take much imagination to understand that if one witnesses a violation of an obligation – for example, that a detainee is being beaten – that one should recommend that the ill-treatment cease, those responsible be punished and the victim provided with appropriate forms of redress. If one sees that facilities are grossly overcrowded or insanitary, or that basic legal safeguards or procedures are not being respected or offered to those in police custody, again, it is not difficult to craft a recommendation to the effect that these situations be addressed; likewise with gaps and inadequacies in the relevant legal and administrative frameworks. Without doubt such recommendations have a preventive potential. Such recommendations, however, still "tilt" in the direction of determining whether there has been compliance with existing obligations, standards and best practices, and tend towards the generation of recommendations which are evaluative and dispositive. In short, adjudicating compliance still leads to judgmental recommendations.

---

72 This being one of the reasons why OPCAT art. 30 provides that reservations are not permitted.

73 Whilst the aims of the mechanisms are to prevent, this is not of quite the same order as the obligation in art. 2 of UNCAT.

74 *Ibid.*, ¶ 5(f).

75 *Ibid.*

The entire point of moving away from the "legal obligation to prevent" and towards the "preventive approach" is to avoid being led down this path. After all, there is something of a pious fiction written into the ECPT, that its role is to help "strengthen existing protections against torture and ill-treatment"[76] rather than seeking to eradicate existing violations – what used to be described in the European system as strengthening the "cordon sanitaire" which already serves this purpose.[77] Of course, that "cordon sanitaire" is often already thoroughly breached – if it ever existed at all – but nevertheless the theory underpinning prevention implies that one is seeking to render the risk of ill-treatment even more remote than it currently is.

The attraction of this fiction is that it frees one from focussing on compliance. After all, the theory implies that the State already is compliant, but recognises that even the most compliant State can still do more to reduce the risk of non-compliance even further. For the preventive body, the focus becomes not so much addressing the potential breach – or even the actual breach if there is one – but considering the preventive potential of the recommendation which is to be made. One is no longer adjudicating compliance by the State but adjudicating the worth of the recommendation one is making against the ideal of seeking to ensure that violations do not happen: the question becomes "will this recommendation help 'prevent'?" If a recommendation cannot not help prevent, or is not the most helpful preventive recommendation that could be made, why should a preventive body make it? This is certainly a non-judicial approach: it is, however, an approach that calls upon the human rights body concerned to focus rather more upon its own contribution to prevention through the recommendations that it chooses to make, and to focus rather less upon assessing and passing upon the levels of compliance with human rights commitments by the State whose obligation it is to prevent.

---

76 This is most evident in the ECPT, art. 1 of which provides that the CPT is to undertake its visits "with a view to strengthening, *if necessary*, the protection of such persons from torture and from inhuman or degrading treatment or punishment," emphasis added. Likewise, art. 10 refers to the CPT "suggesting, if necessary, improvements in the protection of persons deprived of their liberty." The OPCAT is, perhaps, a little less diplomatic, referring to the visits as being "in order to prevent" (art. 1) to the recommendations that it makes (art. 16(1)). It is clearly foreseen that there will be preventive recommendations.

77 For the first few years of its work, each CPT Report included a "Preface" that explained both the non-judicial nature of the mechanism and that its purpose was "to assist them [the State party] to find ways and means of strengthening the 'cordon sanitaire' between acceptable and unacceptable treatment or behaviour."

Index

www.ingramcontent.com/pod-product-compliance
Lightning Source LLC
LaVergne TN
LVHW020652300926
849161LV00004B/913